PRAISE FOR MARLEY BRANT'S
The Outlaw Youngers

"The definitive history on their violent lives."
                                    —*Los Angeles Times*

"Brant has brought the gun-blazing brothers to life."
                                    —*Booklist*

"Brant has carefully crafted a comprehensive and informal account based on the available primary sources and has properly qualified many statements for which definitive proof is lacking. She successfully involves readers in the Youngers' story, making the work especially appealing to a general audience."
                                    —*Library Journal*

"An extremely readable, informed, and even-handed account of the lives and careers of the Youngers."
                                    —*Atlanta Journal-Constitution*

"This full-length study of the Youngers' lives is biography at its best."   —*True West* magazine

"Destined to become a classic . . . one of the best outlaw books ever written."   —*Rocky Mountain House*

"This work is an especially valuable contribution to the outlaw literature as well as the Civil War period and aftermath . . . the work of Marley Brant will stand out high above the other works."   —*The Roundup*, English Westerners Society

"Makes for reading on the edge of one's seat—memorable and thought-provoking."   —*Daily News* (Faribault, MN)

"There is fabulous material inside the pages of this book. . . . An excellent addition to your Civil War and Western history library."   —*The No Quarterly*

Continued . . .

"A dramatic, highly readable account. While meticulously researched, more important, it's simply 'a good read.' Anyone interested in outlaws, or who enjoys any well-written biography, will find the illustrated book worth their while."

—*Daily Mail* (Nevada, MI)

"Hollywood has rarely been accused of portraying history with inordinate accuracy . . . they feel they can 'do it better.' When we filmed *The Great Northfield, Minnesota Raid,* we unfortunately did not have access to the considerable information afforded Ms. Brant. However, by Hollywood standards we did well . . . the only support possibly missing was the scholarship of Ms. Brant . . . with her we might have 'done it better.' "

—Cliff Robertson

"A lively, even-handed, documented account of the famous bandit family, exploring both their dark side and their justifications."

—Elmer Kelton

JESSE JAMES

The Man and the Myth

~~~~~~~~~~~~~~

Marley Brant

BERKLEY BOOKS, NEW YORK

For Dave

———

This book is an original publication of The Berkley Publishing Group.

JESSE JAMES: THE MAN AND THE MYTH

A Berkley Book / published by arrangement with
the author

PRINTING HISTORY
Berkley trade paperback edition / January 1998

The Putnam Berkley World Wide Web site address is
http://www.berkley.com

ISBN: 0-425-16005-X

BERKLEY®
Berkley Books are published by
The Berkley Publishing Group, a member of Penguin Putnam Inc.,
200 Madison Avenue, New York, New York 10016.
BERKLEY and the ''B'' design
are trademarks belonging to Berkley Publishing Corporation.

PRINTED IN THE UNITED STATES OF AMERICA

10 9 8 7 6 5 4 3 2 1

ACKNOWLEDGMENTS

RESEARCHING JESSE JAMES for almost two decades has had its frustrations and rewards. It has been frustrating inasmuch as there were plenty of holes in the chronology of his story and rewarding because I have met dozens of interesting and kind people who have shared their unique information and perspectives with me.

I would like to thank the James family for their friendship these many years: Lawrence, Thelma, and Betty Barr; Ethelrose James Owens; and James R. Ross. I also appreciate the many members of the Younger, Miller, Bronaugh, Hoffman, Shirley, McCoy, Duncan, Jarrette, Rawlins, Settle, and Hall families for their assistance in helping to fill in the blanks.

Historians Chris Edwards, John Mills, Chuck Parsons, Nancy Samuelson, N. David Smith, Phillip Steele, Jack Wymore, Ted Yeatman, and Wilbur Zink have always been helpful and supportive, and I appreciate their friendship immensely. Thanks to Armand De Gregoris and Elizabeth Becket of the Jesse James Farm and Museum for their help with the photos used in this book.

I also want to thank Milton F. Perry and Dr. Bill Settle, Jr., for their special friendship and for always being available to speculate, share, and confirm Jesse stories with me. I am honored and blessed to have had these extraordinary individuals in my life.

Thanks to the many individuals associated with the countless societies, associations, and organizations with whom I have worked over the years as I made my way down the Jesse trail, especially The State Historical Society of Missouri, Columbia; the James Farm; The Minnesota Historical Society; Cass County Historical Society; Jackson County Historical Society; Clay County Archives; Kansas City Public Library; Missouri State Archives; Kentucky State Archives; Tennessee State Archives; the Northfield Historical Society; Emmett Hoctor, the National Association of Outlaw & Lawman History; the Western Outlaw and Lawman History Association; the Friends of the James Farm; and the Friends of the Youngers and the James-Younger Gang.

Special thanks to my agents David Hale Smith and Shelley Lewis of DHS Literary and to Gary Goldstein and Kim Waltemyer of Berkley for allowing me the opportunity to do this book.

I could accomplish nothing without the continued love and support of my family and Jesus. There are no adequate words to convey my appreciation to each and every one of you: thanks to Dave and Tim Bruegger; Gladys Olmstead; Kathie Montgomery; Willie and Carol Olmstead; John, Nanette, and William Olmstead; the O'Neils, Walls, Averys, Barringtons, and Brueggers; and all of my friends who have encouraged me with a simple "How's the writing going?"

And finally, "Hey, Jesse," wherever you are.

CONTENTS

INTRODUCTION

JESSE JAMES IS the most famous outlaw in American history. His fearless exploits and glamorous rebellion continue to arrest the imagination of millions of people, even though he died over a hundred years ago. *Jesse James*. The name itself has a musical, poetic ring. It is a name that captures immediate attention and continues to earn bold headlines in newspapers all over the world as evidenced by the coverage his recent exhumation for an abstruse DNA study received. The names of Jesse and his associates loomed large on the Western frontier at a time when history-making events were occurring almost daily. From simple Missouri farm boy beginnings to an international legend, much of Jesse's story remains a fascinating mystery.

Jesse James was an outlaw. The word *outlaw* itself invites controversy and discussion. To many people, an outlaw is someone who has broken the law in order to somehow serve his own need. To others, the word represents people who embody the American spirit. Society has a deep-seated need for heroes and villains. Outlaws sometimes serve that need as their complexities and conduct reflect the frustrations of those less adventurous but supportive of the cause they claim to serve.

Jesse James was a career rebel. His future was decided once he swore the mysterious oath that aligned him with the Confederate guerrillas. Jesse and his comrades were denied the opportunity to return to lives of normal citizens after The War between the States. The forces that conquered their rebellious activities made it impossible. Their conventional lives were over before they reached the age of thirty. They were bored—and broke. So they did what frustrated, desperate youth have often done. They roamed the country in an effort to participate in adventures of their own creation. They robbed banks and trains and created a chaotic stir of excitement wherever they made their presence known. They thought little of defying the accepted moral practices of their nineteenth-century society. The criminal activities of Jesse and his gang were well supported by many of the people who continued to live within the boundaries of their war-ravaged countryside. Jesse and his friends eventually accepted with honor the role of adversaries to the incoming power elite of the Midwest. In so doing, they assumed symbolic significance in the myths and fables of the American West.

Jesse James possessed an irrepressible need to be known. He enlisted the aid of famed journalist John Newman Edwards and the media to establish himself as a distinctive personality. Jesse found an audience who was both ready and willing to embrace him as their spokesman. Others found his antics reprehensible and wrong. The question of whether Jesse was a Robin Hood or self-centered mercenary continues to be debated today. Jesse has always been portrayed on film by box office stars, most notably Tyrone Power. He has been portrayed as a misunderstood rebel and a cold-blooded killer. His appeal shows no sign of decline. A recent international poll of historians named Jesse James one of America's top three most famous people. The name Jesse James continues to be fertile material for song, theater, film, and television.

Jesse James loved as aggressively as he hated. His personal code of ethics demanded loyalty be paramount. His family grieved at the lifestyle his activities imposed on them, yet they supported his actions with an innate understanding that Jesse was incapable of denying his inner haunting. The war would never be over in the eyes of Jesse James. He suffered greatly at the hands of federal, state, and local governments over the years. Yet that torment mattered little to him as he continued his competition against those whom he had decided were his self-appointed enemies. And Jesse stole money. Lots of money. If we are to believe the reports, the James-Younger Gang alone profited upwards of $175,000 over the ten-year period in which they were active. But what happened to the money? These spoils unexplainably dwindled to nothing. Jesse's wife would be left in poverty by the end of his life.

From his explosive career during The War between the States throughout the tempestuous reconstruction period, Jesse was a political activist who made his mark on the psyche of the American public. People thrilled to recount his outrageous actions and fervent dedication to his long-lost cause. The results of his publicity campaign show that his efforts were perhaps the most successful in American history. The majority of the members of Jesse's two gangs met with murder, suicide, imprisonment, and other unpleasant early deaths by the end of their reign as Midwest terrorists. Whether in spite of or encouraged by the notoriety with which he lived his life, Jesse's assassination by the hand of one of his friends resulted in the continuation and embellishment of his legend. Many of the people who crossed Jesse's path in the course of his explosive career have become famous merely because of their fleeting association with him. Not a day goes by that someone, somewhere, does not claim to be related to Jesse James. Or to one of his gang members. Or to one of his victims. Or at least to someone who touched his elusive shadow for even a brief moment.

The intricacies of Jesse's life must have surprised even the great bandit himself. His success at molding himself into the most famous of outlaws no doubt delighted him. But what was the price he paid? And was it all worth it? Although he died a broken, lonely man, there are few people on the face of the media-fed planet who do not know the name Jesse James. Yet the ride of Jesse James through the history books is muddled with folklore, lies, and assumptions. The Jesse who emerges under the careful scrutiny of the facts may well be a completely different Jesse from the one we think we know. Only by riding alongside Jesse James will we learn the real story. And what a ride he had.

ONE

❧❧

The Family James

*"... train up your children in the nurture and admonition of the
Lord and live a christian life your self."*
—Reverend Robert James
in a letter to his wife Zerelda, April 14, 1815

ROBERT SALLEE JAMES was a man of tenacity. He had
little regard for the disadvantaged circumstances into which he
had been born. From an early age he decided to seize whatever
opportunities might come his way and mold himself into someone of whom his family could be pleased and proud. Robert
believed emphatically in God and country. The precept that an
individual could overcome all obstacles if he worked long
enough and, most important, hard enough was important to him.
Robert's father, John William James, was a respected Baptist
minister and farmer from Goochland County, Virginia. His
mother, Mary (Polly) Poor, was the daughter of a cornet in
Lighthorse Harry Lee's Partisan Legion.[1] Robert was born the
fifth of eight children in Logan County, Kentucky, on July 17,
1818. The Jameses' Kentucky community was family-oriented
and honor-bound. A lifetime of peaceful invulnerability, however, was not to be Robert's reality.

4

Things changed drastically for Robert when he was nine years old. John and Polly James fell ill and died within months of each other that year. Robert's eldest sister Mary had only recently married John W. Mimms, but she refused to see her brothers and sisters separated into the households of her parents' brothers, sisters, and friends. The Mimms would begin their marriage with the ready-made family of Mary's five minor siblings. One thing could be said about the James family, and that would be emphatically handed down to their children: They all had very strong ideas about family loyalty and the tenacity it took to keep the family unit functioning and together.

Robert James refused to succumb to any of the disadvantages he faced. He had a quick mind and had early on acknowledged the importance of education. He was determined to rise above his orphan status and somehow make a contribution to his community. Robert no doubt felt it was what his God, and perhaps his parents, expected of him. Robert managed to obtain a solid secondary education despite the financial obstacles he must have faced. He continued in his pursuit to fulfill his self-proclaimed goals and was ordained as a Baptist minister in 1839. Robert's Christianity was of the greatest importance to him. He also wanted to increase his knowledge and learn to express himself with eloquence and authority. It likely surprised no one when Robert was accepted into Kentucky's Georgetown College as a ministerial student.

Robert approached his education seriously. At the same time he was very attractive and a fascinating conversationalist. He worked hard at his studies yet somehow found time to socialize with other students. During one of Robert's forays out into the community while he was a student at Georgetown, he met a vivacious young woman named Zerelda Elizabeth Cole.

Zerelda Cole knew a childhood of deprivation herself. She was the only daughter of James Cole and Sallie Yates Lindsay. Zerelda was born in Woodward County, Kentucky, on January 29, 1825.[2] She, too, knew what it was like to lose loved ones early in life. Zerelda was two years old when her father fell from a horse and almost immediately died from his injuries. Sallie Cole took the toddler and her baby brother Jesse Richard to live with

James's father, Richard Cole, Jr., at the Black Horse Tavern near Lexington.

The Blackhorse was quite a place. It was established by Richard Cole, Sr., in 1812. At the time of Zerelda's arrival, the Black Horse Tavern was one of the leading gathering spots for the men of the area as well as several prominent local and national politicians. Statesmen such as Henry Clay stopped at the tavern to pontificate during their campaigns. Heated debate often punctuated the inn's casual atmosphere. Most of the men in town would visit the tavern regularly, yet some of the ladies of Lexington denounced the Black Horse as "Sodom." The boisterous atmosphere and the serving of copious amounts of raw whiskey were not to their liking. The activities of those who frequented the inn were fodder for a great deal of conversation and controversy. Zerelda Cole and her brother Jesse grew up in the shadow of the Black Horse and all it offered.

After the eventual death of Richard Cole, Sallie married widower Robert Thomason. Thomason brought six small children to the merging family. Some family members voiced the opinion that Zerelda was not particularly pleased to inherit additional siblings nor did she like Robert Thomason. Sallie and Robert Thomason decided that the new family would benefit in all ways by relocating to the pioneer state of Missouri. Zerelda was completely disinterested in traveling west and obstinately insisted on remaining in Kentucky. Sallie no doubt was eager to begin her new married life with a minimal of dissension from her daughter. She sent Zerelda to live with Sallie's brother James Lindsay in nearby Stamping Ground. Her mother decided that even though Zerelda was not a Catholic, she would be enrolled in St. Catherine's Academy in nearby Lexington.

Zerelda was only fifteen when she met Robert James at a Bible meeting, but she seemed more knowledgeable about life than some of the other young women he had met.[3] Zerelda thrived on fun and excitement. She likely did not expect to fall in love so young, especially with a serious ministerial student. Robert and Zerelda were different in most ways yet quite alike in others. Robert was somber and often quiet. Zerelda was never one to hold her opinion, and she often joked and played pranks.[4] Zerelda and Robert seemed to agree when it came to setting goals, handling responsibilities, keeping promises, and maintaining loyalties, even though their public personalities were very different. They each strived for a personal respectability and each seemed dedicated to finding a comfortable niche in life. Zerelda accepted when Robert proposed that they marry and spend the rest of their lives together.

James Lindsay had to vouch for Zerelda as her guardian because she was underage at the time of her engagement to Robert James. Lindsay agreed to her marriage by written authorization to Scott County officials. He guaranteed the marriage agreement by asking a friend of his to help post a bond of fifty dollars. Robert James and Zerelda Cole were then married by Reverend Y. R. Pitts on December 28, 1841, at the home of her Uncle James in Stamping Ground, Kentucky.

The couple lived between Frankfort and Lexington in a little house on the Frankfort Pike during their first year of marriage. Zerelda decided to introduce her new husband to her family by the time their marriage entered the second year, so Zerelda and Robert traveled to Missouri in the summer to visit her mother and brother Jesse. Missouri was beautiful. It was replete with flourishing communities and the excitement of new enterprises. Life there seemed challenging and full of opportunities. The young couple considered eventually making their home in the pioneer territory. Zerelda stayed on with her family for an extended visit while Robert returned to Georgetown to complete his studies in the fall. Zerelda was married too brief a time to be separated from her new husband and no doubt missed him very much. She wrote to Robert often and shared her observations of Missouri and all it seemed to offer. With each letter she continued to urge her husband to relocate to Missouri. Zerelda remained in Missouri for another reason: she was pregnant with the couple's first child. Robert eventually agreed that Missouri could be promising for both himself and his family. He made plans to join Zerelda when his work at Georgetown was completed. Zerelda began to look for an acceptable farm near her mother in Clay County. Robert knew that he would have to farm in addition to any ministry in which he might become involved. Working only as a preacher would not enable him to earn money to provide the security his growing family would need. Robert had already decided to return to Georgetown in the future. He wanted to work toward a master's degree.

Robert was not able to complete his relocation to Missouri by the time his first son, Alexander Franklin James, arrived. The baby was born at the Thomason house on January 10, 1843. Robert did not reunite with Zerelda or set eyes on his new child until later in the year. Robert and Zerelda leased a 275-acre farm with the option to purchase shortly after Robert arrived in Missouri. The small cabin was originally owned by Jacob Groomer and was located near Centerville (later to be called Kearney).[5] Robert secured seven slaves to assist him in his new enterprise. A beloved slave nicknamed Aunt Charlotte had traveled to Missouri with Zerelda's mother. Aunt Charlotte now joined the James household to help in whatever ways she could. She would remain with the James family for at least thirty years along with another slave named Ambrose. Robert farmed during the week and found places to preach, without pay, on Sunday. Robert and Zerelda worked hard to get their new farm up and running. Robert worked equally as hard building a congregation at nearby New Hope Baptist Church. He eventually reorganized and became pastor in residence at New Hope Baptist. The church became the largest of its denomination in Northwest Missouri. Reverend James was soon riding the circuit and preaching at several other churches and gatherings in Clay County. He established two additional churches in the county: the Providence Baptist Church and the Pisgah Baptist Church of Excelsior Springs. Robert assisted other local preachers in his area as together they created the North Liberty Baptist Association in 1844.[6]

A second son was born to Zerelda and Robert in July 1845. The baby was named Robert after his father but lived only five days. Zerelda and Robert attempted to look to the future and overcome their sorrow. Robert stayed busy with his preaching and Zerelda oversaw the daily operations of the farm. Robert found time for continuing his education by reading books on a variety of subjects. His interests included history, literature, Latin, philosophy, and various sciences. Everyone seemed to like Robert. He was regarded as an educated and dedicated man of the cloth. Reverend James was well respected in his community and his opinion on many local issues was often solicited. He was among those community leaders who founded William Jewell College in the nearby town of Liberty and served on the college's first board of trustees. On the other hand, people didn't know quite what to make of the preacher's wife. Zerelda had a lot of friends as she was outgoing and fun to be around, but sometimes her sense of humor differed from the other young wives and mothers in the area. Zerelda was unlike her neighbors in another way, too. She refused to defer to her husband and the other men of her social circle when it came to voicing opinions. Zerelda thought nothing of joining a conversation or allowing her views on any given subject to be known. Zerelda James had a reputation as a spitfire.

On September 5, 1847, Zerelda and Robert were elated when son Jesse Woodson James was born. The James family seemed to be prospering, yet some of the members of Robert's family later claimed that Zerelda was not at all pleased at the amount of time Reverend James allotted his ministry. She felt that he was not spending enough time with her and the children.[7] Robert must have spent some time with Frank and Jesse. A strong bond between Reverend James and his son Jesse does seem apparent by Jesse's later statements. Zerelda told her grandson's wife many years later that she saw her husband once baptize as many as sixty-five people while she held up young Jesse to witness this momentous occasion.[8] Jesse himself would later be baptized near the same spot as this event. It does appear as though Robert's interests apart from his family dominated his time. His pursuit of his continuing education resulted in Robert's being awarded a master of arts degree from Georgetown College in 1848. He did spend at least some time at home. On November 25, 1849, daughter Susan Lavenia was born to Reverend and Mrs. James. The hard work of someone around the James homestead paid off. Robert and Zerelda owned their farm outright by 1850, as well as a small herd of cattle, some horses, and thirty sheep.[9]

In early spring 1850, Robert James surprised Zerelda by informing her that he wanted to follow his brother Drury west to the California gold fields. Many Clay Countians had traveled to an area called Hangtown to seek their fortunes. Reverend James

The James Farm, Kearney, Missouri.
The author

evidently felt that a representative of God's word might be beneficial to those who had made the expedition. Members of his family later speculated that perhaps Robert wanted a short vacation from the constant nagging of his wife. Zerelda often complained in public about her husband's absences from their home as he traveled in the name of the Lord. Other tales have suggested that Zerelda was not faithful to Robert and that he discovered that Jesse was not his son after all but rather the result of Zerelda's tryst with a local doctor.

Regardless of why he chose to follow his brother, Robert left Zerelda and his young children at home on their farm. He joined his close friend William Stigers on the journey west to California on April 12, 1850. Zerelda later claimed that little Jesse pleaded with his father not to go. The good Reverend told Zerelda that if he had not spent so much money preparing for the trip and had not promised Drury James and Stigers that he would go, he would forget his journey.[10] Nonetheless, Robert James joined his group and left his family in Missouri far behind.

Robert must have retained a certain degree of affection for his wife as letters he sent home from the trail were loving and concerned. Robert wrote a letter just a few days after his departure. He asked Zerelda to "Give my love to all inquiring friends and take a portion of it to yourself and kiss Jesse for me and tell

Franklin to be a good boy and learn fast.'' Other missives written later in his travels contained equally tender remarks.[11] There were some words, however, which would come back to haunt Zerelda James not once but twice in her lifetime. Robert wrote to her from Grand Island, a mile from New Fort Carney, ''Pray for me that if no more [you and I] meet in this world we can meet in Glory.''[12]

Reverend James arrived in Hangtown (later to be called Placerville) on July 14. It is not clear whether he became ill during his long journey or after his arrival in California. On August 18, Robert Sallee James died from one of the several dysentery-type illnesses that plagued so many of those seeking their fortunes in the goldfields. He was only thirty-two years old when he was buried in an unmarked grave.[13] The grave's location was not remembered by anyone who was present at his burial nor would it ever be identified.

Frank James was seven when his father died, and Jesse not even three. Susan was just an infant. It is interesting to speculate what influence the reverend would have had on his two sons were he an integral part of their childhood development. Robert James was an individual dedicated to helping the members of his community and making a positive impression on those with whom he came in contact. He was sensitive, caring, and compassionate. He was educated and well-read, with an interest in many different subjects. Foremost, Robert was dedicated to his Lord and the preaching of the Bible.

Robert James's sons had barely an opportunity to get to know their father in regard to his likes and dislikes, his strengths and weaknesses before he was taken from them. Yet each would develop and possess some of his qualities and traits as they grew to be men themselves. Frank learned to love literature and peppered his speech with quotations from Shakespeare, although he lacked a formal education. Jesse, perhaps in a recognized effort to emulate his father, studied the Bible and quoted from that book regularly. Both young men shared an avid interest in the affairs of their community. The trials and tribulations that awaited both their family and their neighbors, however, would determine the means by which they reacted to the events that colored the evolution of Clay County and Missouri. But when it came down to it, Frank and Jesse were raised by their mother. Her influence would come to be clearly visible as they grew. Frank's personality would reflect Zerelda's perseverance and unflappable approach to any problems life might initiate. Jesse developed her grand sense of humor and love of pranks and horseplay. Both boys would dedicate themselves to their family and each would develop a fierce pride that was obviously drawn from both parents. Jesse and Frank were from the same stock. They each experienced the absence of their father and the overt domination of their widowed mother. Frank and Jesse James would, however, grow to be two very different men. Their names would be forever linked by a commonality of deeds that would result in their fame as foremost American legends.

TWO

꘎꘎꘎

Changes and Turmoil

"A war was waged from 1861 to 1865 between two organized governments: the United States of America, and the 'War of Secession,' for the Southern States seceded without a thought of war. The right of a State to secede had never been questioned. It was not a 'War of Rebellion' for sovereign Confederate States of America. These were the official titles of the contending parties. It was not a 'Civil War,' as it was not fought between two parties within the same government. It was not, independent States, co-equal, cannot rebel against each other. It was a War between the States, because twenty-two non-seceding States made war upon eleven seceding States to force them back into the Union of States. It was not until after the surrender of 1865 that secession was decided to be unconstitutional."

—The Congressional Record of March 2,
Senate Joint Resolution No. 41[1]

TIMES WERE TOUGH for a single mother. Zerelda James had three children to raise in an area still considered to be a new frontier. She must have felt overwhelmed by her responsibilities as a parent alone and the proprietess of a large and somewhat successful farm. Zerelda could certainly not be blamed for want-

13

ing security and a man to be a father figure to Frank, Jesse, and baby Susan. She married a wealthy widower named Benjamin A. Simms on September 30, 1852. Simms was twenty-five years older than his new bride. On the plus side, he owned a sizable farm about seven miles from the James place and another spread near Clinton, Missouri. The Simms family was originally from Virginia and was well respected.[2] Benjamin Simms's father had served at Valley Forge with George Washington, and Benjamin himself had been with the Virginia Militia during the War of 1812. Simms was a good catch for Zerelda. Many of Reverend James's former congregation believed he would be a stabilizing influence on the two James boys. It was the opinion of many that the boys were spoiled by their mother since the death of their father. Perhaps Benjamin Simms could bring them into line as Robert James might have done had he still been an influence in their lives.

Such a development was not to be. It appeared to Robert James's family that there were difficulties between Zerelda and Simms almost from the beginning. Zerelda treasured her children. She would not stand for anyone correcting or admonishing them in any way. Frank and Jesse resented any man attempting to act as their surrogate father. They did not obey or even try to get along with Simms. Folklore claims that the James boys were mean-spirited. It has been written that they would often torture animals and frighten their playmates with the excessive use of firearms, but no evidence of this seems to exist. Frank and Jesse were simply headstrong young men who, encouraged by their mother, wanted their own way. The problems between Zerelda and Simms escalated quickly. Very early in the marriage, Zerelda reluctantly agreed to send Frank, Jesse, and Susie to her relatives while she and her new husband adjusted to their partnership. The couple went so far as to leave the James farm. They moved to Simms's 380-acre farm in northern Clinton County. Friends and family left behind by Zerelda chastised her for abandoning her children. She retaliated against their gossip and unwanted opinions by withdrawing her membership in the New Hope Church.

The relocation did not help the relationship. Zerelda was miserable without her children. The records of Dr. Absolam Kerns indicate that she suffered a miscarriage in early 1853.[3] Zerelda returned to the James farm and reunited with her children there a few months later. Simms remained in Clinton. The marriage was at an end. On January 2, 1854, Benjamin Simms was killed in a horse accident before Zerelda could obtain a divorce.

Zerelda no doubt saw that her children desperately needed a father figure in their lives as they grew. Life was rough on a farm in rural Missouri and there was much that her two boys needed to learn. Zerelda had become acquainted with a doctor from Liberty named Reuben Samuel shortly after her return to Clay County. Samuel had set up an office over the general store of Robert James's brother William in 1854. Reuben was the son of a pioneer named Fielding Samuel. He and his family had relocated to Clay County in 1840 from Owen County, Kentucky. Reuben attended the Ohio Medical College in Cincinnati from 1850 to 1851. He returned to Clay County after college. Although he intended to practice medicine, Samuel eventually bought a small farm near the James farm. His roots were in agriculture, and he enjoyed farming as well.

The dispositions of Zerelda and Reuben Samuel were as different as had been the personalities of Zerelda and Robert James. Nonetheless, the two enjoyed each other's company and began to formally see each other. The imperturbable Dr. Samuel liked Zerelda's children and enjoyed keeping company with them. Slowly and with caution, Frank and Jesse learned to respect Reuben Samuel. The twice-widowed Zerelda secured her boys' approval and married Reuben Samuel on September 12, 1855. The bond between Samuel and Reverend James's boys would grow to be a strong one, and they soon loved their new stepfather as an important member of their family. Jesse and Frank eventually even called Dr. Samuel "Pappy." Zerelda and Samuel ultimately delighted the James children with four half-brothers and sisters: Sallie, John, Fannie, and Archie.[4]

Young Jesse James was beginning to settle into a comfortable family life by the late 1850s. His day-to-day life was characterized by the same routines that most of the other children of his time experienced even though he had a turbulent early childhood. He went to school, helped on the farm, attended church, and engaged in the camaraderie a large family and close community

typically enjoyed. Many of his neighbors would later say that
Jesse was not extraordinary as a child. They found him engaging
and polite. It was noted that the boy possessed his mother's sense
of humor. Jesse did not appear to be quite as intelligent as his
older brother but certainly was smart. There didn't seem to be
too much sibling rivalry between Jesse and Frank, even though
it appeared that their mother favored her firstborn. Zerelda had
called her eldest Mr. Frank from the time he was a little boy.

Jesse enjoyed people and he liked to be in their company. He
would entertain other children and adults alike with stories or
Bible quotes whenever he felt encouraged. Generally well liked,
he was quite good-natured and was known to be generous.[5] On
other occasions he would become unaccountably despondent and
easily agitated. He did not suffer fools and was quick to get
angry if things did not seem to be going his way. He was impulsive and liked immediate results, regardless of whether he
was working or playing. Jesse seemed to enjoy these multifac-
eted sides to his personality. He no doubt felt that his unpre-
dictability drew attention to him and made him interesting. Jesse,
abandoned by his father and made to play second fiddle to his
brother in his mother's affections, loved and craved attention.

Events were evolving in western Missouri and Kansas that
would transform the future course of Jesse and Frank's lives
throughout their childhood. Missouri farmers who lived near the
eastern border of the territory of Kansas in counties such as Clay
read in their local newspaper that all was not peaceful in the
borderland. A situation was brewing that was causing increased
animosity between the two states. Missouri had been the state
farthest west in America's expansion for quite awhile. Pioneers
had begun their journeys west to California and Oregon from
various points in Western Missouri. The Territory of Kansas for
the most part was populated by Indians who had been relocated
from the East. Few white pioneers had settled there. By the time
Jesse was a young boy, the demographics were beginning to
change. New laws and directives needed to be made in order to
supervise the actions of the new immigrants as homesteaders
from the East began to arrive and build towns. In 1854, the
Missouri Compromise had proclaimed that slavery be prohibited

in the new territory of Kansas. It was presumed that while the new territory of Nebraska would be slave-free, Kansas would eventually choose to allow the continuation of slavery. The decree was overturned by the Kansas legislature in 1854 when it was decided that homesteaders should determine this matter for themselves through an election. The Missourians who lived near Kansas began to feel threatened. It seemed to them that those who would be drawn to Kansas under a ban on slavery would soon try to influence the way Missouri conducted its business. Although the percentage of slaves in Missouri was less than 10 percent of the population, nearly 80 percent of the Missouri settlers had slave-state backgrounds. The use of slaves was the way their business and enterprises had been run for generations. The less affluent farmers did not want to be dictated to on the subject even though many of them did not own slaves. They wanted the right to choose how they conducted their business and had already decided by moving west that less government was their preferred way of living. Additionally, they felt strongly that Missouri's economy would be greatly affected were a ban on slavery to be enacted.

The Missourians' concern increased when settlers began to infiltrate Kansas. Many of them were brought west from the Northeastern states by those wishing to advance the antislavery agenda. The Missouri farmers feared they would have to protect their property from encroachment by those who had been encouraged to move into the area. Missourians themselves were persuaded by the local press to relocate to Kansas in order to increase that state's population and force the Northeasterners to establish their new homes farther north in places such as Nebraska. Many Missourians eventually did take up residence in Kansas. This was done both to squeeze out the Northeasterners and to influence the election that would decide the matter. Most of those living along the borderland remained in Missouri attempting to protect their interests.

The antislavery group in Kansas was not happy with the interference of their neighbors to the east. There was a great deal of resentment by the residents of both Kansas and Missouri. The Northeastern antislavery contingents along with the newly formed Republican Party committed to step up the protest through the use of the local and national press. The controversy was presented as solely an issue of slavery (as the coming war between the states would be promoted).

The occasional physical clashes were reported as full scale warfare. Missourians and Kansans were soon engaged in verbal combat as a result of what each side perceived to be the other's answer to the problem: violence. The media-invented brutality became an ugly reality. Northern abolitionist John Brown soon appeared in Kansas full of explosive rhetoric and accusations. Shortly after his arrival, he amassed his Free-Soil demonstrators. Brown was soon appointed captain of a local militia company. Almost immediately he and six of his followers murdered five proslavery men. A group of outraged Missourians took it upon themselves to retaliate against Brown and his force with vengeance of their own. Evidently most of the people who may have supported Brown's oratory did not support his manner of demonstration. Brown and his group were soon run out of Kansas but not before violence became commonplace along the borderland.

Dissension over land claims and political sponsorship soon eclipsed the slavery issue. Hatred between the residents of the two states intensified. Such action impacted all of the people along the border, although those who taunted or reciprocated with violence were not the majority of the people at odds. Malice and suspicion intensified throughout the late 1850s and continued into the '60s. The discord between the North and South over issues that included but were not limited to slavery was also escalating within the eastern regions of the country at this time. The atmosphere of internal hostility could not be denied.

The James and Samuel families were Southerners who naturally sympathized with those advocating Missouri independence. The opinionated Zerelda James Samuel was, as usual, outspoken about her view of the situation.[6] Her children were quite naturally drawn into the unpleasantness, as many of the strikes occurred within miles of their home and school. Zerelda encouraged her boys to stand up for their beliefs, or at least those beliefs that she encouraged them to have, by pronouncing their resentment of the Kansans and Northerners. The introspective young Frank James came to believe that the integrity of the people of western Missouri was on the line. Though Jesse was still just a boy, he listened to his mother's political exclamations with great interest and assured her that he agreed wholeheartedly.

By 1861, the increasing animosity in the eastern part of the country magnified the problems with which Missouri had been dealing. The Missouri legislature decided to put the issue to a vote by its citizens when the succession issue finally reached the Midwest. Pro Union representatives from eastern Missouri had been voted into majority during the winter election, although the legislature was composed mostly of Southerners. It was decided that Missouri would remain neutral for the time being and see what developed.

Missouri Governor Claiborne F. Jackson was a champion of the people of the western areas. He was a vocal supporter of the Confederacy. Jackson believed that the pro-Confederacy people of Missouri would be threatened with this new movement in Kansas. He quickly began efforts to raise and arm a state guard after the firing on Fort Sumter. Meanwhile, John C. Fremont, Frank P. Blair, and others representing the voters in eastern Missouri campaigned to allow Missouri to join those states supporting the Union. Before long, a confrontation occurred between Jackson's state guard and a group assembled by Fremont. This physical discussion was won by the Fremont/Blair group. Jackson was outraged. He promptly called for fifty thousand men to take up arms against the likely onslaught of Northern representatives. In turn, Blair requested Union troops.

An opportunist named James H. Lane was elected United States senator from the new free state of Kansas in January 1861. Lane was known for his vitriolic tirades against Missouri during the Border War. He had gained favor with Abraham Lincoln by organizing protection for the United States capitol after the firing on Fort Sumter. Lincoln acknowledged Lane's contribution to his country by quickly granting Lane's request that Lincoln allow him the authority to raise troops in Kansas to deal with any problems the nearby pro-Confederate west Missourians might create. Lane gathered troops of men who had made themselves available to represent Kansas during the Kansas and Missouri troubles. These men, who had become known as Jayhawkers, proved themselves to be ruthless and aggressive fighters. Lane formed the third, fourth, and fifth Kansas Regiments by relying on the Jayhawkers as the backbone of his new organization. These soldiers would soon become known as redlegs due to the blood-colored leggings they wore.

An eastern abolitionist named Charles R. Jennison appeared on the scene early in the Border War, ready to offer his expertise to Lane and his forces. Jennison had recently been commissioned a colonel in the Union Army as a means to establish his murderous group of volunteer troops under military discipline and control. One of Jennison's seventh Kansas Volunteer Cavalrymen was a young man named William Cody. Cody would go on to become known in history as Buffalo Bill.[7]

The origins of the coming conflict were deeply rooted in the border disagreements. It was to become known as the Civil War in Missouri or The War between the States. All the earlier trepidation of the people along the Kansas/Missouri border was surpassed. The James-Samuel family was to become deeply ensconced in the political battle of their lives.

Several Missouri communities formed local militia units when the people of Missouri had been caught in the middle of the legislature's infighting. Frank James was eighteen years old when he pledged his support of the Confederacy and joined the Home Guard unit of Centerville on May 4, 1861. Zerelda Samuel was no doubt gratified and proud as she watched her eldest son march off in defense of her Southern principles. Jesse was only thirteen at the time of Frank's departure. Unlike later, when a dying Confederacy would welcome combatants even that young, none of the organized associations welcomed a boy of Jesse's age, regardless of his determination to become involved in the armed conflict. Jesse was frustrated that he was to remain at home while Frank proudly defended the family honor as a soldier. Jesse vowed to join in the fight as soon as he was old enough to be accepted. In the meantime, he would remain on the farm doing all he could to help protect the interests of his family.

The Missouri state convention met in July to remove Jackson and to appoint a governor whose sympathies were clearly with the Union. By August, Frank James had participated in his first major Missouri battle. He had been present when the troops of Confederate General Sterling Price defeated the Union forces at Wilson's Creek. Price and his men marched north as they basked in their victory. James Lane promptly sent 1,500 of his Jayhawkers into Missouri, thereby sending a clear message that those who defended his cause would not be so easily defeated. The Jayhawkers' spree of protest resulted in the destruction of hundreds of farms and businesses. The middle-western Missouri town of Osceola was ransacked and burned by the Kansans. Over a dozen townspeople were murdered when they attempted to save their homes and possessions. During these raids, a Cass County merchant and landowner named Henry Younger was robbed of over $4,000 worth of fine horses, carriages, and wagons from his livery. As with the James family, the politics and acts of the Kansans would long be remembered by the members of the Younger family.

Between the Jayhawkers, Confederates, redlegs, and Union soldiers, there were many factions at work in the tormented borderland. Many of the men expressed their sympathies to be with the Confederacy, but they were not eager to leave their families behind. They knew their loved ones would be extremely vulnerable while they traipsed over the state with the organized Confederate Army. These men began to form into loosely knit area watches. They guarded their families, retaliated when necessary, and were accountable to no one. Before long, a young man named William Clarke Quantrill offered his organizational services to the Confederate cause.

Strangely enough, Ohio-born Charlie Quantrill had spent time in Kansas during the Border War. During that time he had been aiding and abetting the Jayhawker movement.[8] It is not clear what caused the twenty-four-year-old to convert to the Missourians' way of thinking. Quantrill suddenly appeared eager to establish himself as a leader among the disenchanted young men of the western border. There were many who were fervent to assert themselves against a government and movement that they found to be favorably representing all that their hardworking families and ancestors opposed. Quantrill responded to the demand for action by the young rebels and quickly secured his place as a leader among them. He provided the loosely knit group with immediate opportunities to participate in raids against Kansas and Union supporters. Quantrill excelled in organizational skills, and those men not affiliated with the Confederate Army converged to join his group of protesters to defend their homes and farmland. The group's reputation grew with each merciless attack against their enemies. Quantrill's guerrillas were soon recognized by their opponents as an organization of unsophisticated and rebellious border youths who had quickly been molded into one of the most proficient and deadly bands of guerrillas to fight in a war.

One of Quantrill's early recruits was seventeen-year-old Cole Younger. Union Captain Irvin C. Walley vowed to have Henry Younger's son arrested after an altercation with the young man at a birthday party. Cole ignored John C. Fremont's orders forbidding anyone outside of an organized group of recognized militia to bear arms when Walley appeared at the Younger's Cass County home to make good his promise. Cole grabbed one of the family's shotguns along with a revolver, and he and his brother-in-law John Jarrette were welcomed into the ranks of Charlie Quantrill that night.[9] Younger's reputation as a fair and reliable soldier grew throughout the war. His name would be well-known in Confederate circles by the end of the conflict.

Life was as unpredictable for those away from the front line as the men who were actually participating in combat. Cole Younger's father Henry was struck in the back by three bullets fired by Irvin Walley and his men as he traveled unaccompanied down the Westport Road on his way home from a business trip to Kansas City. Cole Younger's antagonist was charged with the murder when the Union captain confessed to it during questioning by officers of the Missouri State Militia.[10] Although Brigadier General Benjamin Loan ordered a court trial, the soldiers of the Fifth Regiment Missouri State Militia who were to testify against Walley were bushwhacked and killed before they could arrive to witness. Because of the ambush, the men could not testify, and the trial was not held.

Frank James did not immediately have the opportunity to distinguish himself as a mighty warrior. He came down with chicken pox in February 1862 and was left in the field to be "captured" by Union soldiers. Frank was allowed to return home on parole as long as he signed the Union's Oath of Allegiance. On April 26, he swore with his signature that his days as a Confederate had ended. Frank's name appeared in a local newspaper in May 1862 as having been one of several who had posted bond and taken the oath to Colonel William Penick.[11] The public Frank James had surrendered. The private Frank James would continue the war someplace other than in the Home Guard. Frank was satisfied to recuperate from his chicken pox and relive his brief military career for the time being. He filled young Jesse's head full of stories of the glories of being a combatant along the front line.

In April 1862, the Congress of the Confederate States of America passed the Partisan Ranger Act. The act authorized President Jefferson Davis to commission officers and raise troops. Quantrill and his men were sworn into Confederate service under the act on August 14 by Colonel Gideon W. Thompson. Quantrill's troops were considered irregulars but were recognized as an important part of the Confederate cause.

The Confederate Army could not hold Missouri, even with the addition of the guerrillas into their ranks. Harassment of the Confederate people along the western Missouri border increased as ruthless advancements were made toward those who sympathized with the South. Many of the young men who had joined the army to represent the Confederate cause returned home to protect their families and assets in the wake of the destruction of their farms and the disruption of family businesses. The Union leadership made an offer to those who wanted to surrender. They pledged amnesty to those whose participation had not resulted in serious war crimes. This was on condition that the rebels swear their allegiance to the United States government and give a bond with good security representing their vows to stay out of any future conflict. Many men grudgingly accepted the Union's offer as they saw no other choice if they were to remain on their farms in order to protect their interests. As others considered whether the amnesty offer was something with which they could live, the provisional government decreed that every man of military age must enroll in the state militia and be subject for service if called. Those men who had already accepted the offer and its stated conditions were infuriated as they felt that they had been tricked into surrendering under false pretense. To change the rules after their surrender and demand that they serve the cause of those they adamantly opposed was unthinkable to a large number of the young men who had returned home. They refused to become affiliated with the Union Army and took the only way out that they knew: they took to the bush and joined Quantrill.

Quantrill and his men enjoyed several successful skirmishes up and down the state of Missouri and into Eastern Kansas during the remainder of the year. Having proved their mettle, a large number of the irregulars were assigned to General Jo Shelby's Confederate Army brigade in Arkansas. The irregulars were not supposed to act alone on any military matters while they were in the company of the Confederate Army. Yet the Army liked to employ them as partisans to increase the number of troops at any given engagement. Quantrill's guerrilla fighters had participated in battles at Cane Hill and Prairie Grove, Arkansas, by the end of 1862.

General Jo Shelby was nearly captured by Union forces on the night before the battle of Prairie Grove in the winter of 1862. There was an exciting eleventh-hour recovery of the leader said to have been led by John Jarrette and others of the guerrilla contingent. A popular piece of folklore handed down in the years after the event names Frank James, having rejoined the Confederate irregular troops, as being one of those involved in Shelby's rescue. On the other hand, the account of one of the other guerrillas present that day placed Frank in Missouri at the time of the rescue.[12] Shelby had great respect for the efforts of Quantrill's guerrillas during the war. He admired the fearlessness and commitment of the individuals who became part of the organization. An attachment was formed during the war between Frank James, Cole Younger, General Shelby, and Shelby's adjutant, John Newman Edwards. It could be possible that the friendship Shelby and Edwards bestowed upon the boys years later was a direct result of Frank and Jarrette's involvement in the rescue of the general. Yet there is nothing concrete that places Frank James at the event.

During the winter of 1862–63, Quantrill and his men made their way down to Mt. Pleasant, Texas, to regroup before their return to Missouri in the spring. The James-Samuel family was experiencing harassment at home in Clay County during this time. One of the stories that has been repeated throughout the years by popular biographers of the James boys has been that Frank reaffiliated himself with the Confederate Army in some manner. He was said to have been arrested at his family's farm for parole violation and subsequently jailed for three days in Liberty.[13] Frank evidently decided that he could not simply watch the destruction of Missouri from the sidelines. By late May 1863, he had joined the ranks of Quantrill's guerrillas. It was during his time with the irregulars that Frank would continue the war and meet his lifelong best friend, Cole Younger.

THREE

⁓⁓⁓

Quantrill and Anderson

"You have voluntarily signified a desire to cast your fortunes with us; by so doing remember that our purpose is to tear down, lay waste, despoil and kill our enemies; mercy belongs to sycophants and emasculated soldiers, it is no part of a fighter's outfit; to us it is but a vision repugnant to our obligations and our practices."
—Said to be the Guerrilla Oath, J. W. Buel,
The Border Outlaws: An Authentic and Thrilling History of the Most Noted Bandits of Ancient or Modern Times, the Younger Brothers, Jesse and Frank James, and Their Comrades in Crime

NEIGHBOR-TO-NEIGHBOR warfare was heating up in Missouri. The animosity between the Union supporters and the Confederate sympathizers grew increasingly volatile. The militia was keenly aware of those men who had taken to the bush to serve with Quantrill and his men. Frank James's association did not go unnoticed. Union soldiers often appeared at Zerelda Samuel's farm demanding to know where Frank and his buddies were camped. They knew that the feisty and loyal Zerelda would never reveal such secrets. By making periodic visits to the farm, they let her know that the families of those fighting against the Union

26

would be subject to constant harassment until the irregulars got the message and gave up their fight. Prevailing thought seemed to be that since the men had initially been attracted to the guerrilla movement by a desire to protect their families, they would surely give up their association if they felt that the lives of their families were in danger because of their involvement. The Union representatives seriously underestimated the commitment of the irregulars. Zerelda's family would bear their secrets in silence, yet no amount of caution could keep her from castigating her enemies in no uncertain language. His mother directed Jesse to ignore the questions and goading of the soldiers, but Jesse would sometimes be overcome with the need to give them a piece of his mind as well. This would result in Jesse being roughly pushed aside, hit, or kicked. Even then the stubborn young man's pride would not allow him to keep his mouth shut and wait for the soldiers to simply tire of the game and leave.

It didn't take long for the militia to figure out that Zerelda, and probably her contemptuous son Jesse, was providing information and taking supplies to Quantrill's men. During Frank's first year with the guerrillas, a small group of soldiers appeared at the farm on May 25, 1863. They were fairly certain Zerelda would never give them the information they wanted. They decided to see what Zerelda's husband might know and perhaps divulge. Zerelda was asked once again for information regarding her son's or Quantrill's whereabouts. As usual, she had little to say, other than to lambaste the militia. The pregnant woman was jostled and shoved as the soldiers shouted obscenities at her and accused her of being a Confederate spy. The group then turned their attention to Jesse and his stepfather, both of whom they found in the fields at work. They questioned Reuben Samuel and found him equally resistant. The frustrated soldiers decided to take the game a step farther and threw a rope around Samuel's neck. Dr. Samuel was hoisted four times from the branch of a tree as his tormentors attempted to get him to tell them what they wanted to know, but he did or could not. Failing to shake loose anything from the resolute Samuel, the irritated and persistent soldiers turned to Jesse. The boy was chased through the field at bayonet point until he was finally caught. He was then thrashed to a bloody pulp with a rope. Had Jesse witnessed the

Reuben Samuel sitting under the coffee tree from which he was hanged by Union soldiers. *The Jesse James Farm*

manhandling of his mother by the militia, he probably would have been shot. Even at his young age he would not have allowed his mother to be so mistreated without rising to her defense with whatever means were available to him, even if it was his bare hands. The local soldiers were well aware of Jesse's temperament. They likely attempted to locate him before they threw a branch over a tree to hang his stepfather. As Jesse lay defeated in the field, the soldiers dragged the stricken Dr. Samuel before a hysterical Zerelda, telling her to say good-bye to her husband because she likely would not see him again. Fortunately, Dr. Samuel was found by Zerelda the next day in the Liberty jail, and he was released.[1]

The consequences of the incident would have a major impact on the James-Samuel family. The multiple hangings decreased the oxygen flow to Dr. Samuel's brain every time the rope pulled up against his carotid artery. Even after recovering from the physical trauma, his mental abilities were seriously diminished.[2]

Jesse was enraged by the events of that day. His hatred for his enemy intensified far beyond the ordinary emotions of a teenage boy. He swore that he would soon find someone within the Quantrill organization who would allow him the opportunity to avenge the atrocities to which his family had been subjected.[3]

Such treatment of their families caused an increase in the fury of the guerrillas. They confronted the militia at every opportunity with even more effective tenacity. Their enemy grew increasingly frustrated and perplexed as to how to put an end to their assaults. Union Brigadier General Thomas Ewing was finally directed to use whatever means necessary to put a stop to the guerrilla movement. Ewing thought that perhaps by undermining the guerrillas' morale with a relentless assault against their families they would realize that their opponents held the upper hand as long as they were not around to protect their interests. It was decided that a sampling of the wives, sisters, and mothers of known guerrillas would be arrested and jailed. Ewing felt that the women would not only be unable to continue to assist the guerrillas but would also serve as hostages. Josie Younger Jarrette, Caroline Younger Clayton, Sally Younger, and several of the Younger cousins were among over one hundred frightened young women who were taken into custody at Kansas City. Zerelda Samuel, along with fourteen-year-old daughter Susan and possibly five-year-old Sallie, was taken to a makeshift jail in St. Joseph. They remained there for perhaps as long as twenty-five days.[4] Zerelda must have felt that she had to do whatever it took to try to protect her family. She signed the oath of loyalty and was paroled on June 5, 1863. Reuben Samuel would support his wife's decision and sign himself on June 24.[5] All of this could not have set well with Jesse.

The guerrillas were infuriated by this latest offensive and refused to be intimidated. Fate intervened before they could devise a plan to liberate the women. On August 14, 1863, the three-story building in Kansas City where the women were being held suddenly collapsed. Though most escaped injury, several of the young women were killed. Many others were seriously hurt. The Younger sisters escaped injury, but their cousin, Charity Kerr, was killed. One of guerrilla Bill Anderson's sisters had been killed and another seriously injured during the collapse. Ander-

Susan Lavinia James Parmer, Jesse's sister. *The Armand De Gregoris Collection*

son demanded immediate deadly revenge with a wrath that would result in him soon earning the nickname Bloody Bill.

The guerrillas could not help remembering how Kansas Senator James Lane had orchestrated the disastrous assault on the town of Osceola earlier in the war as they contemplated each new attack on their families. The guerrillas held Jim Lane as responsible for the death and destruction at Osceola as they blamed Thomas Ewing for the unrestrained assaults on their families. They now decided that the tables would be turned on those who would so callously harm women, children, and noncombatants. The men of Quantrill selected Lawrence, Kansas, hometown of their enemy Jim Lane, as their next target in the escalating hostilities.

On August 19, 1863, over 450 of Quantrill's men made their move. They gathered in Johnson County, Missouri, to begin their two-day ride toward the prosperous town of Lawrence. The leaders of the group consisted of Quantrill, Bill Anderson, John Jarrette, and George Todd. Frank James and Cole Younger were present in the ranks of men who followed their leaders.

What happened in Kansas at seven o'clock on the morning of August 21 made the raid on Osceola look like child's play. A bloodcurdling rebel yell announced the arrival of some of the fiercest men ever to walk the face of the earth. The guerrillas had decided that any males remaining in the town were to die, regardless of whether they might be old men, young boys, or noncombatants. The targets were rousted from their hiding places. They were chased and thrown into the streets to be slaughtered as their mothers, wives, and children looked on in horror. Homes and businesses were relentlessly ransacked. The guerrillas whooped and cheered as they stuffed their saddlebags and loaded larger items onto the backs of their horses. The plan was to torch the town. Those who had pulled this assignment followed their orders with delight. The smell of smoke from the burning stores, public buildings, hotels, and houses was nauseating. The stench of death was even worse.

Cole Younger had been one of those who had been assigned to locate Jim Lane. Younger's efforts were in vain. Lane had bolted from his bed and run into a cornfield immediately after he heard the first rebel yell. He was able to hide and successfully elude those who pursued him. After hours of torture and depravity, the guerrillas were alerted to approaching Union troops. They gathered their booty and began their return to Missouri. Revenge had been theirs.

Frank James was only a minor player in the Lawrence incident. He never publicly discussed that day, so his exact role in the massacre is not known. What is known is that the teenager was present and an eyewitness to the horrendous events that unfolded. How what he had seen or possibly had done that day would affect the young man would remain to be seen.

It was the Union's turn to be outraged. With the cooperation of President Lincoln, Lane devised General Order #11. This order would permit Ewing to enforce the mass evacuation of all Confederate sympathizers within the border counties of Missouri. If anyone suspected of being an insurgent could prove their loyalty to the Union, they would be allowed to move their family and some of their belongings to the closest military post. Those who refused or who were not believed were to leave the area within fifteen days. Most of those who fell into this category would be forced out of their homes long before the deadline. They would watch in disbelief as their homes and farms were burned to the ground. Cole Younger's mother Bursheba was to fall victim to this retaliation. The Younger farm was destroyed. The fragile woman and five of her minor children were left homeless. Fortunately, the James-Samuel farm was located in an area outside the designated boundaries of the order. That family would only have to be subject to the continued authorized harassment by the militia.

The butchery at Lawrence did not set well with the troops or leadership of the Confederate Army. When Quantrill and most of his men returned to Texas for the winter of 1863–64, they found that they were not graciously received. There were many among the irregulars who were disgusted and guilt-ridden by what they and/or their comrades had done. Many of the men would search their souls that winter to determine if they should continue to be a party to what Quantrill and Anderson, in particular, advocated.

Watching his beloved Missouri go up in flames had to have profoundly affected the fifteen-year-old Jesse James. He grew increasingly frustrated that he was not yet considered old enough to join the guerrillas. It was no secret in his community that when the opportunity finally arrived, Jesse would grab it with both hands.

The disintegration of Quantrill's group continued down in Texas. Quantrill himself was tired of the constant battle and stress. He decided to temporarily hand over his leadership to George Todd and Bill Anderson while he spent time with his mistress in Missouri.[6] Many of the men decided to join or rejoin the Confederate Army. Since the army had for the most part moved out of Missouri, the diehard Missouri patriots decided to stick it out. They would remain with Anderson and Todd when they returned to their home state.

FOUR

꙰꙰꙰

Jesse Takes to the Bush

"Jesse James had a face as smooth and as innocent as the face of a school girl. The blue eyes—very clear and penetrating—were never at rest. His form—tall and finely molded—was capable of great endurance. On his lips there was always a smile, and for every comrade a pleasing word or compliment. Looking at his small white hands with their long tapering fingers, it was not then written or recorded that they were to be become with a revolver among the quickest and deadliest in the West."
—John Newman Edwards, *Noted Guerrillas*[1]

THERE WERE PROBLEMS and changes even within the ranks of the Confederate guerrillas by early 1864. The uncertainty on the home front was mirrored by the strife and confusion within the ranks of the irregulars. Bill Anderson was leading his own group of guerrillas after the winter of 1863–64 and was no longer taking orders from Quantrill. His determination to make the Yankees suffer had not diminished after he returned to Missouri. Bloody Bill plainly saw the hatred and fearlessness in the eyes of the young teenager who asked to be allowed to continue the fight with him. Anderson must have been delighted to enlist the services of such a committed recruit. The boy's name was Jesse James. Jesse participated in one of Anderson's skirmishes within days after joining the guerrillas. He quickly learned the dark side of battle when he was shot and seriously wounded in the right side of his chest in August of 1864. Jesse was taken to the nearby home of John Rudd to recover.[2] He was back with Anderson by September.

The personal agendas of Bill Anderson and George Todd reached a despicable low on September 27, 1864. The two leaders descended on the small Missouri town of Centralia with approximately two hundred twenty-five men that day. The guerrillas terrified the people of the town with primitive celebration. As a civilian train approached the Centralia station, Anderson gave the order to bring the train to a halt. Among the passengers on board were twenty-five unarmed Union soldiers on furlough. The soldiers were ordered off the train by Anderson's men and told to strip off their uniforms. The guerrillas confiscated the jackets and pants and awaited their next order. Anderson glared at the humiliated representatives of the hierarchy he despised. He hardheartedly ordered the men to be executed one by one where they stood. Anderson and his men returned to their encampment outside the town after leaving the soldiers dead and mutilated on the ground. Union Major A. V. E. Johnston arrived with his troops shortly after the guerrillas left Centralia. Johnston could not believe that unarmed men could be so callously eliminated. He ordered his men immediately back into the field to locate the barbarians responsible for the slaughter. When Johnston's troops met up with Anderson's, both sides wasted little time concluding that any kind of dialogue would be fruitless. Over one hundred Union soldiers lay dead after the physical confrontation that occurred that day. Anderson's men had barely been touched. It is not known for certain, but Missouri legend has it that Jesse not only participated in the combat that day but managed to make a name for himself. It has been written that he was the teenage guerrilla who fired the round that ended the life of Major Johnston. If the story is indeed true, Jesse James was already on his way to becoming a legend.

In an effort to further Jesse's wartime reputation, John Newman Edwards would later tell the story of another event that was

Jesse Woodson James, seventeen-year-old Confederate guerrilla, 1864. *The Jesse James Farm*

alleged to have taken place shortly after Centralia on November
22. Edwards recounted how Fletcher Taylor's command of
twenty-seven guerrillas, including Jesse and Frank James, encountered a Union force of thirty-two commanded by Captain
Emmett Goss somewhere near Cane Hill, Arkansas. Edwards
tells a thrilling story of how young Jesse singled out Goss and
shot him repeatedly. Jesse, wrote Edwards, paused only briefly

before quickly dispensing with Reverend U. P. Gardner, the chaplain of the Thirteenth Kansas.[3]

Jesse had been given the nickname Dingus by his guerrilla buddies sometime around the Centralia incident. He had pinched off the tip of his finger while cleaning his gun. The boy reacted to the injury by claiming that the weapon responsible for the accident was the "dodd-dingus pistol" he had ever seen. The nickname would stick to Jesse for the rest of his life.[4] Frank, in the meantime, continued to be called by his boyhood nickname of Buck.

The battle of Centralia was Anderson and Todd's last military victory. Only a few additional encounters took place between his men and the enemy before Todd was killed during an engagement near Independence in October. Anderson and his men were ambushed by Union Major S. P. Cox a week after Todd's death. Anderson was killed, although Jesse and others of the group were able to make their escape. Jesse was to remember the incident and fall of Bloody Bill with venomous accuracy. The guerrillas were forced to retreat so quickly from the scene of the conflict that the Union troops had been able to procure Anderson's body before it could be rescued by his men. The jubilant Yankees beheaded the despised rebel leader and displayed his remains. Everybody could see that Bill Anderson was now nothing but a memory.

The guerrilla forces were quickly being depleted. The irregulars returned south to rest and regroup during the winter of 1864. Frank and Jesse arrived in northeast Arkansas by November, although they did not remain together past this point. Jesse continued on to Texas with one group of guerrillas; Frank reunited with Quantrill and crossed over into west Tennessee headed toward Kentucky. Jesse remained with the band led by Dave Poole and Arch Clements. His group returned from Texas in early May.[5] Quantrill was not ready to surrender the cause. He decided to resume leadership of the troops and expand his base of operation east of Missouri in the spring of 1865. Folklore has it that he thought he might take his group to Washington and assassinate President Lincoln. The plan was to so terrorize the Union that their leaders would feel threatened enough to abandon the fight. It was a lofty plan that was never put into motion. By

May 7, Jesse's group had arrived back in Missouri. On that day they raided the Johnson County town of Holden. Shops and businesses were burned and one man was killed. The guerrillas pillaged the railroad town of Kingsville shortly after. Eight men, including four railroad teamsters, were killed there.[6] The bloodshed was not over yet.

Frank James was moving eastward through Kentucky with Quantrill during this time. After engaging in several scuffles along the way, Frank's group stopped at the farm of a Confederate sympathizer named Jeremiah Wakefield near Louisville on May 10, 1865. The men were exhausted and it had started to rain. A large group of the ragtag soldiers took refuge in Wakefield's barn and some climbed up into the hayloft to sleep. Others camped nearby. It was nearly the end of the road for Quantrill and his last remaining outfit. The men were fatigued and demoralized. Deep into their exhaustion, they failed to adequately respond to the approach of Union Captain Edwin Terrill and his men. Wakefield's farm exploded with the latest Union offense. The guerrillas were caught asleep and by surprise. They attempted to mount their horses and skeddadle off into the brush rather than try to organize an offensive. Many of them succeeded in getting away from the federals while others were not so lucky. Several of the guerrillas lay dead or wounded by the time it was over. William Clarke Quantrill fought to the end. Shooting into the onslaught of Yankee soldiers, he bolted from the barn to face his enemy. His previous good luck didn't hold. His horse reared and ran away when he attempted to mount it and join the others in their escape. Quantrill chased after his men, shouting for them to help him. Dick Glassock and Clark Hockensmith returned to Quantrill to help their distressed leader, Hockensmith attempting to pull Quantrill up on his horse. Just as a rescue looked possible, the horse was shot and reared out of control. Then it happened. Quantrill was shot in the back and fell to the ground. One of the Union soldiers rode by and fired again as he lay in the mud. This time Quantrill's right index finger was shot off. Both of his men were shot and killed as they continued to try to help him. William Clarke Quantrill was finally a prisoner of his enemies.

The guerrilla leader responded that he was Captain Clarke of the Fourth Missouri Cavalry when later questioned as to his identity. Captain Terrill then allowed the paralyzed leader to remain at Wakefield's farm. Wakefield sent for a doctor but was told shortly after the doctor's examination that the wound was fatal. Quantrill remained at Wakefield's for two days. Many people called at Wakefield's house to visit with the incapacitated Confederate hero. Terrill returned on the second day not to visit but to conduct some business. He had learned the identity of Captain Clarke as he listened to the buzz throughout the area after the skirmish at Wakefield's barn. Terrill arranged for Quantrill to be taken to the military hospital in Louisville. He died there on June 6, 1865. Those who had been with Quantrill when he had been wounded were jailed in Lexington and eventually taken to the federal penitentiary at Alton, Illinois. One of those men was Cole Younger's teenage brother Jim. Jim Younger had been with Quantrill only since the group had been in Kentucky.

Frank James was not with the group that spent the night in Wakefield's barn. Frank and his comrades had been lucky and had been able to get out of the area without a fight. They continued to elude Terrill's group and other Union troops for over a month. But they soon realized their efforts to continue would be in vain and that they had little chance for escape back to Missouri. They surrendered to the Union Army at Samuel's Depot, Kentucky, on June 26. A frustrated and beaten Frank James swore the oath of allegiance and pledged to no longer bear arms against the United States government. He and the other guerrillas were soon paroled and sent back to their families in defeat.

Jesse and the guerrillas who had remained back in Missouri with Poole and Clements were dismayed to hear of Lee's surrender at Appomattox on April 9. They knew that their time was running out, too, but refused to simply deliver themselves into the hands of their enemy. Arch Clements demanded that the Union forces within the town of Lexington surrender to him. His directive was ignored.

Union Colonel Chester Harding, commander of the District of Central Missouri, soon after received word that approximately one hundred of Clements and Poole's guerrillas wanted to surrender. Harding was told that the irregulars feared they would be killed if they did turn themselves in but felt they had little choice if they were to survive at all. Harding's officers negotiated for a peaceful submission and guarantee of safety for those who decided to come in. The order given, however, stipulated that until the guerrillas surrendered, they would be treated as the enemy. Harding then ordered the Johnson County commander to hunt and "exterminate" any guerrillas who might be in his area.[7] The guerrillas did not all agree as to how they wanted to proceed. Some just wanted to surrender and get it over with. Others wanted to leave Missouri for Mexico with their dignity intact. On May 15, a skirmish between the Third Wisconsin and a band of guerrillas occurred south of Lexington that caused some of the Union officials to believe that the request by the guerrillas was insincere.[8] It is likely that Jesse was included in the small group who took part in this offense.

By late May 1865, Jesse could no longer deny that it was time for him to give up the fight. Several years later, Jesse gave his version of the day's events to his boyhood friend, Judge Thomas Shouse. Jesse claimed he was on his way to Lexington to surrender on May 21. He and the small guerrilla group he was with were fired on by drunken Union soldiers before they had the opportunity to formally approach the Union representatives. Jesse was shot in the chest but still managed to shoot the horse of one of the soldiers. That action ended the attack. Jesse was left alone, presumably dead. He crawled to nearby Taho Creek, where he passed the night. In the morning, he was somehow able to crawl up a bank. He was seen by a farmer who helped him to the Virginia Hotel, where he was able to receive medical attention. Jesse said he knew that he had no choice but to surrender to the Union, even though he was gravely ill. He swore the oath of loyalty while lying in his sickbed.[9] There is at least some credibility to Jesse's story. His name does appear on a roster of Confederates who surrendered at Lexington.[10] Only his illness and fight for survival would be greater than the young soldier's humiliation at having to admit defeat.

The surrender of Lee, the death of Quantrill, and the surrender of the renegade units brought an end to the war in Missouri. Some of the guerrillas were not in Missouri when the last efforts to save the dying Confederacy were made. Cole Younger was making his way back to Missouri from a Confederate mission to the West Coast at the time the war ended. He was in San Jose,

California, on April 9, 1865. Younger never surrendered. Those who did only felt compromised. The promise contained in the terms of surrender meant little for the men who had felt that they had no choice but to take the oath if they were to stay alive. The events of the past five years would remain locked in their psyches forever. For many, if not most, the war would continue to rage in their hearts and souls for the rest of their lives.

The people of Missouri were exhausted and overwhelmed. They had suffered violent conflicts and witnessed savage combat almost daily. Their lives would never be the same. Their families had been crippled by loss and emotional and physical injuries. Their farms had been demolished and their lifestyles destroyed. The futures of the people of the borderland were clouded and uncertain. Apprehension and fear dominated their every waking moment as they attempted to look ahead to tomorrow. Their options seemed few and any forecast for happiness indeterminate. An infertile wasteland awaited those returning to their homes from the exiles forced upon them by General Order #11. The men had been unable to provide income during their absence and had little or no seed money to restart farming operations. Their economic suffering was almost as great as their personal grief at the events to which they had been subjected. The Union claimed that the Confederate sympathizers were the ones who should be punished, yet those who had supported the federal government were made to suffer as well. The productive power of Missouri had essentially been fractured for all citizens. The once-bountiful fields had been destroyed, and few people had the money to spend to rebuild the economy or ease the problem. Institutions and wealthy individuals from the Northeast descended on the state. They offered financing to those farmers who could qualify and who were willing to pay outrageous interest on restorative loans. These men were called carpetbaggers for the carpet-covered, money-laden valises they carried. Bankers and individual loan sharks signed outrageous contracts with the desperate families whereby farms could be rebuilt and families fed. The reestablishment of the communities would take some time. The people of western Missouri struggled to find the money to both pay the interest rates to their lenders and come up with the money necessary to plant their crops. They may have been conquered on paper, but they would not allow their enemy to conquer their spirit. The pioneer essence of the Missourians enabled them to lift their heads high. They dedicated themselves to reconstructing their lives on the land that they had learned to hold in such great regard. They would not be defeated.

No one was surprised at the regulations and restraints that were placed on Confederate sympathizers by the victorious Union. It was proclaimed by the Missouri legislature through the Drake Constitution in 1865 that those known to have Southern sympathies or who had participated in the armed conflict could not vote, hold public office of any kind, nor be employed in any professional position. There would be no amnesty for those who had taken up arms against the United States government. These restrictions made life even more difficult for those who chose to stay in Missouri and try to rebuild their lives. Few of those who attempted to restore their farms would be allowed to supplement their incomes with jobs outside agriculture. They would also have no voice in the affairs of their community. Some things did not change. The militia continued to harass its former enemies. Those who had fought with the Confederate Army or irregular groups were threatened by the possibility of arrest and imprisonment regardless of whether or not they had taken the oath of loyalty and been paroled. Not only did this hamper economic progress, it angered and frustrated the farmers even more.

Many of those who had served the Union during the conflict believed that the Southern sympathizers actually were being treated far better than they should expect. Many people were resentful enough to believe that it would have been completely within bounds for the Union leaders to order the execution of any and all of those who had served the Confederacy. The people of western Missouri continued to be at war.

Zerelda and Reuben Samuel had been driven out of their Clay County home during the final months of the war. They had taken their family to live near Zerelda's brother in Rulo, Nebraska.[11] They had a good idea what punishment would await the conquered Southern protesters. Zerelda taught one term of school in nearby Burt County once she was safe in Rulo. Nebraska folklore speculates that Dr. Samuel attempted to start a medical practice while there.[12] The family would wait and watch until they felt it was safe for them to return home to their beloved Missouri.

Frank James traveled west from Kentucky after his parole and reunited with his family in Nebraska. On June 13, 1862, friends had seen to it that Jesse was taken by steamboat to the boarding house of his uncle, John Mimms, in Harlem, Missouri. Mimms was a Kentuckian who had traveled down the Ohio, Mississippi, and Missouri Rivers to make his home across the river from Westport Landing, the site of the future Kansas City. Mimms and his wife Mary had been the family who raised young Robert James. The couple would now care for Robert's son as he lay broken and ill. Eventually it was decided that Jesse could be moved, and so he joined his family in Rulo on July 15. Jesse's lung wound was serious. It was not known if he would recover enough to ever leave Nebraska. Jesse remained with his family for about six weeks. His mother assured him that he would get better in time, but Jesse grew increasingly despondent. He was certain that he was going to die. Jesse finally convinced his mother that if he was not going to recover, he wanted to return to Missouri. Zerelda Samuel reluctantly agreed that no harm would likely come from the trip and that Jesse might actually benefit by being back in the state that he loved. The rest of the family would soon return home to their farm in Clay County.

Jesse's prostrate body was placed on a boat that then made its way down the Missouri River to Kansas City. Jesse was returned to the home of Mary and John Mimms on August 26. The Mimms assigned their twenty-year-old daughter Zerelda Amanda the task of caring for her cousin Jesse's daily needs while he was recuperating. Zerelda was a quiet young woman who demonstrated a great deal of compassion and tenderness as she sat with Jesse and anticipated his every need. Jesse fondly bestowed the nickname Zee upon his nurse, cousin, and friend since she shared the same name as his mother. Jesse continued to suffer periods of deep depression that were brought on by his illness and the fear that he would never recover. Zee rarely left his bedside. She continually encouraged Jesse to draw on his faith and keep up his spirits.[13]

Jesse remained with the Mimms family from August until late October 1865. Zee and Jesse spent many days sharing their hopes and dreams for their future individual lives. They soon found their feelings for each other growing beyond the love of one cousin for another. Jesse realized that he was in love with Zee Mimms and she with him. By the time his aunt felt that it was physically safe for Jesse to return home to the James-Samuel farm in Clay County, Jesse had made a pledge to Zee. He swore that someday, when things were better for him, he would make her his wife.

By November 1865, Jesse had finally been reunited with Zerelda, Frank, and the family when they arrived back in Missouri. Jesse was much healthier than he had been when they had last seem him in Nebraska. Although he was still a long way from complete recovery, his health continued to improve and he grew stronger. Frank helped Reuben Samuel rebuild their farm, and Jesse helped with whatever chores he was able to handle. Jesse and Frank spent most of their free time exchanging war stories and enjoying each other's company. They also enjoyed the attention they received from their family. Their sixteen-year-old sister, Susan James, doted on her older brothers. Their Samuel half-sisters, seven-year-old Sallie and two-year-old Fannie Quantrill, loved to have the young men play with and fuss over them. Four-year-old John Samuel idolized his two big brothers. Zerelda was pregnant with her fourth son, Archie Peyton, by the time Jesse arrived home. The James-Samuel farm was somewhat peaceful for the first time in many years.

Having suffered his near-death experience, Jesse decided that it was time he was formally baptized. He had been attending the Baptist Church in Kearney and had joined that congregation shortly after his return home.[14] Jesse spent a lot of his time studying the Bible and attempting to be the good neighbor his father had been. He soon learned to quote the Good Book randomly and would often extol the virtues of his maker to family and friends alike. He enjoyed the company of those in the area who had returned to take up where they all had left off. The people of Clay County attempted to put the war behind them and rebuild their lives. Even so, the former Confederate farmers were visited on numerous occasions by the militia and those wishing to continue the harassment. It was no secret that the James boys had been with the Quantrill organization, and they were subject to more than one threat of lynching from those who had supported the Union. Jesse and Frank would take to the fields or hide up in the farmhouse loft when an unwanted posse appeared. Zerelda berated the soldiers for badgering her boys and advised them that it would be best if the family were allowed to exist in peace. Although they initially attempted to make light of their situation, the constant threats and harassment began to irritate Frank and Jesse. They did not like it at all that they were made to feel unwanted in their own community. They had, after all, technically surrendered. They felt that they should be allowed to live on their farm in armistice as long as they were no threat to their neighbors or the new government. They had never forgiven their enemies, but at least they were making efforts to live with them. But the Yankees continued to make it hard for them. Their patience and tolerance, not at an all-time high to begin with, eventually gave out. Their previous animosity returned, and their hostility intensified when the harassment continued. They felt that the persecution was neither fair nor right. Something would have to be done to stop it. Frank and Jesse had lived lives of excitement and adventure the past few years. The two young men now had many long and boring hours to ponder the fate of their enemies whether or not those enemies were real or imagined. Frank and Jesse planted and plowed the fields and attended to their daily chores. But as they did, they privately discussed ways in which their adversaries could be punished. Eventually, they came to the conclusion that the ordeal and distress that they and their family had suffered would be avenged.

FIVE

〜〜〜〜

A Town Called Liberty

"The other robber had me in tow outside the vault and demanded the Greenbacks. I pointed to a tin box on the table and told him they were in that box. He hoisted the lid of the box, took out Greenbacks 7/30 and UM bonds and told the robber in the vault to put them in the sack and to be in a hurry."

—Greenup Bird's statement given after the Liberty bank robbery,
February 1866

BY JANUARY 1866, the people of Missouri had still not been able to dig their way out from beneath the rubble of the war. They tended to their farms and attempted to rebuild their lives, but the former Confederate sympathizers continued to be domineered and harassed. For the most part, they accepted that they had lost the war. They knew they would be subject to the demands of the winner. Since the winner claimed to have fought the war for their mutual country's unity, the loser did not understand why continued hostility was allowed to dominate their every move. In Clay County as elsewhere, the carpetbaggers thrived and brought huge amounts of Yankee dollars into the community. A great deal of it was sitting in the Clay County Savings Association.

It is impossible to say who first had the idea to rob the Clay County Savings Bank. It has been accepted folklore in years past that not only did Jesse James make his first appearance as a bank robber there but also that the robbery was his brainchild. It seems unlikely that Jesse was well enough to travel to the bank and endure the necessary escape. It does seem credible that he was in on the planning. Jesse and Frank's anger against their former enemies increased as they watched the struggle of so many of their neighbors. They continued to feel the sting of defeat. It annoyed them that their mother and their family continued to be hounded by small groups of militia who periodically showed up looking for them. Somewhere along the line they decided that they were not going to take the continued persecution without fighting back. They looked some ten miles south of their farm to the town of Liberty.

Jesse was still weak as he continued to heal, but that didn't stop him from spending a lot of time rehashing the war and expressing his hate for the Northerners to Frank and members of his family.[1] Frank was not as verbal, but he apparently felt the same loathing as his brother. Frank had kept in touch with his guerrilla friend Cole Younger. Younger was another young man driven toward revenge for the atrocities his family suffered at the hands of the Union. It seems most likely that Jesse, Frank, and Cole somehow formulated the plan to rob the Liberty bank, then recruited the manpower to make the raid successful.[2]

No records seem to exist of Jesse or Frank James having been involved with the law prior to February 1866. William A. Pinkerton wrote in his 1907 book that an incident occurred during "1865–1866" in which the boys were arrested. Pinkerton claimed that Jesse, Frank, Clell Miller, Jim Poole, and George White had some drinks at Meffert's saloon and fired their revolvers outside while acting "like a lot of Indians." Pinkerton declared that "Sheriff Rickerts" arrested them, had them arraigned at the courthouse, and threw them in the county jail.[3] No substantiation has been found for this allegation, however.

Whether Jesse alone, Jesse and Frank, or Jesse and Frank together with Cole Younger thought of the idea to rob the bank, the notion took root. A plan was put into action. The men who had ridden with Quantrill continued to be friendly, and the guer-

rilla network of information remained intact. Most of the guerrillas retained a high degree of bitterness over the events of the
past few years. They continued to be frustrated by the restrictions
that had been placed on them by the new government. Additionally, these were men who had lived with their lives in jeopardy and the heated rush of adrenaline every day for over three
or four years. There had been no stimulation like the excitement
of battle for some time. Many of the guerrillas were frustrated
and bored tending to their farms. When the leaders of the Liberty
robbery brought some of them an adventurous plan, it didn't take
much to get them to say yes to participating.

The selection of the Clay County Savings Association as the
target for the first peacetime bank robbery is interesting. If the
James boys were indeed the masterminds, it was within their
county but far enough away to allow them an escape. Reverend
James had been well known in Liberty and various parts of Clay
County, yet his sons had stuck pretty much to the area around
Kearney since they had returned home from the war. They likely
wouldn't be recognized in Liberty if they took some precautions.
They would be able to get back to their farm easily and unnoticed. Another factor that may have been a part of the selection
process was the fact that the town square was known to the
guerrilla movement from two events in its recent history. A band
of forty guerrillas led by Colonel Ben Parker had held the town
of Liberty for several hours in March 1862. It would also have
been remembered that a public meeting was held in Liberty in
July 1864. At that time some prominent Clay Countians denounced the guerrilla movement by calling those who participated in it "monsters of society." Only those who were involved
knew why Liberty was chosen, but once the target was selected,
the plan described, and the recruits in place, the game was on.

At 2:00 on the cloudy afternoon of February 13, 1866, a non-
chalant group of young men numbering between ten and fourteen
rode into Liberty's square. A few more waited outside town. The
men wore assorted pieces of Union Army clothing such as pants
and jackets. The only thing that could be presumed from their
apparel was that due to their ages, the men had likely served as
soldiers. It was a cold, wintry day, and not too many people
were on the street. A trial was in session inside the Liberty

Courthouse. Those who had been in town who had not hurried home to escape an imminent snowstorm were inside observing the proceedings. No one became suspicious of the riders. Several of the men dismounted from their horses near the bank and stood talking quietly among themselves. Two men who were later described as being tall entered the bank. They wore blue soldier's overcoats. It is probable that these two men were Frank James and Cole Younger.

The two men nodded a greeting at Cashier Greenup Bird and his son William who were both at work at their desks. One of the men warmed himself in front of the stove. The other approached the counter and announced that he wanted to change a bill. William Bird left his desk to help the customer. Before another word was exchanged, a revolver was shoved in young Bird's face. The second man drew his revolver and jumped over the counter. The Birds were directed to keep quiet and do as they were told. It was then demanded that the clerks quickly hand over all of the money in the bank. William Bird hesitated to obey the directive and was hit in the back with a pistol. He was then shoved inside the vault and ordered to place all coin in a proffered wheat sack. The other robber trained his gun on Greenup Bird as the captive watched him grab paper currency and shove it into the sack. A tin box full of government bonds was soon discovered by this bandit. Those went into the sack as well. When the two bandits determined that there was nothing left for them to steal, they ordered Greenup Bird to enter the vault where his son was standing. Bird claimed, "He told me that if I did not go in instantly he would shoot me down."[4] The door was slammed closed with the two clerks left inside in the dark. The robbers quickly left the bank to join their associates in the street.

The robbers had failed to secure the lock on the door of the vault in their haste to leave the building. Greenup and William Bird pushed open the door and ran to the window yelling that the bank had been robbed. Two young men, S. H. Holmes and college student George "Jolly" Wymore, were walking down the sidewalk across the square. They heard the call from the window of the bank. One of the bandits noticed the boys and fired a warning shot. He yelled to them to stay where they were.

Cashier's desk inside the Liberty bank. *The author*

Whether by accident or on purpose, Jolly Wymore was shot and killed as he stood frozen to the spot in front of the Green House hotel. Shots were also fired at Holmes. Holmes barely escaped being seriously injured when the bullet tore a hole through his coat. By then, the entire group had mounted their horses. The command was given to withdraw from the square. The robbers headed east down Franklin Street in a thunderous retreat, shouting the familiar rebel yell.

The compensation for the short, illegal visit to Liberty was some $60,000 in currency and bonds. Three bags of silver and gold that had been placed in the bank for safekeeping had been taken as well. Those who had participated now held more money than they had seen in the past five years. There had been few eyewitnesses, yet speculation about who may have been involved ran rampant. Some of those subsequently named were former guerrillas Oliver Shepard, Bud and Donny Pence, Frank Gregg, James Wilkerson, Joab Perry, Bill Wilkenson, Ben Cooper, Red Monkers, and John Jarrette. Another man mentioned as possibly being involved was Allen Parmer, the future brother-in-law of the James brothers. Most of these men were from Clay or Jackson County. Only years later would it be speculated that Cole Younger and Jesse James had anything to do with the robbery and that Frank and Cole were the men who had gone inside the bank.

It remains debatable as to whether or not Jesse was well enough to participate in the robbery, even if he was one of those who planned it. It does seem likely that Jesse and his brother at least concocted the plan. Jesse's personality would not allow him to idly observe while Frank and Cole hatched so ingenious a scheme. He would have been compelled to offer his two cents at the least. Cole Younger later maintained that he did not even know Jesse at that time except by reputation and from the stories of Frank. Younger claimed in his autobiography that he met Jesse for the first time at a meeting at Blue Springs, Missouri. Attorneys from Independence had offered to defend, free of charge, anyone having anything to do with the raid on Lawrence. Jesse's attendance at such a meeting would have been peculiar, as Jesse had not been present at Lawrence. Younger's remarks as to Jesse's physical condition at the time of the Liberty robbery may have been more accurate: ''. . . when I saw him [Jesse] early in the summer of 1866 he was still suffering from the shot through the lung he had received in the last battle in Johnson County in May, 1865.''[5] It is very possible that even if he had a great desire to be present and involved in the Liberty holdup, Jesse was just not strong enough to make the ride.

It was reported in the *Liberty Tribune* on February 16 that after leaving Liberty, several of the men crossed the Missouri River by ferry. Others headed in the opposite direction. A snowstorm began almost simultaneously with the outlaws' exit from town, and their tracks were soon obliterated. Frank James's absence from the Kearney area was not noted. It is possible that he returned home to the farm almost immediately after the robbery. He would undoubtedly have been eager to share the details of the escapade with Jesse as soon as possible and to present his brother with his share of the haul. It was never determined who killed Jolly Wymore. Several of those whom speculation placed in the band of robbers that day were virulent, unpredictable men. Killing a civilian had probably not been part of the plan, but these were men who were trained to immediately react when threatened. If, on the other hand, the shooting of Wymore had been deliberate, there were certainly a few of the suspects who would have been capable of cold-blooded murder if it suited their needs. Regardless, the guerrillas stuck to their code of silence and alliance. The name of the man who shot Jolly Wymore would be a secret held forever and known only to those who had been there.

A former Union captain named Garth came upon the scene after the outlaws left Liberty. He immediately formed a posse of approximately thirty men to chase after the robbers. Another twenty to thirty men followed the original group when they could assemble. The robbers were well on their way by that time and were able to cross the Missouri River well ahead of the posse. It was obvious they were well versed in quick and efficient departures. Because of the snow, there could be no real pursuit. The men recrossed the river near Sibley when it was safe. Again, according to the *Liberty Tribune*, they rode northwest to the Mount Gilead Church to divide the money that had been taken from the bank. It was an interesting touch that the spoils of the robbery were taken to the Mt. Gilead Church if Frank and Jesse James had indeed been involved in the planning of the robbery. Mt. Gilead had been on Reverend James's circuit. Were the

James boys avenging themselves in the name of their devout Christian father?

A $5,000 reward for the apprehension of the robbers was immediately offered by the Clay County Savings Association. The Liberty Savings Association and Clay County Sheriff James M. Jones kicked in an additional $2,000. Warrants were issued within the next few days for the arrest of Aaron Book, William Easter, and James Couch: three men who were likely nowhere near Liberty that day. Why these three men were named as suspects is anyone's guess, as none of the eyewitnesses claimed to have recognized any of the bandits. R. L. Raymond later stated that no one in the posse knew the identity of any of the men being chased.[6] Posse members David Duncan of Cedarville and Captain Minter of Liberty both claimed that they recognized Frank James and Bud Pence but later said they could not be certain.[7] Warrants were not issued for James and Pence. Couch was arrested within a short period of time but was almost immediately released due to insufficient evidence. Apparently, it was then obvious that Book and Easter were not involved, either, as they were never charged with the crime.

Popular speculation was that the robbers had obviously been some of Quantrill and Anderson's men. The citizens of Liberty named guerrillas whom they felt might have been capable of such an act. The list of suspects grew to include Anderson Tate, Jim White, Bill Chiles, J. F. Edmundson, Arch Clements, George Shepard, Dick Burns, William Clay, Arnold Foster, Bill Ryan, Andy McGuire, Jim Anderson, L. S. Smith, and Payne Jones. Nearly two dozen men were now suspected of a crime in which only twelve to thirteen robbers had originally been counted. Several of the men mentioned as possibly having been involved, including Wilkerson, Gregg, and Monkers, gave sworn statements as to their whereabouts the day of the robbery. Joab Perry escaped from the Independence jail where he was being held on another charge. The others apparently stayed out of sight until the authorities all but admitted that it was impossible to know who had been in the square that day. Any further investigation of the matter was dropped.

The cash had been divided at Mt. Gilead. The bonds were apparently awarded to Cole Younger and Frank. Younger later wrote that he was visiting his great-uncle in Howard County the day of the robbery. He admitted however that "At one point I was happy to cash bonds given to me by friends who had not had the opportunity to cash them. I never knew where the bonds came from as I never asked it of the friends who had given them to me to cash."[8] Frank made no public alibi. Younger cashed the bonds throughout the Midwest and East over the next few years. Only once before when a Vermont bank had been robbed by Confederates during the war had such a robbery occurred during the day. The robbery at Liberty, Missouri, was definitely a precedent.

SIX

⌒⌒⌒

Copycats

"Who of these men, if any, were guilty will most likely never be known, but it seems that eventually all settled down to the belief that the Jameses and Youngers were not concerned in it, though at first almost universally suspected."

—Frank Triplett,
The Life, Times and Treacherous Death of Jesse James

THE LIBERTY ROBBERY certainly grabbed the attention of the people of western Missouri. The brazen and defiant pillaging of the bank was a hot topic of conversation throughout the state for months to come. Frank James made no public statement about the events at Liberty, although he obviously knew that speculation as to his participation might be less if he was not in the Clay or Jackson County area. In June, Frank set off to visit family in Kentucky until the excitement from the robbery diminished. His trip would not be an uneventful one. Frank had an altercation with four federal soldiers near the town of Bradenburg. Guns were quickly drawn and the quarrel rapidly escalated into bloodshed. Frank was alone, yet he managed to kill two of the soldiers and wound a third. The fourth soldier man-

55

aged to shoot Frank in the joint of the left hip before the fracas
had ended.[1] Frank was able to make it to the home of his uncle,
George Hite. Once there, he asked his aunt and uncle to send
for his brother. Jesse was still quite weak from his own injury,
but he rushed to Frank's side. Jesse stayed with his brother until
the fall while Frank recovered.

John Jarrette evidently had money from the robbery. Jarrette
bid on a parcel of land that was offered at auction by a bank in
Lexington, Missouri. He was unsuccessful in obtaining the property. Jarrette and his brother-in-law, Cole Younger, then decided
to become partners in a cattle venture. Younger would drive the
cattle south into southern Kansas and Louisiana while Jarrette
remained in Missouri with his family. It seems that Jarrette may
have had plans of his own.

The prosperous riverside town of Lexington, Missouri, was
visited by another group of strangers eight months after the Liberty robbery. About 12:30 P.M. on October 30, 1866, two of the
men entered the banking house of Alexander Mitchell and Company. One of the men asked to have a bill changed while the
other chuckled and wondered aloud what the "discount" on it
might be. The men made cashier J. L. Thomas uncomfortable,
and he decided that he did not want to do business with them.
Thomas informed his would-be customers that the bank was not
presently buying such funds. Two other men entered at this time
and immediately approached Thomas. They pointed their revolvers at Thomas's heart and demanded $100,000. One of them
told Thomas that they knew the bank had the funds on hand.
They wanted the key to the vault. The cashier claimed he did
not have the key. The robbers threatened to kill him if he would
not comply with their order. Thomas coolly informed them that
even if they were to shoot him, they would not find a key. The
frustrated bandits eventually came to the conclusion that the
cashier wasn't lying, and they set about ransacking drawers.
They found a little over $2,000. The men grabbed the money
and calmly left the bank. They mounted the horses they had left
tethered in a nearby alley and headed out of town as unobtru-
sively as they had entered.[2]

Thomas gave the alarm and watched as a posse was formed
within minutes. Interestingly, four of the locals who responded

to the call first were former guerrillas: John and Dave Poole, Jesse Hamlett, and Hedge Reynolds. The posse returned after only a short time. They claimed that the robbers had disappeared into the countryside. Questions were raised by bank officials and some of the citizens of Lexington about the legitimacy of the posse since John and Dave Poole were two of the most dedicated of Quantrill's men. The observation was made that the posse had not seemed too eager to catch the robbers. It seemed a good possibility that the robbers might have been their former colleagues. It was suggested that perhaps the Pooles had been in on the robbery. The four men who rode in the posse had been seen before and during the robbery casually standing near or in view of the bank.[3] It was possible that the Poole brothers had led the posse so that they could control the makeup of those who would inevitably chase the bandits.

As before, the men were not recognized. The speculation as to who it was that robbed the bank at Lexington was as futile as had been the suppositions made in Liberty. Who committed the robbery can only be theorized since no one was ever charged with the crime. John Jarrette had possibly been present at Liberty and so was no stranger to bank robbery. If Cole Younger had been one of the men who had entered the Clay County Savings Association, it is likely that he discussed the technique with his brother-in-law. Jarrette would have had a motive if the Alexander Mitchell and Company Bank was the bank that had denied him a loan. Jarrette may have decided to create his own gang while Younger was out of the area, since he had served as one of Quantrill's lieutenants all those years and was adept at plotting strategies. Many of the men who may have been present at the Liberty robbery were used to following his command. The name of guerrilla leader George Shepard has also been mentioned over time as a possible participant. It was never determined whether or not the Poole boys were in on the scheme. It remains a distinct possibility that they were somehow attached to the event given the fact that they were former guerrillas. As to the involvement of Jesse, Frank, and Cole Younger at Lexington, their presence does not seem likely. It is possible that Jarrette planned the robbery and asked the three of them to participate. That theory would place Jarrette, Younger, and Frank and Jesse James as the robbers. Jesse would likely have been quite disappointed to have missed the Liberty robbery. It is possible that he could have executed another plan when he was well enough to actively participate. But Jesse had not ridden under Jarrette and would have wanted to be the leader himself. More importantly, Jesse was exhausted and weak when he returned from taking care of Frank in Kentucky. His own wound had begun to hemorrhage, and Jesse's health briefly took a turn for the worse after his arrival back in Clay County. It does not seem likely that Jesse would have planned and executed a second robbery without including his brother Frank at that point in time. It doesn't seem plausible that Frank had recovered enough from his Brandenburg injury at that point to ride with his brother into Lexington. If Jesse and Frank were involved, however, it is likely that Cole Younger was as well. Younger would have been willing to once again collaborate with his close friend Frank James and his respected brother-in-law Jarrette on a second robbery. Then again, Younger may have been out of the state cashing some of the Liberty bonds at this time. While it certainly is possible that the four robbers may have been Jesse, Frank, Cole Younger, and John Jarrette, it doesn't seem likely.

Jesse was definitely home at his mother's farm in Clay County on the night of February 18, 1867, regardless of whether or not he was one of the robbers at Lexington. Winters were hard on him. Jesse was often bothered by congestion and breathing problems brought on by the weakness in his lung from his wartime wound. He often felt lethargic and on many nights would retire early. Such was the case on one particular evening. Five men appeared on the porch of the James-Samuel farmhouse and demanded to be let in according to an account Jesse gave later. Reuben Samuel asked the men what they wanted and they insisted he open the door. Jesse looked out the window of his loft. Even in the dusk of the night he could see the calvary saddles on the strangers' horses. This clearly identified the men as militia. It only took Jesse a second or two to figure out that the men were looking for him. The soldiers knew that enough time had passed that Jesse had likely been alerted to their purpose. They began to beat on the door with their rifles. They commanded Jesse to surrender. Jesse grabbed his revolvers and silently crept down from the loft. The soldiers were taken completely by surprise when Jesse fired a revolver through the door. One of the soldiers was critically wounded where he stood on the porch. Jesse then threw open the door. He fired both revolvers into the cluster of men who had gathered on the porch. Two more of the men were wounded. A fourth was killed as he ran down the front steps. The group picked up their fallen associate and fled into the yard. They scrambled to mount their horses and escape from the young man who refused to be abducted from his home. When the men were out of sight, Jesse grabbed a horse himself and left the farm. He knew that the militia would be back in the morning.[4]

John Jarrette might also have been the mastermind for the next robbery that occurred in Missouri. At least six men were involved this time. From the way the events unfolded, it seems that some of them might have been involved in such an adventure for the first time. On March 2, 1867, robbers entered the private banking house of Judge John McClain in Savannah, Missouri, and demanded the key to the vault from McClain. The intrepid old judge refused the order. He pushed past the would-be bandits in an attempt to break a window and alert the town that he was being robbed. He was promptly shot in the chest. The frustrated gang panicked. They fled the building empty-handed.[5]

Cole Younger wrote, ''. . . the five who did this were identified, and there were no Younger boys in the party.''[6] Younger didn't say who the identified men were. R. McDaniels, Robert Pope, and someone known as Fitzgerald were believed to be suspects in the robbery, according to the *Liberty Tribune*, yet no warrants were issued.[7] Who these men were is uncertain as none of these names appear in any of the guerrilla rosters. Jim White, Bill Chiles, J. F. Edmunson, Arch Clements, Oliver and George Shepard, and Bud McDaniels have been mentioned as possible suspects by several authors, but there has been no substantiation of their involvement. It is unlikely that Frank or Jesse James had anything to do with the robbery if it is a fact that Cole Younger did not participate. This robbery may have been thought up by John Jarrette and his gang, but it's also quite possibile that Jarrette wasn't involved whatsoever. The robbery may have been inspired by the Liberty robbery but with an entirely different cast of characters. Judge McClain evidently survived his wound. Who it was that shot him remains an unanswered question.

The vengeful thefts were far from over. The next robbery to take place in Missouri seems most certainly not to have been the work of the James boys and Cole Younger. As few as eleven and as many as twenty men were involved in the attempted robbery of the Hughes & Wasson Bank in Richmond.

At about 3:30 on the afternoon of May 22, 1867, a group of strangers entered the town of Richmond from the east. They traveled down three different streets: South Main, College Street, and North Main. They stopped in front of the M. E. Church South and all but one dismounted.[8] Bookkeeper Willis Warriner looked up to see four men enter the Hughes & Wasson Bank shortly afterward. It didn't take Warriner long to determine that the strangers were up to no good. The bookkeeper rushed to the vault, but a shot was fired at him before he could shut the door. Warriner fell to the floor. He remained there throughout the following ordeal, even though he was uninjured. The men directed cashier George Wasson to open the vault and hand over the money as they kept an eye on Warriner. Thirty-five hundred dollars was delivered. Robert Sevier, Ben Chipeze, and Ephraim January, who were evidently customers, observed the proceedings while held at gunpoint. The outlaw who had remained on horseback reined his mount in a circle outside the bank. In this way he was able to see in every direction as he fired into the air to keep the citizens of the town away from the area. Nonetheless, the robbers were fired upon as they left the building. Mayor John B. Shaw was one of the first men to arrive at the bank. Within seconds, he lay facedown in the dirt with a fatal bullet in his chest. Frank S. Griffin fired from behind a tree in the courthouse yard. When the mounted robber spotted Griffin, he was shot through the head. As town jailer William Griffin tried to drag his son Frank away from the area under siege, he was viciously shot in the forehead. There would be no consideration of those who attempted to stop the robbery this time.[9]

Deputy Sheriff Tom Reyburn and his posse chased the robbers south. They got close enough at one point to exchange fire. The outlaws were soon out of sight as they split into two groups near the Missouri River. One group of the robbers crossed the Missouri River near Sibley while the other headed east. The posse was able to get close to one faction of the gang near the Holt Station of the Hannibal & St. Joseph railroad. One of the bandits' horses was shot, but they all managed to escape. They were not seen again.[10]

There had been too many witnesses this time. If names could be joined with the faces, arrests could be made. A horse thief named Felix Bradley bragged from his jail cell that he knew the identities of the Richmond bank robbers. The local law enforcement considered this flimsy information yet issued warrants for eight men. Those named were former guerrillas Payne Jones, Dick Burns, Ike Flannery, Andy McGuire, Tom Little, James and John White, and Allan Parmer.[11]

The number of bandits would naturally affect the take of each man. Jesse, Frank, and Cole were all quick studies. They could see how easily a robbery could be accomplished with just a couple of men. It doesn't seem too probable that they would have reverted back to the use of such a large gang. The additional risks that existed when so many were involved far outweighed the amusement a large group of bored guerrillas could have bragging about their exploits. As events unfolded, it was demonstrated that the robbers this time were careless and seemingly without a plan. They were quite unlike the demonstrated personalities of Cole Younger and the James boys. Jesse was likely in Nashville, Tennessee, when the Richmond bank was robbed. Jesse had arrived in Tennessee some time in late May or early June to have his lung examined and treated by Dr. Paul Eve. On his way back home, Jesse stopped in Kentucky to visit family. He probably didn't return to Missouri until November, long after the Richmond robbery.[12]

Allan Parmer had been seeing Susan James. Folklore relates that Susan's brother Jesse did not like Parmer nor did he want Parmer involved in his sister's life. This seems unlikely, as Parmer was one of Jesse's guerrilla comrades, and it is probable that Parmer was involved in the Liberty robbery with Frank James. Also, Jesse continued to associate with Parmer until Jesse's death. Parmer immediately let it be known that he was not present in Richmond on May 22. He sent a letter to the editor of the *Missouri Democrat*. The letter claimed that Parmer knew nothing of the robbery and was at work in the employ of J. E. Shawhan & Co. when the robbery occurred. Included with his letter was an affidavit from Shawhan supporting his claim.[13]

Most of the others who had been named either didn't have a good alibi or simply did not have the time or opportunity to produce one. A posse in search of Payne Jones was led by Captain P. J. Miserez. Information led them to the house of Jones's father-in-law near Independence. When Miserez and his posse arrived there at 6:00 in the morning, Jones charged from the house, blasting away with a double-barreled shotgun. A member of the posse named B. H. Williamson was fatally wounded. An eight-year-old girl was killed in the cross fire. The posse pursued Jones as he ran through the cornfields. He was shot in the shoulder when at one point he lost his footing. Jones managed to disappear into the foliage and escape capture, even though he was wounded. The posse decided to continue their search and located Jones several weeks later. He was immediately lynched.[14]

The people of Richmond were furious that a bank in their town had been held up and three innocent men killed. A $500 reward per robber was offered by the sheriff of the county. The bank officials posted a reward in the amount of the money taken from the bank. Missouri officials offered $300 for each of the bandits. Every man known to have been with the guerrilla movement was suspect as the authorities gathered information that might lead them to the perpetrators of the crime. Two of the first to be arrested were Tom Little and a friend of his named Fred Meyers. The authorities in Johnson County charged the two men with participating in the Richmond robbery in addition to other crimes. While Little and Meyers were being held in jail in Warrensburg, friends of Little were quick to come to his defense. They presented affidavits that certified that Little had been in Dover at the time of the robbery. This enraged some of the people of Warrensburg and a mock trial was held. Little and Meyers were both promptly lynched. The same fate awaited Felix Bradley when he was eventually found and jailed. Andy McGuire was arrested in St. Louis, but no one was able to identify him as one of the robbers when he was returned to Richmond for trial. Bud Pence was arrested in July when cashier George Wasson said that Pence was in on the robbery. Pence claimed that he had been living in Kentucky since 1865 and was subsequently released. The search for the robbers then took a peculiar turn. The body of Dick Burns was found laying wrapped in a blanket in a field near Independence on November 22. His head had been crushed. Former guerrilla Jim Chiles was named as a possible suspect in Burns's murder.[15]

Another robbery took place on November 27, 1867, at the banking house of P. Roberts in Independence. Two men entered the bank and pointed their guns at the president. They demanded he give them the contents of the vault. The president and the teller were then locked in the vault as the robbers made their escape. Former guerrilla Jim Cummins later claimed that Jim White was present.[16] It is possible that Cummins himself was one of the robbers. A local newspaper account suggested that a man named Jim Devers was involved in the Independence event. Andy McGuire informed authorities in Richmond that Devers was involved in that town's robbery. McGuire told the sheriff that Devers could be found in Crab Orchard, Kentucky. A posse soon arrested Devers there. After his arrest, Devers foolishly admitted to having been involved in illegal activities, yet he vehemently denied being in on the Richmond robbery. Nonetheless, Devers was taken to Richmond and thrown into a cell with McGuire. A vigilante group forcibly removed McGuire and Devers from their cell at midnight on March 17 and hanged them.[17] The White brothers fared much better than the others who were mentioned as suspects. They were able to evade the authorities completely and were never caught.

SEVEN

⌒⌒⌒

Back in Business

"Having served in Kentucky with Quantrill, Jim Younger and Frank James were well known through that state, and it being known that the previous bank robberies in Missouri were charged to ex-guerrillas, similar conclusions were at once drawn by the Louisville sleuths who were put on the case."
—Cole Younger, *Cole Younger by Himself*

FRANK, JESSE, AND Cole Younger no doubt paid keen attention to the aftermath of the Richmond robbery. Most of the men who had been made to answer for the sacking of the Hughes & Wasson Bank were friends of theirs. The James brothers and Younger had little to be concerned about. They were not named as suspects in the Richmond robbery. Frank James offered no alibi but apparently had been visiting family in Kentucky with Jesse around the time of the robbery.[1] Younger decided later to provide an alibi anyway, since the people of Richmond found all of the former guerrillas suspicious. He wrote that he was staying at the Bass Plantation near Lake Providence, Louisiana, with the well-respected Lea brothers of Independence.[2]

Frank traveled to Kentucky during the early months of 1867,

according to a letter written by Jesse at a later date. He had been staying with a friend of his named Alexander Sayer in Nelson County when he decided to go to New York City.[3] Some of the bonds taken from the Clay County Savings Association were cashed in that city around this time.[4] It is possible that Frank and Cole Younger made this trip together. Jesse wrote that Frank sailed from New York City but didn't mention where his brother was going. Frank may have left New York to travel to California in search of his father's grave at Hangtown. Both Jesse and Frank later said that they searched for Reverend James's burial site a couple of times unsuccessfully. This might have been the brothers' first attempt to locate Robert James's grave.

Family accounts place Frank on his uncle Drury James's ranch in Santa Margarita, California, during the spring of 1867. Drury James and his partner J. L. L. Blackburn had built first a stage stop and later an elegant hotel near a spring in the town of Paso Robles. People traveled from all over the country to avail themselves of both the spa and the atmosphere surrounding the beautiful hotel and its grounds. Jesse later wrote that Frank found work on the Labousu Ranch in San Luis Obispo during this time. The Labousu was owned by Drury's friend J. D. P. Thompson. Jesse in the meantime stayed near the home of his aunt Nancy Hite west of Adairville, Kentucky, at the Chaplin Hotel.[5] Frank apparently wrote to Jesse from California telling him that he ought to consider joining him at Drury's ranch. Frank felt that the treatments that were available at the spa might help heal Jesse's lung. He also felt that it would be good for Jesse to get away from the Midwest. Frank felt Jesse would enjoy the resort. Jesse replied that he liked his brother's idea, but he didn't have the money to get to California. Jesse suggested Frank return east and meet him at their aunt's. Once they were together, they could discuss how he might develop the funds he would need to get to California.

Evidently, at this point, Frank contacted Cole Younger, and Younger agreed to meet Frank and Jesse in Kentucky. The trip from California was longer than the trip Younger had to make from Louisiana, and Cole arrived in Kentucky before Frank James. Jesse had already apparently decided that the nearby Nimrod Long Banking Company in Russellville, Kentucky,

Jesse James, taken in Greenville, Illinois, 1869.
The Armand De Gregoris Collection

would be ripe for robbery. Jesse's selection of this bank as a
target is interesting indeed. Robert James had attended Georgetown College on a scholarship that had been funded by the
bank's former owner, George Norton, and by Nimrod Long himself. Why Jesse would want to repay Long for the kindness

shown his family by robbing Long's bank is odd. Jesse may have had inside knowledge of the bank or he may have felt that because of his father's association with the bank he would have a ready alibi. It was not an alibi that was ever used if that was the case. It is possible that the selection of this bank arose out of some long-buried resentment of Jesse and Frank toward their father for his desertion of them, but they never voiced any animosity. The motivations behind the selection of the Nimrod Long Banking Company by the James-Younger Gang will likely never be known.

Jesse and Cole Younger were probably uncomfortable around one another without Frank James to mediate. They had always been friendly but did not always agree. Jesse assumed that he should be designated as leader of any gangs formed for the purpose of robbery, since it was he who had the initial idea to visit the Liberty bank. Younger had a hard time awarding that position to the younger and less-experienced man. Younger participated because his closest friend, Frank James, was involved. Younger might never have gone to Liberty had Frank not been a participant. Younger thought Jesse had a tremendous ego. He was amused by Jesse's grandiose plans.[6] Younger relied on Frank to bring Jesse down to earth and fine-tune his schemes into workable plans. Only out of respect for Frank would Cole Younger even listen to Jesse and tolerate his pretensions.

The planning of the robbery escalated after the arrival of Frank James in Kentucky. The three men felt that they needed accomplices if they were to be successful. There is little hard evidence pertaining to who actually was included, but it seems from most accounts that John Jarrette was once again in the fold. There were several other friends of Younger and the Jameses who were later suggested as possible accessories. George and Oliver Shepard were suspects almost from the day of the robbery. Oliver Shepard was a friend of both Jesse and Cole Younger. His cousin George Shepard had served as a captain in Quantrill's unit. A tinner originally from St. Louis named Arthur McCoy has been mentioned. McCoy also was a former guerrilla and had served as a captain in General Jo Shelby's Cavalry division.[7] Jim White was later named as possibly being involved, but there is no evidence that places White in Russellville. Another person speculated to have been in the robbery was a fellow named Alex Henderson.[8] It seems likely that the four men who entered Nimrod Long's Southern Deposit Bank on the day of the robbery were Jesse, Frank, Cole Younger, and John Jarrette.

A man identifying himself as Thomas Colburn from Louisville appeared at the bank and asked to convert a bond a week before the robbery. Colburn claimed he needed immediate cash to buy cattle and offered Long a discount. A suspicious Long refused to cash the bond. The unhappy Colburn left the bank empty-handed that day. He returned with a friend a few days later. This time he asked to change a $100 note. Long once again refused. He was still uncomfortable with Colburn. For some reason, Colburn's friend made him ill at ease as well.[9]

Colburn returned a third time on March 20, 1868. This time he was in the company of two men and not of a mind to have Long refuse to do business with him. Clerk Hugh Barclay and cashier Thomas H. Simmons were eating their dinner at the back of the bank. Long was standing at the counter when the men entered the bank. Colburn walked directly up to the counter and threw down a $50 note. Staring hard at Long, he demanded to know if this note was acceptable to the bank president. Long was not intimidated. He replied that he thought the note might be counterfeit. Again he refused to cash Colburn's bond. Colburn was outraged and immediately drew his revolver. He pointed his gun at Long's head while his companions drew their revolvers. Colburn then demanded Long surrender all of the money in the bank. Long said nothing. He turned from the bandit and suddenly bolted to the back door. A fourth man entered through the side door and ordered Long to stop right where he was. Long ignored this robber as well, and continued toward the back door. The fourth man grazed the side of his head with a bullet when Long disregarded yet another warning. Long fell to the floor but was determined to make his way out the back door. He was struck in the head with the bandit's revolver when he attempted to rise. The robber must have thought that Long was down for the count. He turned his attention away from the banker in order to see how the others were faring. Long used that opportunity to jump up and rush out of the building. He ran to the street in front of the bank. There he faced two additional mounted strangers who had been waiting behind some trees at the intersection of Main and Bethel Streets.[10] The strangers fired at Long as he ran down the street.

Barclay and Simmons were being held inside at gunpoint while the robbers threw money into a wheat sack. The outlaws quickly and efficiently left the bank when their task was completed. They joined the two men in the street where they mounted their horses and rode down the Gallatin Road. A man named O. C. "Matt" Owens was shot in the side when he attempted to stop the robbers by shooting at them. A small group of men from the town chased after the bandits, but the robbers were soon on their way toward Franklin and out of sight. They may have met up with a sixth companion just outside town, but the firepower wasn't needed. The robbers had successfully stolen between $9,000 and $14,000 from Nimrod Long's company.[11]

This time the men had been seen a little more clearly than in past robberies. Some of the people of the town had a look at them as well as Nimrod Long and his two clerks. The local newspaper described the bandits as ". . . very good looking, stout young men."[12] Long would not forget Colburn's face any time soon. A detailed description of the three robbers, the fourth man at the door, and one of the men who had waited outside was given to the Logan County sheriff after the robbery. The *Louisville Daily Journal* described the robbers, although it appears that several errors were made in the descriptions, especially when it came to the heights of the men:

"One, riding a bay horse with Morgan saddle, 26 years old, black hair and whiskers, florid complexion, 5 feet 8 inches tall, weighs about 140 pounds, wore a felt hat, sack coat, vest made of velvet, and silver spurs. [Jarrette?]

"One, 5 feet 7 inches in height, short, curly, sand hair, round bull-dog head, prominent eyes, red face, and weighs 160 pounds. [Jesse?]

"One, 5 feet 6 inches high, thin visage, 32 or 33 years old, shabbily dressed in light clothes, defect in one eye, light hair and whiskers, weighs 150 pounds, had on a white hat much worn. [Frank?]

"One, 6 feet high, weighs 140 pounds, 33 or 34 years old,

light hair, inclined to curl, thin whiskers, was shabbily dressed in dark clothes.'' [Younger?][13]

It is probable that the first three men in the bank were Cole Younger, and Frank and Jesse James, considering these descriptions together with other available information. John Jarrette would have been the fourth man. Oliver and George Shepard may have been the men outside the bank while Arthur McCoy waited just outside town in case he was needed.

The gang eventually rode toward Bowling Green, where they were seen by some farmers. They then headed westward to Glasgow. It appears that there they split up with at least one of the groups riding toward Gainesville. Nimrod Long meanwhile asked Louisville detectives D. T. ''Yankee'' Bligh and John Gallagher to investigate the robbery. Bligh's invitation by Russellville's bankers and city fathers would mark the first time that a professional detective had been involved in the hunt for the Midwest bank robbers. Bligh questioned all of those who had any personal knowledge of the robbery. He eventually concluded that Oliver and George Shepard had been involved as well as some other young men from Missouri: Jesse and Frank James, Cole Younger, John Jarrette, and a man named McCoy. Bligh determined that George Shepard was in the town of Chaplin, Kentucky, through good detective work. Chaplin was in Nelson County up near the Hite farm. Shepard was in custody within days after he had been arrested in a Chaplin store. Shepard told Bligh that he had been away trading horses and had been nowhere near Russellville at the time of the robbery. Bligh claimed to have some kind of paper that was said to have been in the custody of the robbers where Shepard's name had been mentioned.[14] George Shepard was taken to Russellville where he was identified as having participated in the robbery. He was eventually tried and sentenced to three years in prison. The detectives tracked Oliver Shepard to his father's home in Missouri. Ol Shepard was not as lucky as his cousin. He was shot and killed while resisting arrest.

Jesse, Frank, Cole Younger, John Jarrette, and Arthur McCoy apparently were not actively pursued by Bligh at this time. The issue of the identity of the other robbers seems to have been dropped after the death of Oliver Shepard. Jesse made no effort to deny being in Kentucky at the time of the robbery. He claimed later that he was staying in Chaplin near his relatives and that Frank was there with him before traveling to California in search of work. Jesse contended that his health was once again a concern. He said that his brother had been with him in Kentucky earlier but had already left for California by March. Jesse later wrote, "If Mr. Tom Marshall, Proprietor of the Hotel at Chaplin, Nelson Co., Ky., will say I was not at home March the 20th 1868 the day of the Russellville, Ky, Bank robbery, I will acknolledge I was in the Russellville robbery, and if D. B. Blackburn, ex Sheriff of San Luis Obispo co. Cal. will say Frank James was not at work on Mr. Thompson's Ranch on that day in Cal. I will say Frank James is guilty."[15]

Cole Younger later wrote a letter concerning the Younger brothers' involvement in the affair. He did not deny having participated in the robbery but rather proclaimed the innocence of his brother Jim. Jim Younger must have loved that. He had never been mentioned as a suspect in the first place.[16] The Youngers' brother-in-law, Richard Hall, gave an interview to the *Kansas City Commercial Advertiser*, which appeared on June 3, 1868. Hall claimed that the robbery was the brainchild of John Jarrette and the Shepards. He alleged that Jarrette approached Cole Younger while Younger was working on his family's Jackson County farm and essentially talked the younger man into going to Russellville. He said that Younger had never participated in a robbery before Russellville. Richard Hall clearly implicated Cole Younger while attempting to lay the blame on another brother-in-law he evidently didn't like.

This may have been the last robbery for John Jarrette. Members of their family claim that John and Josie Jarrette were ambushed by enemies sometime between 1867 and 1868. The Jarrette home was set on fire while the couple and their two young children, Margaret and Jeptha, slept inside. Family members say Cole and Jim Younger were able to rescue the children, but John and Josie expired in the fire.[17] The story of John Jarrette's death was complicated when guerrilla Jim Cummins wrote in his autobiography years later that Jarrette died in the "Frisco Mountains" of California in 1891. The Jarrette family, however, claims otherwise.

EIGHT

༺～ོ～ༀ

A Score Is Settled

"As boy and man, he [Jesse] could smile at slightest provocation;
he could smile, and he did, in a certain manner, when putting a
bullet through head or heart of soldier or citizen."
—Robertus Love, *The Rise and Fall of Jesse James*

THE RUSSELLVILLE ROBBERY was a success. Jesse, Frank, and their friends enjoyed the satisfaction of having pulled off another noteworthy public exclamation of their Rebel dissatisfaction. Once again their pockets were full of the hard-earned money of other people. Frank James again asked his brother to join him in California. Jesse told Frank that he would consider California after he made a trip to New York. Frank James and Cole Younger had enjoyed that city and evidently Jesse wanted to see it for himself. Jesse had been examined and treated by Dr. Joe Wood of Kansas City before he went to Kentucky. The doctor suggested that some rest and recreation would be good for the young man's health. Jesse knew just where to go. He probably enjoyed expanding his horizons by meeting some of the people he found in New York, but within a week, he was eager to leave the city. He booked passage on a ship bound for

72

Panama. He likely did not stay long in that country and soon boarded a ship that would take him to San Francisco. Apparently, Frank joined Jesse in Northern California upon Jesse's arrival there since later accounts by the brothers indicate that they looked for their father's grave together sometime in 1868. Jesse and Frank were still not able to locate the grave of Reverend James.

The James boys left the Hangtown area and traveled south to their Uncle Drury's hotel and spa in Paso Robles. The spa no doubt helped Jesse's lung. The time they spent at Drury's La Panza ranch afforded them another opportunity to visit with their family and renew their roots. It is doubtful that the two brothers needed much money while they were visiting their relatives. Jesse's trips to New York City, Panama, San Francisco, and then Paso Robles, on the other hand, must have cost quite a bit. Jesse and Frank must have been broke by the time they returned home to Missouri sometime in the fall of 1869.[1]

One of the legends of Jesse James revolves around the time period of this trip. In an area known as the Devils Nest in northern Nebraska, the locals have claimed for years that Jesse and Frank passed through the territory. The two brothers were said to have enjoyed the company of the Indians they met there and established a trading post. The story goes that they lived there over a year, using the aliases of Jesse and Frank Chase. It has been told that the two outlaws married two Indian girls who were the daughters of a man named Thomas Wabasha. Both of the men parented children. Jesse had a son he named Joe Jesse and Frank had a daughter named Emma. The legend continues that the two brothers had some kind of trouble with a French trader on July 4, 1870. The brothers were said to have killed the Frenchman. They left the area and never returned. Family of Joe Jesse Chase claimed that while Jesse wrote to his "wife," her mother would not allow her to reply. That was the end of the marriage. Joe Jesse was raised by his mother and stepfather, William Good Teacher. An interesting story, but likely untrue.

Cole Younger returned to Texas after the Russellville robbery. He and his brothers had relocated there after the war and had been making an effort to create a successful cattle operation. Younger made trips to Louisiana and Florida with his cattle but

The Hotel Paso de Robles and stage stop (foreground). *Ethelrose James Owens*

mainly stayed at the family's new home near Scyene. Younger may not have been aware of Frank and Jesse's return to Missouri.

The next robbery to occur in the Midwest was unlike any before it. On December 7, 1869, a stranger asked cashier John Sheets of the Daviess County Savings Association in Gallatin, Missouri, to cash a one hundred dollar bill. A second man entered behind the first and offered to buy the bill himself. The two men whispered together before any business could be transacted. With either little or no conversation, the unarmed John Sheets was shot. One bullet entered his head near the bridge of his nose and the other lodged firmly in his heart. A lawyer named William A. McDowell was in the bank transacting business of his own. He was shot in the arm as he ran from the building. McDowell shouted, "Captain Sheets has been killed!"[2] The robbers quickly scooped up $700 from the cashier's drawer and bolted from the bank. Before McDowell had yelled his announcement, the shots fired within the bank alerted passersby that something was wrong. When the two men attempted to mount their tethered horses, they were fired on by some of the townspeople. One of the bandits attempted to mount his horse only to have his hand become tangled in the reins. Someone in the crowd of onlookers hollered "Let's get him!" Those gathered quickly backed off when the bandit pointed his gun menacingly at the crowd. The outlaw jumped on the back of his companion's mount as shots were fired and joined his partner in fleeing from the town.[3]

The outlaws encountered a farmer named Daniel Smoot not far out of town. They leveled their guns at Smoot and demanded he surrender his horse. Smoot immediately complied. The bandits headed toward Kidder now that they each had their own mount. They stopped within a few miles to ask directions from a Reverend Helm. They then continued in the direction of Honey Creek, Hamilton, and Breckinridge. The robbers were eventually swallowed up by the back roads and farmland. They could not be tracked beyond that point. Sixteen-year-old Edward Clingan, a brother-in-law to Sheets, joined the posse as they chased after the robbers. Clingan was a lifelong resident of Gallatin, yet as he rode after the robbers, he was accompanied by a man he had never seen before. Clingan found a way to separate himself from his riding companion and rode to where the posse was returning to town in frustration. Clingan's suspicions seemed to have been confirmed. The man whom he had suspected might be a spy for the outlaws was nowhere to be seen in the following hours.[4] The Daviess County Savings Association, prominent citizens of Gallatin including Sheets's widow, and the State of Missouri offered a $3,000 reward for any information on the identity of the robbers.[5]

Attorney McDowell claimed that when the two men had whispered together, he had heard one of them mention to the other that the man behind the counter (Sheets) was a fellow named S. P. Cox. The stranger had claimed that Cox had been one of those responsible for the death of Bloody Bill Anderson. Another man who had been in the bank maintained that the men knew who Sheets was and had accused Sheets of being with Cox when Anderson was killed. Someone who saw the bandits leave the bank claimed that he recognized one of their horses as belonging to "a James of Clay County." He believed that the two bandits looked like the owners of the horse. Jesse and Frank James were officially declared suspects in a bank robbery for the first time after descriptions of the two men were provided by McDowell and those who had encountered them during their escape.[6]

Two Gallatin men named Alec Irving and Jess Donohue mounted their horses and headed for Clay County when they heard that the James brothers had been mentioned as suspects. They enlisted the help of Deputy Sheriff John S. Thomason and his son Oscar when they arrived in Liberty. This group of four rode to the James-Samuel farm outside Kearney. Thomason knew right where the James boys lived. Thomason got down from his horse and approached the front door of the house. A small boy darted past him. The boy ran to the barn and threw open the doors. Frank and Jesse burst out, mounted on horses. Thomason quickly remounted his horse and the small posse chased after the James boys. Frank and Jesse shot at Thomason and his companions while rapidly guiding their horses around the known obstacles of their farm. Thomason's mount was the only horse able to jump one of the fences. The others of the sheriff's posse stopped to dismantle the top rails of the fence so that they could continue while the sheriff proceeded after the James boys. Thomason drew close to Jesse and Frank. He leaped from his horse in order to shoot more accurately. One of the outlaw brothers shot the horse through the neck as it ran toward them. Now Thomason would not be able to chase them any farther. Thomason returned to the James-Samuel farm where he grabbed a horse and returned to Liberty. Thomason was surprised to hear upon his arrival that it had already been rumored that he had been killed in the pursuit.[7] Frank and Jesse had by now disappeared. In the meantime, Daniel Smoot received a letter from the robbers. They informed him that since they had taken his horse, he was welcome to keep the Kentucky mare they had left behind.[8]

It seemed to the people of Missouri that the robberies not only had turned bolder but were now deliberately vicious. It was time for the state government to become involved lest the desperadoes continue their deeds and wreak havoc throughout all of Missouri. When the James brothers had been mentioned as suspects, the local newspapers were quick to point out that both of them had a guerrilla background and should be considered dangerous men. The *Liberty Tribune* editorialized that "if innocent of the crime charged against them, they acted very foolishly in resisting the sheriff."[9] Missouri Governor Joseph W. McClurg notified the counties surrounding Clay that posses should be organized. McClurg felt militia units should be placed on alert in case their assistance was needed to locate and arrest the two outlaws. The *St. Joseph Gazette* predicted that the outlaws responsible for the death of Sheets would be "shot down in their tracks" before being allowed the luxury of a trial.[10] No sightings of the outlaws were reported, however.

Jesse decided to attempt to clear his name by addressing the public in regard to his suspected involvement in the Gallatin robbery. He enlisted the assistance of Jo Shelby's former adjutant, John Newman Edwards. Edwards was now editor of the *Kansas City Times*. The *Times* published an open letter addressed to Governor McClurg. It was dated June 1870 and signed by Jesse. The letter read:

I and my brother Frank are charged with the crime of killing the cashier and robbing the bank at Gallatin, Missouri, December 7, 1869. I deny the charge. There is not a word of truth in it. I can prove, by some of the best men in Missouri, where I was the day of the robbery and the day previous to it, but I well know if I was to submit to an arrest that I would be mobbed and hanged without a trial. The past is sufficient to show that bushwhackers do not have any show in law in Missouri. Several bushwhackers have been arrested in Missouri since the war, charged with bank robbery, and they most all have been mobbed without trial. I will cite you to the case of Thomas Little of Lafayette county. A few days after the bank was robbed at Richmond, in 1867, Mr. Little was arrested in St. Louis, charged with being one of the party who perpetrated the deed. He was sent from St. Louis to Warrensburg under a heavy guard. As soon as the parties arrived there they found out that he could prove, by the citizens of Dover, that he was innocent of the charge. As soon as these scoundrels found out that he was innocent a mob was raised, which broke in the jail, took him out, and hanged him.

Governor, when I think that I can get a fair trial, I will surrender

myself to the civil authorities of Missouri. But I will never surrender to be mobbed by a set of blood-thirsty poltroons. It is true
that during the war I was a Confederate soldier, but since that I
have lived a peaceable citizen, and obeyed the laws of the United
States to the best of my knowledge. The authorities of Gallatin
say the reason that led them to suspect me, was that the mare left
at Gallatin, by the robbers, was identified as belonging to me; that
is false. I can prove that I sold the mare previous to the robbery.
It is true that I fought Sheriff Thomason, of Clay county, but was
not my brother with me when I had the fight? I do not think I
violated the law when I fought Thomason, as his posse refused to
tell me who they were.

Three different statements have been published in reference to
the fight that I had with Thomason. But they are all a pack of
falsehoods. Deputy Sheriff Thomason has never yet given any
report of the fight, that I have seen. I am personally acquainted
with Oscar Thomason, the deputy's son, but when the shooting
began his face was so muffled up with furs that I did not recognize
him. But if I did violate the law when I fought Thomason I am
perfectly willing to abide by it. But as to them mobbing me for a
crime that I am innocent of, that is played out. As soon as I think
I can get a just trial I will surrender myself to the civil authorities
of Missouri, and prove to the world that I am innocent of the crime
charged against me.[11]

The letter regarding Gallatin would be the first of many mes-
sages that Jesse sent to various people through his use of the
press. John Newman Edwards would prove himself to be not
only Jesse's greatest ally but his public relations mentor. The
two men discovered that they could mutually benefit one another
while staying true to their objectives and beliefs. John Newman
Edwards had remained with Shelby after the war. The two traveled to Mexico where they joined forces with Maximillian to
assist the leader with his own rebellion. Edwards chronicled their
adventures in a book he titled *Shelby and His Men* that was
published in 1867. Edwards joined the staff of the *St. Louis Missouri Republican* as a reporter upon his return to Missouri. He
remained friendly with the guerrillas whom he had come to know
through their association with Shelby. He also continued to support the Confederate cause, although not in such an overt manner
that it might lead to his arrest. Edwards's flowery musings cham-

pioned those who had participated in the guerrilla movement by relating his experiences during the War between the States. These men of tenacity were touted as mighty warriors who took up the battle only when they were forced into the protection of their families and homeland. In 1868, Edwards and two friends of his founded the *Kansas City Times*. Jesse likely approached Edwards to ask that he be allowed to publish an alibi letter addressed to Governor McClurg, but it could be that the idea was Edwards's. Regardless, Edwards not only saw to it that the letter was published but helped Jesse write it. Jesse wanted his say on whether or not he and Frank were involved in the Gallatin robbery. It could be that Jesse wanted to disassociate himself from the robbery for the sake of his family. More likely, he simply enjoyed the controversy and liked having a reputation. Edwards was able to keep the men of the "lost cause" before the eyes of the public and advance his own agenda through his involvement with Jesse. The Gallatin letter would be the beginning of a significant alliance between John Newman Edwards and Jesse Woodson James.

Another of Jesse's letters was published a week later in the *Times*, dated July 1870. Jesse again addressed his letter to the governor. He reiterated his innocence as to any involvement in the Gallatin affair:

Since my letter to you of June, I have been influenced by my friends to prove an alibi, and let those men who accused me of the Gallatin murder and robbery know that they have tried to swear away the life of an innocent man.

Governor, the testimony of my witnesses will be published through the columns of the Kansas City Times in two or three weeks, and will be such as you and all men can believe.[12]

Several affidavits from prominent men in Clay County were published in the *Times* on the heels of this second epistle. Jesse's testimony was supported. John S. Groom and James M. Gow said that they had known Jesse since he was a boy. They maintained that he had been in their stores in Kearney the day before the robbery. Alfred R. McGinnis claimed that he had seen Jesse the day after the robbery at the home of a woman named Fox.

Jesse's family signed affidavits proclaiming that Jesse was at his farm on the day of the robbery. Susan James and Zerelda and Reuben Samuel further attested that the horse that had been identified as having been Jesse's had been sold the previous Sunday for $500 to a man from Topeka, Kansas.[13] Jesse was further vindicated when a writer for the *Liberty Tribune* announced in that paper, "Those who have read Jesse James' defense generally believe him innocent—at least all I have heard speak of it."[14] Jesse no doubt gloried in the attention. Frank was likely happy to have been left out of it. There was no mention of Frank in the affidavits.

Cole Younger was still in Texas with his family as the James boys were being recognized as outlaws. He had yet to be mentioned as a suspect in any robbery. Although he was considered an outlaw in Missouri for his failure to take the loyalty oath, Younger had no reason to hide in Texas. He and his brother Jim worked their cattle and even took temporary jobs as census takers for Dallas County. A posse came looking for Cole and Jim almost immediately after the Youngers took their ailing mother back to Jackson County to live out the remainder of her numbered days. The men of the North had a score that they wanted to settle with Quantrill's captain and his brother. The Youngers' teenage brothers John and Bob were assaulted at their family farm in front of their mother when they claimed not to know the whereabouts of Cole. Their assertion was likely true, but that didn't matter. John Younger was hoisted from the rafters of the barn four times until he was released unconscious. Bob Younger was knocked senseless when he attempted to go to the aid of his brother. This was an event the Younger boys would not forget, especially in view of the fact that their traumatized mother died within the month. The boys returned to Texas after the death of Bursheba Younger. Sixteen-year-old Bob was eager to continue his relationship with the daughter of a local preacher. The romance would be short-lived. Rumors that Cole may have been involved in the Russellville robbery caused the girl to break off their engagement without allowing Bob an opportunity to explain. Bob was not amused.

By December 1870, Jesse and Frank realized that it was best for them to stay away from the family farm until accusations surrounding the Gallatin affair died down. They traveled out of the area, visiting family and friends in other parts of the Midwest. There is a prevalent bit of folklore regarding an incident in which Jesse was involved that took place about this time. Jesse was visiting the Hites in Kentucky when one night a doctor was called to the house to care for him. The popular story is that Jesse was so distressed by sister Susie's marriage on November 24, 1870, to Allen Parmer that he tried to commit suicide. The premise of this story seems unlikely. Parmer was a former guerrilla and friend of both Jesse and Frank James. Jesse would visit Susan and her husband several times in the future. Jesse himself may have been responsible for this tale. Several writers have reported that Jesse's claimed unhappiness over the marriage is what caused the doctor to have to be called to the Hite home that night. A more likely scenario is that Jesse accidentally took too much of the pain medication he used to keep the distress from his chest wound at a minimum. Jesse continued to be plagued by the damage to his chest. The resulting pain would trouble him for the rest of his life. Jesse frequently took the opiate laudanum to help him deal with his discomfort. It is possible that Jesse was made ill by too much of this drug and that this story was circulated by him in an attempt to cover up his addiction.[15]

The Youngers were back in Texas by this time. Their peaceful existence there was about to be made complicated. On the night of January 15, 1871, John Younger was involved in an incident in Scyene that would cause him to become a wanted man. Younger got drunk one night and while engaging in some horseplay with pals of his from Missouri attempted to shoot a pipe out of a slow-witted man named Russell's mouth. After Russell swore out a warrant for John Younger's arrest, a heated argument broke out between Dallas Deputy Sheriff Charles H. Nichols, Younger's friend Tom McDaniels, Nichols's friend James McMahon, and Younger. When it was all over, Charles Nichols was dead, the first lawman to be killed in Dallas County.[16] Warrants were issued, but the Texas law never caught up with John Younger.

Another young man was about to become an outlaw. Clelland Miller was a friend of the James boys. He had been born in

nearby Holt, Missouri on January 9, 1850. Miller had met Jesse
when both had been affiliated with Bloody Bill Anderson. Miller
had been captured by Union soldiers during the skirmish that
took Bill Anderson's life three days after he joined the outfit.
He was only fourteen years old when he was taken to the Jefferson Barracks in St. Louis as a prisoner. He was held there for
the next six months and was released at the end of the war. The
young man was no doubt frustrated that he had not had the opportunity to make a valuable contribution to the Confederate
cause. Miller was probably quite excited when his pal Jesse
James presented him with a plan to get even with the Yankees.
Jesse, Frank, and Cole Younger would have a new companion
to take the place of John Jarrette by the time they rode to their
next robbery. Clell Miller was in for the long haul.

NINE

༄༅

Enjoying a Reputation

"These bold fellows only laugh at the authorities, and seemingly invite their sleepy enterprise, by bearding the legal lion in his lazy lair."

—*Lexington Caucasian*, August 30, 1873

IT WAS NOT uncommon for travelers to ask to stay in the homes or barns of farm families that they encountered away from home. Four sophisticated wayfarers spent the night in the barn of the Alcorn family on the night of June 2, 1871. The farm was located near Allerton in southern Iowa. The Alcorns' son Miles was given the gift of a silk handkerchief by one of the men when they left the barn the next morning. Miles watched as they headed north toward the small, bustling town of Corydon.[1] The presence of four strangers was not extraordinary that day. The local dignitaries and members of the Corydon Methodist Church were busy welcoming visitors from other nearby towns and villages. Soon they would all gather to listen to distinguished speaker Henry Clay Dean address the issue of a proposed new railroad that would serve their area. All of Corydon's visitors were not interested in the information and opinions Clay would offer. The four men who had stayed at the Alcorn farm the night before rode quietly over to the Ocobock Brothers' Bank. The bank was open for business, and the cashier was alone. Guns were drawn, and the cashier was bound to a chair while Dean held the attention of the citizens of Corydon. Somewhere between $6,000 and $10,000 was taken from the bank. The bandits calmly left the building without difficulty or intervention. It is almost certain that the robbers were Jesse, Frank, Cole Younger, and Clell Miller.

There were two things that Jesse James loved: attention and a good joke. One of the bandits, probably Jesse, could not allow the opportunity for further sport to go by without taking advantage of it. One of the robbers ducked his head in to interrupt Dean's speech as they passed the church on their way out of town. The outlaw informed the assembled audience that their bank had just been robbed. Neither Dean nor those attending the meeting were amused by the disturbance. Some members of the conference thought maybe the young man was boorishly attempting to disrupt the gathering.[2] The bearer of the unwelcome comment was soundly told to be quiet. Frowns and hard stares accompanied his departure. A small boy named Adam Ripper had been sitting outside, watching the group of strangers. They threw him a coin as they left the town square. "We've just robbed the bank. Go tell everyone," the boy was told.[3] Someone thought that although the information was likely untrue, perhaps the bank ought to be checked anyway. Good thing. The cashier was found bound and gagged. The men who left him that way were long gone.

A posse was quickly formed from some of the men who had been present at the meeting. Preliminary information indicated that the bandits had headed south. A farmer named Tom Stevens lived halfway between Corydon and the Missouri border in an area called Woodland. Stevens reported to the Corydon sheriff that someone had exchanged a heated horse for a horse that he had left tied to a hayrack near his road.[4] The mare that had been stolen had a colt with her. Stevens speculated that when the mare was taken, the colt must have followed. A farmer who lived near the town of Woodland told the posse he found a bunch of pennies under a tree in his grove. It looked as if that was where the group had divvied up the spoils from the robbery. Since the trail indicated that the outlaws had retreated to Missouri, the names of Jesse and Frank James were once again mentioned as possible suspects. By the time the posse questioned people in northern Missouri, it was suggested that the other men might be guerrilla captain Cole Younger and a Clay County fellow irregular Clell Miller.[5] Other names that were mentioned included Jim White and a man named James Koughman.[6] Younger was known to have been a close friend of Frank James. Younger was also considered a dangerous outlaw who had chosen not to surrender at the end of the war. Miller had been seen in the company of Jesse James shortly before the robbery. Authorities were optimistic that since they actually had leads this time, they might get lucky and nab the robbers.

The search for the Corydon bandits was more organized than the posses that had been formed to hunt robbers in the past. William A. Pinkerton of the Pinkerton Detective Agency out of Chicago later claimed that the company's assistance was requested by the Corydon sheriff and local civic leaders.[7] The small size of the town suggests that perhaps instead it was Pinkerton who made the offer to help find the robbers. The Pinkertons were obviously hired by someone since their employees were not permitted to accept rewards for any of the criminals they might catch. Soon after the detective agency took on the case, Pinkerton's son Robert was sent to Corydon. He followed the trail of the bandits into Missouri. The posse was supplemented there by a contingent of men from Lafayette County. The *St. Joseph Morning Herald* reported on September 7 that these men chased the trail of the James and Younger brothers down to St. Clair County without success.

Nonetheless, a Pinkerton detective named Westphall eventually arrested Clell Miller as a suspected participant in the robbery. Miller was returned to Corydon where he was charged with the crime. He was held on $5,000 bail and made to stand trial in Wayne County. Things did not go as smoothly as the people of Corydon and the Pinkerton Detective Agency had hoped. Miller was released when he was able to produce several witnesses who testified that he was nowhere near the town of Corydon on the day the bank had been robbed. In addition, it was determined that those who had traveled to Iowa to witness on Miller's behalf would be entitled to have their expenses paid. The transcript from the trial reads:

"... the said motion of defendant that he recover costs of his witnesses in this case, is sustained by the court to the extent that the court holds that one hundred and fifty dollars of the cost named in said motion is witness fees for witnesses whose testimony was material."[8]

Following Miller's acquittal, a letter from Jesse was published in the *Kansas City Times:*

I have just seen in the Lexington Register, copied from the Caldwell Sentinel, charging myself and my brother Frank with robbing a bank in Iowa of seventy thousand dollars. And as I believe the editors of the Kansas City Times to be honest men and inclined to do justice to every one, I have concluded to drop a few lines to them for publication.

As to Frank and I robbing a bank in Iowa or any where else, it is as base a falsehood as ever was uttered from human lips. I can prove, by some of the best citizens in Missouri, my whereabouts on the third day of June, the day the bank was robbed, but it is useless for me to prove an alibi. One year ago I proved an alibi by some of the best citizens of the State, and proved enough to satisfy every honest man that I was innocent of the killing of Captain Sheets, at Gallatin, but the degraded Radical party criticised my alibi and insinuated that I had bribed my witnesses, and just so it would be in this case if I was to prove an alibi. But I don't care what the Radical party thinks about me, I would just as soon they would think that I was a robber as not; but they don't think so, they know it is false when they say so.

As to Frank and I defying the civil authorities, it is perfectly absurd. We have never defied the civil authorities. I have no doubt but the authors of some of those pieces published against Frank and I are the perpetrators of the crimes charged against us.

From what I can learn, I have been indicted at Liberty for resisting the civil authorities on the 11th of December, 1869. If times ever get so in Missouri that I can get an impartial trial, I will voluntarily go to Clay County and stand my trial. But I am satisfied that if I was disarmed at present, that those brave Radical heroes in Missouri would try to mob me.[9]

Missouri governor Silas Woodson apparently did not believe Jesse. On October 13 Woodson responded to the requests of his constituents to end the Missouri outlaws' reign of terror. He posted a $2,000 reward for the arrest and delivery of Jesse and Frank James to the sheriff of Daviess County, Missouri.

John Younger had recently returned from California. He had attempted to escape from his Texas trouble by relocating there with his uncle, Jeff Younger. John's new life didn't last long. The young man decided that he was homesick and, in the company of his brother Jim, he soon headed back to Missouri where he had friends and family. John quickly became bored after he arrived home and began to crave some kind of excitement. Cole Younger had previously suggested to his brothers John and Jim that they might like to join the little group he had put together with the James boys. Jim Younger had been disgusted by the idea when he had been approached by Cole. He refused to even consider such a thing.[10] Cole had not solicited his youngest brother Bob as he likely, and correctly, assumed that their mother would have been appalled. Anyway, Bob was currently employed on the docks of New Orleans loading seabound ships. Cole probably had second thoughts about including either of his younger brothers by the time John returned from California. It appears as if he chose not to include John in the group's next escapade.

Cole left Texas in late April 1872 to visit Frank James in Missouri. No warrants stemming from the Corydon robbery had been issued for the arrest of Cole Younger and the James boys. Clell Miller had not yet been arrested in relation to the crime. Jesse, Frank, and Cole were used to being careful about their friends and associates. They had learned quickly to check each other's backs lest someone decide to sneak up on them and turn them in to the authorities. They were growing accustomed to outlaw life.

On the morning of April 29, 1872, Jesse, Frank, Cole Younger, and Clell Miller evidently decided to press their luck and embark on another adventure. Four or five men rode into the town of Columbia, Kentucky. They posed as cattlemen and asked a variety of questions about the community. They stayed at a farm called Green Acres just outside town on the evening of April 28. Three of them used the names John Wilson, William Wilson, and John Warren.[11] In the morning they quietly rode into town. Within minutes, two of the men were walking into the Bank of Columbia. The other two stood guard outside on their horses. Most of the patrons of the bank were not yet in town since the bank had just opened. The bank was fairly quiet. Judge James Garrett, James T. Page, W. H. Hudson, and Major T. C. Winfrey were sitting at a round table in the front of the room. Cashier R. A. C. Martin was at the counter preparing for the day. One of the strangers walked over to the seated group and drew his revolver. He announced, "Consider yourselves under arrest."[12] Judge Garrett figured out immediately that the men were there to rob the bank. "Bank robbers!" he cried. Hudson threw a chair at the man with the revolver. The bandit fired his gun at Judge Garrett in response. Garrett was able to slam his hand against that of the outlaw. The bullet lodged in the judge's hand as it exited the gun. Cashier Martin repeated Garrett's cry of "Bank robbers!" He was immediately shot dead. Page, Hudson, and Winfrey had no problem seeing that the robbers meant business. They reacted quickly while Garrett and his attacker wrestled. The three men were able to jump through a window when the outlaw was thrown back into the fireplace. A third robber entered the bank when he heard the sound of the gunfire. Garrett pushed his way past the outlaws and ran out the door. The bandits dragged Martin's body back toward the vault. They quickly grabbed a sum of money from the safe. It was later said to have been between $600 and $1,500. They then ran from the bank into the street.

The men quickly mounted their horses. An eighteen-year-old boy named Isaac Cravens was at work at a mercantile store across the street from the bank. Cravens bravely took a shot at one of the outlaws. Cravens's employer guarded against unwelcome intruders by locking the door of the store once Cravens was outside. This forced Cravens to seek shelter in the law office of William Stewart. A bullet hit the door casing as Cravens ran through Stewart's door. The bullet barely missed the young man. The outlaws rode south out of the town where they encountered a farmer named William Conover. Conover was ordered to open the gate of his farm. Conover didn't have a clue as to who it was who addressed him so rudely. The feisty farmer barked back, "Open it yourself." Conover was dumbfounded to suddenly be staring down the barrels of four guns. The farmer quickly recovered. He lifted his hat and ushered the unwanted visitors through the gate.[13] The band of robbers circled the farm and exited to the north. A posse of townspeople led by Captain J. R. Hindman was quickly formed but was soon riding around in confusion. Unbeknownst to them, the outlaws had circled back around the town.

Louisville detective Yankee Bligh was again called upon to investigate. Bligh began his inquiries immediately. He listened intently as various people reported that they had seen the men who had robbed the bank in the area posing as cattle buyers. This time, descriptions were offered. It didn't take Bligh long to name Jesse and Frank James and Cole Younger as suspects. A report in the *St. Louis Missouri Republican* a few days later relayed the story that a man answering the description of Frank James had spent the night at Green Acres the night before the robbery. Frank borrowed a copy of *Pilgrim's Progress* from the farmer's mother and returned it to her the following morning, according to the story. The placement of the bookmark indicated that he had read nearly the entire book in one sitting. The woman stated that a man with such breeding and interest in literature could not possibly be one of the bank robbers.[14] Cole Younger's alibi had him in Neosho Falls, Kansas, with a herd of cattle at the time of the robbery.[15] Jesse had used his relatives in Kentucky to provide an alibi when robberies occurred in Missouri. He now claimed that he was not in Kentucky at the time of the Columbia robbery. Jesse later wrote:

As my attention has been called, recently, to the notice of several sensational pieces copied from the Nashville Union and American, stating that the James and Youngers are in Kentucky, I ask space in your valuable paper to say a few words in my defence. I would treat these reports with silent contempt, but I have many friends in Kentucky and Nashville that I wish to know that these reports are false and without foundation. . . . There are desperadoes roving around Kentucky, and it is probably very important for the officials of Kentucky to be vigilant. If a robbery is committed in

Kentucky today, detective Bligh, of Louisville, would telegraph
all over the United States that the James and Younger Boys did
it, just as he did when the Columbia, Kentucky, bank was robbed,
April 29, 1872. Old Bly, the Sherman bummer, who is keeping
up all the sensational reports in Kentucky, and if the truth was
known, I am satisfied some of the informers are concerned in
many robberies charged to the James and Younger Boys for ten
years. The radical papers in Missouri and other states have charged
nearly every daring robbery in America to the James and Younger
Boys. It is enough for northern papers to persecute us without the
papers of the south, the land we fought for four years, to save
from Northern tyranny, to be persecuted by papers claiming to be
Democratic, is against reason. The people of the south have already heard one side of the report. I will give a true history of the
lives of the James and Younger Boys to the Banner in the future;
or rather a sketch of our lives . . . [16]

The Columbia robbery was not soon forgotten. On August 30
an indictment was filed against the robbers. Unfortunately, no
one in the town knew the true identities of the bandits. The
indictment read:

The grand jury of Adair County in the name and by the authority
of the Commonwealth of Kentucky accuse John Warren (alias
John James), John Younger (alias John Wilson), William Younger
(alias William Wilson), Thomas Jenkins and William Willoughby
(alias Thomas Wilson) of the crime of murder committed as follows, to-wit: The said John Warren (alias John James), John
Younger (alias John Wilson), William Younger (alias William
Wilson), Thomas Jenkins and William Willoughby (alias Thomas
Wilson), heretofore, to-wit: On the 29th day of April, 1872, in the
Commonwealth and county aforesaid, did then and there unlaw-
fully, willfully, maliciously, feloniously mad of the malice afore-
thought kill and murder one R. A. C. Martin by then and there
shooting him to death with pistol then and there loaded with a
leaden bullet or other hard substance and against the peace and
dignity of the Commonwealth of Kentucky. [17]

Where or how the officers of the court came up with the additional names listed in the indictment is anybody's guess. It's
unlikely that John Younger ever knew that he had been men-

tioned as a suspect in a murder in which he probably had no part. The town of Columbia would long remember the day the bank was robbed. Judge James Garrett would later lose his hand due to complications from his gunshot wound. William Conover would forever be known to people in the town as Open-the-Gate Conover.

The James boys and Cole Younger would soon have something else to deny. Cole and John Younger visited their sisters in the Kansas City area after the Columbia robbery. The James brothers were likely at home with their own family in nearby Clay County. The annual Kansas City Exposition was being held at the fairgrounds. Three men on horseback approached the ticket office on September 26, 1872. One of them jumped off his horse and grabbed the money box away from cashier Benjamin F. Wallace. A large group of people stood in line waiting to purchase tickets and witnessed the exchange. The robber threw the box to the ground after packing the money into a sack affixed to his waist. He then turned away from the box office and started to get back up on his horse. Wallace darted out of the booth and attempted to snatch back the money. He backed away when he saw one of the other bandits point a gun at him, but the robber fired at him anyway. The crowd was stunned when the bullet missed Wallace but hit the leg of a little girl who was standing in line with her mother. The three men disappeared into the crowd as those assembled screamed, ran, or fell to the ground. The money taken was a mere $978.[18]

Some of those present speculated that this deed was perpetrated by the James brothers as well since the names of Jesse and Frank James had been mentioned in conjunction with other robberies. The story took on folktale proportions years later when an article published in the *Neosho (Missouri) Times* claimed that the robber who grabbed the box was overheard to announce that he was Jesse James.[19] Cole Younger's name was suggested as being a participant somewhere along the way. It does not seem likely that the three robbers would have been the James boys or Cole Younger. They had many friends in the Kansas City area and would have been quite easily recognized. The flagrant disregard for the safety of innocent bystanders who were primarily children and families does not seem in character for Jesse, Frank, and Cole. It is ridiculous to think that Jesse would announce himself, since he was going to such great pains to deny any wrongdoing on his part through the use of the newspaper.

It seems that the gang's greatest supporter, however, thought there might be a good chance that the Kansas City Fair robbery was the work of his boys. John Newman Edwards wrote a sermonic editorial in support of the outlaws in the October 20 edition of the *Kansas City Times*. He denounced the crime and the shooting of the little girl, but he praised the robbers as heroes for their daring. Edwards wrote, "These men are bad citizens but they are bad because they live out of their time. The nineteenth century with its Sybaric civilization is not the social soil for men who might have sat with Arthur at the Round Table, ridden at tourney with Sir Lancelot or won the colors of Guinevere. . . . men who could have met Turpin and Duval and robbed them of their illgotten booty on Houndslow Heath." Edwards claimed that the men who robbed had been victims of their society. As such, they were acting in a manner that best conquered their enemies but did not separate them from the wartime traumas their fellow Missourians had experienced. These men reacted in the way in which they did "not because honest Missourians have less nerve but because freebooting Missourians have more." Perhaps the Jameses and Cole Younger would not have been so quickly named as suspects were it not for Edwards's defense of the men who had committed the crime. The supposition that Jesse, Frank, and Cole Younger had been involved increased when Edwards published another fervent editorial glorifying the guerrillas two days later.

On October 25, the *Times* published a letter that was said to have been a communication from the robbers. The contents of the letter mirrored Edwards's words. The authors expressed the belief that the men who robbed the ticket office should be admired for their bold stunt. They further claimed that the actions of the robbers were certainly more moral than some of the acts perpetrated in the name of the Union government. The writers of the letter expressed regret for the injury of the little girl by offering to pay her medical bills. The signatures were not those of any members of the James-Younger Gang but rather three well-known historic figures: Jack Shepard, Dick Turpin, and Claude Duval. Jesse apparently read the letter and decided that his usual denial of involvement should be issued. In a letter published on October 20 he wrote:

I have just read an article in the Independence Herald charging Frank and myself with robbing the ticket office at the Kansas City Exposition grounds. This charge is baseless and without foundation, and as you have always published all articles that I have sent you for publication, I will just write a few lines on the subject, and here is what I have got to say to the public: I can prove where I was at the very hour the gate was robbed, and, fortunately for me, there were several persons close by with whom I am very well acquainted, and who will testify that I was miles away from Kansas City. I will meet Marshal Page and any two men who say that they know the robbers, and convince them that I am innocent.

The Herald says further that Frank and myself have been in Fort Osage township very frequently during the spring and summer, and have been hiding from no one. I have been in Independence very frequently, attending to legitimate business, and have harmed no man, and taken nothing from no man.

As the matter now stands, however, I cannot be arrested. A man charged with robbery these days is most invariably set upon by a mob after he is captured, and hung or murdered without judge or jury. If I could have a fair trial I could prove my innocence before any jury in the State.

It is generally talked about in Liberty, Clay County, that Mr James Chiles, of Independence, said that it was me and Cole and John Younger that robbed the gate, for he saw us and talked to us on the road to Kansas City the day of September 26th. I know very well that Mr Chiles did not say so, for he has not seen me for three months, and I will be under many obligations to him if he will drop a few lines to the public, and let it know that he never said such thing. If the civil authorities have anything in reply to this let them answer through the TIMES.[20]

A letter from Chiles did indeed appear a week later. Chiles denied seeing Jesse or the Youngers at any time near the date of the robbery.

Cole Younger was infuriated that Jesse had taken it upon himself to offer an alibi for himself and his brother. John had not

been a suspect prior to Jesse's letter. Cole himself wrote a letter
that was published in the *Pleasant Hill (Missouri) Review*. Cole
stated, "My name would never have been used in connection
with the affair had not Jesse W. James for some cause best
known to himself, published in the *Kansas City Times* a letter
stating that John, he and myself were accused of the robbery."[21]
Cole claimed that it was true that he and his brother John had
been visiting their sisters in the area at the time of the incident.
Yet he claimed that the two Youngers had nothing to do with
the robbery. Cole later wrote in his biography that he and Jesse
were not on good terms at the time of the episode. Cole claimed
that Jesse's public claims at this time were the key elements in
the future public connection of the James and Younger names.

Jim Younger returned to Dallas during the winter of 1872–73.
He joined the Dallas police department under Marshall Tom
Flynn. Jim likely hoped that such employment would distance
him from his brother Cole's tarnished reputation. Unfortunately
for Jim, such an attempted disassociation proved fruitless. A robbery took place in Dallas in February 1873. Jim Younger and
fellow officer J. J. L. Hollander were named as suspects and
indicted. It is unlikely that Younger was involved. There exists
the possibility that Hollander shielded his accomplice by maintaining that Jim Younger was involved with him. Younger's
brother, after all, was a known wartime outlaw and was suspected of having been involved in a couple of robberies himself.
Jim did not believe that he would be given a fair trial. He fled
Texas before he could be arrested. Hollander was found guilty
and was sentenced to five years in prison. Jim Younger was now
an outlaw, too, through no fault of his own.

John Younger was likely amused by the fact that he had been
named as an accomplice in the Kansas City Fair robbery whether
or not he had actually participated. The time was right for John
to officially join the gang and get in on some of the excitement,
since he was suspected of being a member of the outfit anyway.
Cole welcomed his brother as did Jesse and Frank.

The quiet riverside town of Ste. Genevieve, Missouri, was
visited by Jesse and his friends on May 27, 1873. Two men
entered the Ste. Genevieve Savings Bank that day while another
two waited outside on their horses. Inside the bank the would-

be robbers approached cashier O. D. Harris. They drew their guns and demanded Harris hand over whatever money he had on hand. Harris handed them some $4,000. A young man who had been in the bank at the time they entered sneaked out the back door unbeknownst to the outlaws. He quickly alerted those whom he saw that the bank was being robbed. When the bandits heard him shouting, they pulled the cashier in front of them. Harris was used as a shield as the outlaws pushed their way out the front door. Once outside, they grabbed their horses from their comrades in the street and attempted to mount. One of the horses bolted and ran down the street. The robbers saw a farmer who had been watching their attempted escape and ordered him to hand over his horse. The robbers had obviously thought ahead. A local Confederate named Sam Hildebrand had served the guerrilla cause loyally and ruthlessly. The outlaws evoked his name and reputation as they fired their guns into the air. They raced from the town shouting "Hurrah for Hildebrand!"[22] The robbers of the Ste. Genevieve Savings Bank were very likely Jesse, Frank, and Cole, along with their latest recruit, John Younger.

The James brothers apparently escaped to Clay County after traveling east across the state of Missouri. The Youngers returned south to St. Clair County. When Cole and John arrived home, they found that their younger brother Bob had returned from Louisiana eager to start up a farm in Missouri. Bob's brothers scoffed at his idea of living a normal life in Missouri. Bob ignored them and expressed an interest in joining Cole and the James boys in one of their escapades. He felt he might earn the seed money needed to realize his dream. Bob had met Jesse James while living in Texas. He had been quite taken by Jesse's charisma and intelligence.[23] Cole and Jesse had the power to make young Bob a wealthy man. Besides, robbing banks of Yankee money seemed to him the ethical thing to do.

The Union representatives and those who supported them continued to express the belief that Missouri would be better off without those who had defended the Confederate cause. Carpetbaggers from the East made up the primary framework of the banking community. For the most part, it was they who controlled the money needed for the rebuilding of farms destroyed or damaged during the war and through Order #11. The pro-

Confederate farmers were forced to find new Missouri homes when they failed to raise funds to rebuild. Either that or initiate farming in a more politically friendly environment. The farmers did not embrace the idea of leaving the land for which they had fought. They attempted to eke out an existence where they were. They made every effort to hold on to their land and their pride and to demonstrate to those who had seemingly won that they were in Missouri to stay. They would live side by side with their enemies, if that's what they had to do, although their animosity ran deep. They would not be run out from the land that they loved. With this in mind, the actions the James-Younger Gang took against the establishment were supported by many of their former comrades-in-arms. They felt the gang made a strong and direct statement on their behalf. Getting even with the Yankees for the way they had been forced to live for the past several years seemed righteous and just. When the boys of the James-Younger Gang needed an alibi or a place to hide or rest, they could find such succor from the other families they represented. There seemed little quarrel among the widespread Missouri community of former Confederates that if their former comrades-turned-bank robbers needed help, that's what they would get.

The Eastern power elite decided to expand its domination of the area after they had gained control of the majority of the Midwest banking institutions. They branched out by entering into the Western frontier development of the railroad. It appeared that many of the people involved in this venture were the same as those who had been forcing their will on the Confederate supporters. This action in the Midwest seemed a continuation of the attempts to usurp the rights of the landowners. Jesse, Frank, and Cole Younger may have agreed with this thinking, but they quickly recognized that this new enterprise would involve great amounts of something they had grown to love: easy money. Robbing small-town banks had been profitable, but it was obvious to the boys that the transfer of huge amounts of money to the West through the use of the railroad raised the stakes. They could increase their profits considerably. The Ohio and Mississippi Railroad had been robbed of over $12,000 in September 1866 by bandits who were later determined to be the Reno brothers. Such a robbery had never been attempted west of the Mississippi. The James-Younger Gang had been very successful with the banks. It seemed appropriate that they should be the ones to rectify that oversight. The boys were once again ready to ride.

TEN

⌒⌒⌒⌒

A New Line of Business

> *"Individual daring, more perfect the nearer the man approaches the pastoral life, is a peculiar feature of Western Civilization. It existed in a latent but easily aroused condition before the war, now and then breaking forth into deeds of sudden yet antique heroism; and since the war—quickened by all of the tremendous energies of the strife, and given a new phase because of a society that in losing its homogeneity lost its power to entirely regulate an element so dangerous—it has become a part of the character of the people itself, often made prominent, rarely cruel or vindictive, never brutal, and always more or less serious or tragical."*
> —John Newman Edwards, "A Terrible Quintet," *St. Louis Dispatch*

PART OF THE gang's excitement in robbing banks had been in the planning of the adventure. Robbing trains was quite different from anything they had done before. The founding members of the James-Younger Gang carefully studied the situation. They decided that if they were to venture into the robbing of trains, they would need to add a few more men to their operation. The Chicago, Rock Island and Pacific Railroad was selected as their first target. This would be no minor venture, and they would have to plan carefully. Each man involved would need to be dependable. First they would look to their families. Cole's younger brothers would be polled to see if they wanted to be counted in the number since both of the James boys were already involved. If it had indeed been John Younger who had filled out the group at Ste. Genevieve, his loyalty and enthusiasm would have been welcomed again. Bob Younger was only nineteen years old, but his allegiance to his brothers, his admiration of Jesse, and his desire to obtain money to start a farm made him a desirable recruit. Clell Miller was asked to return. Cole suggested another candidate. Charlie Pitts was the young man who had found and guarded Henry Younger's murdered body after Younger had been shot in the back by Union Captain Irvin Walley. Cole thought he would do well with the group. Pitts was smart and aggressive. His dedication to both the Youngers and the Confederate cause had already been demonstrated.[1]

Jesse and Frank agreed to allow Pitts into the gang. Someone, probably Jesse, proposed a man named Bill Chadwell. It isn't clear how the members of the gang came to know Chadwell.[2] Cole Younger apparently felt obligated to again ask his brother Jim if he wanted to change his mind and join them. Jim had by now seen for himself that trying to live within the law in Texas had rewarded him with nothing more than a warrant for his arrest in conjunction with a robbery he didn't commit. Initially, Jim again refused. Eventually, the frustrated and disillusioned former guerrilla apparently agreed to go only so far as to hold the horses. The new members of the James-Younger Gang were now in place. The robbery of the Chicago, Rock Island and Pacific Railroad would be the first and only time that all four of the Younger brothers would participate in a robbery together.

Frank James and Cole Younger visited Omaha, Nebraska, in early July 1873. They learned there from friends that a shipment of gold worth over $75,000 would travel by rail from the Cheyenne region later that month. The two men arrived in Adair, Iowa, with their brothers, Miller, Pitts, and Chadwell on July 21 after formulating a plan. This time they posed as businessmen. Two of the men ate dinner with Mrs. Mary Grant at the railroad section house. Mrs. Grant's husband oversaw the activities of the Adair railroad station. The men complimented Mrs. Grant on her pie while they attempted to casually obtain information regarding the schedule of the Chicago, Rock Island and Pacific. The others of their group, in the meantime, broke into the handcar house and took a spike bar and tie hammer.[3] All of the men met later on the tracks a mile and a half west of the town at a place called Turkey Creek. By that time, the people of Adair were eating their supper. The spike bar and hammer were used to pry off the fishplate that connected two of the rails. The spikes were then removed. A rope was tied to the west end of the disconnected north rail and a rope was passed under the south rail. The men then hid in a cut they had made in a bank. They held tightly to the rope while they waited for the targeted train to make its appearance.

The outlaws watched and listened as the train approached Turkey Creek a short time later. The remaining rail was jerked from in front of the train seconds before the train reached the disconnected rail. The gang had intended for the suspended rail to cause the train to come to a halt. At that time they would board the train and conduct their business. Unlike most of their robberies, this robbery would not go according to plan. Engineer John Rafferty from Des Moines spotted the displaced rail from his perch in the locomotive. He quickly reversed the engine while applying the air brakes. It was too late. The engine slammed into the break in the rail with a roar of indignation. The engine, tender, and two baggage cars plummeted into a ditch and overturned. The first passenger car was thrown off the track. Engineer Rafferty was killed instantly. Fireman Dennis Foley was thrown beneath Rafferty as the huge iron horse made its descent. The boys on the bank took no chances and commenced firing at the train. They did not want anyone to leave the remaining cars and cause a panic. Such an action would have made it impossible for them to get on with the robbery. Conductor William Smith cringed as two bullets pierced his coat, but luckily did not penetrate him.[4] The quiet evening came alive with the confusion, panic, and fear of the passengers. Two of the outlaws leaped up into the express car and demanded that guard John Burgess open the safe. Burgess handed over the strongbox. It contained only about $2,000. The robbers must have been confused and frustrated at the destruction they caused. They somehow missed the three-and-a-half-ton bullion shipment that was on board.

Previous victims had been carpetbaggers and their institutions. This time that would not be enough. The gang boarded the train and walked through the cars. They directed the distressed passengers to hand over their valuables. The disreputable actions of the James-Younger Gang would result only in an additional $1,000.[5] Passenger O. P. Killingsworth later reported that the apparent leader of the group claimed that they hoped nobody was killed as they didn't want to kill anybody. All they wanted was money. The man who voiced those words was later described as above medium height, well-built, red-faced, and sandy haired. Many of those who later heard that description believed Killingsworth to be talking about Cole Younger. This same bandit expressed sorrow when Rafferty's body was discovered. According to Killingsworth, the outlaw "spoke as if he meant it." The robbery was over in less than ten minutes. This was probably not the way the James-Younger Gang had intended to establish themselves as consummate train robbers.

An alarm sent by railroad employee Levi Clay flew to Omaha and Des Moines over the telegraph wires from the nearby town of Casey. Armed men quickly boarded a train in Council Bluffs and were rushed to Adair. These men were dropped off to mount horses that were being held for them. The trail of the robbers was tracked into Missouri. The gang, in the meantime, stopped in some timber belonging to a family named McCall. There they investigated the contents of the mail bags that they had taken. Then they split up and disappeared into the countryside. The posse had no choice but to return to Iowa empty-handed. Mrs. Jennie Bang later recalled what happened in Adair after the departure of the outlaws:

> The McCall boys found the mail sacks which had been looted and which contained unwanted mail as well as some jewelry. They brought the sacks and contents to our place as my father was keeping the post-office in our home. . . . My father proceeded to get the mail in circulation by sending it to Summit post-office, now Adair, and from there the mail was carried on foot to Casey by Levi Clay.[6]

It appears that the Younger boys returned to their temporary
home in St. Clair County and Jesse and Frank headed west. The
James boys probably once again turned to the haven offered by
their friends and family in Nebraska. Jesse wrote another of his
letters to the editor in December. His return address was proclaimed Deer Lodge, Montana Territory.

Will you permit me a little space in your columns to say a few
words on my own behalf, and in that of my brother, Frank? I
know that we are outlaws, and that there is big money on our
heads; but even though we were to be hung tomorrow, a newspaper that wanted to give a man a fair chance to put himself right
before those who he cared for, would not hesitate to let him print
the truth.

I see from the newspapers of Missouri that one of the Jameses
was recognized with the party who robbed the store in Cass
County some weeks ago, and that later, at Monagaw Springs,
when the prisoners were captured, a James said to a prisoner, "Do
not look at me, damn you, for if you go away and report on me
I will follow you up and kill you if it take me a year."

Perhaps nothing that I might say in way of denial would change
any man's opinion of me, either one way or the other: but this I
do say, that neither Frank nor myself has been in Missouri since
the third day of October, 1873, nor any nearer Missouri than Denver City. Neither of us was in Cass County at the time mentioned,
nor any time within the past year. I am as guiltless of this Cass
County store robbery as a child unborn, and knew nothing whatever of it until I saw it in the newspapers.

This proposition, however, do I make, and will stick to it. I
made it to McClurg when he was Governor, and he said it was
fair and manly, although he did not pay attention to it, and now I
make it to Governor Woodson, who has offered a large reward
for my head. If he will gurantee me a fair trial, and Frank also,
and protect us from a mob, or from a requisition from the Governor of Iowa, which is the same thing, we will come to Jefferson
City, or any other place in Missouri, except Gallatin, surrender
ourselves, and take our trial for everything we have been charged
with. I do not know that Governor Woodson can do this thing,
but if he can and will, we are ready to surrender ourselves. All he
will have to do is give us his word that we shall not be dealt with
by a mob, as we would most certainly be if the militia of Daviess

County could get their hands upon two of Quantrill's and Anderson's best men, or if the Iowa authorities could get us for a crime that we never committed.

If everything said about a man who had a positive character was true, all the jails and penitentiaries in the country would be full. We have many enemies in Missouri because of the war—many who want to see us killed if they can get other people to do the killing; but for all that, if the Governor of our state will guarantee us a fair trial, we will surrender. If we do not, then let public opinion brand us as highwaymen, and do it truthfully, for I will never again write a line to defend myself. But surely we should have a little credit in trying to put ourselves right, and in seeking to have protection while doing it.

We have been charged with robbing the Gallatin bank and killing the cashier, with robbing the gate at the Fair Grounds at Kansas City, with robbing a bank in Ste. Genevieve, with robbing a train in Iowa and killing an engineer, with robbing two or three banks in Kentucky and killing two or three men there; but for every charge and on every charge we are willing to be tried. If Governor Woodson will just promise us protection until we can prove before any fair jury in the state that we have been accused falsely and unjustly. If we do not prove this, then let the law do its worst. We are willing to abide by the verdict. I do not see how we could well offer anything fairer. We do not mean to be taken alive, and those who know us will believe this, even if we do say it ourselves; but we would delight in having a fair trial, and in having this sleepless vigilance on our part broken up. Any communication addressed to me at Deer Lodge, Montana Territory, will be attended to.[7]

It is not known how Jesse, Frank, and Cole Younger felt about the deaths they had caused in Iowa. Jesse likely reasoned that although the engineer's death was unfortunate, the fact that he worked for the railroad made him fair game. Jim Younger was likely repulsed by what had happened. Young Bob Younger was probably upset but likely chose to see it Jesse's way. The boys seemed to put the incident quickly behind them.

After the Adair robbery, the gang heard through the grapevine that the Pinkerton Detective Agency had once again been hired to find them. Even so, none of them saw or heard anything out of the ordinary after they returned to their respective homes. The

Youngers spent Christmas together at the home of their friend Theodrick Snuffer in Roscoe, Missouri, in late December 1873. Sometime after the holiday, Jesse visited them there. Jesse was not overly concerned about his safety, even though by now he had been named as a suspect in more than one robbery. Few people other than his friends or family were aware of what he looked liked. Those who were his family or friends went out of their way to shield him from those who would be his enemies. Most of the people of western Missouri knew by reputation the men who made up the James-Younger Gang. Yet most of the people who could identify them were either friends, supporters, or those who feared whatever repercussions the men might take against them should they speak out.

When Jesse visited the Youngers that winter, the boys likely shared a good laugh. On November 22, John Newman Edwards had published a special supplement to the *St. Louis Dispatch*. He titled his lengthy essay "A Terrible Quintet." Edwards attempted to enlighten his audience as to the true natures of Jesse and Frank James, Cole and John Younger, and a friend of theirs named Arthur McCoy.[8] Edwards shared biographical material relating to each of his subjects. He claimed to have obtained such information by interviewing their families and friends. Edwards attempted to provide detailed alibis for every bank robbery that had occurred in the Midwest since Russellville. He patiently explained that while these particular men had not been involved in the aforementioned robberies, they nonetheless would have been justified in taking such action against their former oppressors. Edwards maintained that the Jameses, Youngers, and McCoys of Missouri's society had been driven to their participation in the war because of the constant persecution of their families. They were "brave and gallant men" who had served the Confederacy "loyally and selflessly." They had felt compelled to take a violent stand only because of the evil deeds of the Union forces. These men battled to reinstate the basic human rights of their families, friends, and neighbors. Edwards went on to pronounce that these same men would have been leaders within their community instead of being classified bank and train robbers had they never been forced to pick up the gauntlet. He decreed that society should be ashamed for allowing such an odious campaign as that which was being waged against these courageous sons of the South. He felt it was wrong to accuse them of stealing the hard-earned money of their neighbors. The outlaws no doubt enjoyed every word of Edwards's diatribe. In December another supportive missive appeared in the *Osceola Democrat*. This one was authored by a friend of the Youngers. St. Clair publisher Augustus C. Appler took up the same refrain. This time the information was supplied by the Youngers' friend, Owen Snuffer. Appler's series of articles in defense of the Youngers was later published in book form.

On January 8, 1874, a mail stage was stopped between Monroe and Shreveport, Louisiana. Approximately $700 was taken from the passengers. The robbery was later rumored to have been the work of the James-Younger Gang. On January 15, a stagecoach was robbed between Malverne and Hot Springs, Arkansas. The bandits demanded the money and jewelry from all of those on board. They asked the passengers if any of them had served in the Confederate Army. Money and a watch were given back to Memphis resident G. R. Crump when Crump replied that he had served as a Confederate soldier. The possessions of the former governor of the Dakota Territory, Union supporter John A. Burbank, were not returned.[9] Other passengers told of how the bandits seemed to think that one of the men riding on the train was a reporter for the *St. Louis Democrat*. The outlaws had great sport at this man's expense as they made jokes about their ability to shoot the hat off his head without mussing his hair.[10] Again in Louisiana, on January 30, five men boarded a steamboat that was anchored at Point Jefferson. They robbed the safe of over $1,500. Whether or not any or all of these robberies were a lark of the members of the James-Younger Gang is doubtful. The James and Younger brothers' reverence for supporters of the "lost cause" notwithstanding, anyone could stop the stage, spout either anti-Union or pro-Confederate sentiment, and be presumed to be the James and Younger brothers. The members of the James-Younger Gang were by now well-known. Lesser-knowns would have delighted getting in on the excitement. They would be able to enjoy the spoils but would also be able to lay the blame of the crime clearly at the feet of their more celebrated colleagues.

Never had a train been robbed in the state of Missouri. It seems that being the first to do so was a challenge that the James-Younger Gang could not ignore. The Iron Mountain Railroad was selected as the target for this performance. The outlaws evidently decided to poke fun at both the railroads and those who would pursue them by selecting as the site of the robbery a station with a serendipitous name: Gad's Hill. Perhaps those who had established the site had taken its name from the epic of *Robin Hood*, perhaps not. Some residents said that the little town was named by founder George W. Creath after Charles Dickens's country residence. Regardless, the irony appealed to the outlaws who fancied themselves modern-day Robin Hoods and the plans for the robbery were laid. William Pinkerton would later claim that the James boys, Younger brothers, Clell Miller, and Jim Cummins were the men involved in the events that were about to unfold.[11]

The flag station of the Iron Mountain line was located some one hundred miles south of St. Louis on the downgrade into Piedmont. All was normal on the evening of January 31, 1874. Several men were socializing around the platform when five strangers approached with their guns drawn about 5:30 P.M. One of the interlopers held the surprised witnesses at gunpoint. The others quietly set fire to a pile of brush near the platform. They then placed a signal flag on the track to alert the engineer of the expected train so that he would stop at the station. Over $700 was confiscated from the tiny town's storekeeper in the meantime.

The Little Rock Express, with twenty-five passengers aboard, had left St. Louis early that morning. At 4:45 in the evening, the train pulled up to the Gad's Hill platform as the engineer followed his directive. Conductor C. A. Alford stepped down to investigate the trouble and was immediately apprehended by one of the outlaws. Alford observed that the man before him was wearing a hood with holes cut for the mouth and eyes. He immediately understood the nature of the delay. The outlaws had planned ahead. They sent the train down an abandoned spur on the track. Two other of the bandits boarded the engine and retrieved engineer William Wetton, fireman A. Campbell, and brakeman Ben van Stumit. One of the robbers ran alongside the passenger cars, ordering those aboard to keep their heads inside, lest they lose them. He informed those who might entertain the idea of becoming heroes that the crew of the train were being held as hostages. The crew members would lose their lives if there was any gunplay. No one fired a shot. Two of the other bandits jumped aboard the express car. They ordered baggage master Louis Constant and a mail agent by the name of Martan to hold their hands in the air. The outlaws quickly found registered mail that Constant had attempted to hide. They ripped open the envelopes and stuffed anything of value into their wheat sack. The express manager pointed his gun at the robbers. He was firmly ordered to gently lay it down. Then the order to surrender the key to the safe was delivered. The bandits carefully and thoroughly removed the contents. One of the robbers chuckled as he wrote in the messenger's receipt book, "Robbed at Gad's Hill."[12]

The outlaws apparently enjoyed themselves. They were satisfied that this time their robbery of a train proceeded much more smoothly than their previous attempt. At this point, the three men jumped down from the express car and entered the passenger cars. They sauntered through the train with their guns pointing to the ceiling. Every so often they stopped to examine the hands of the male passengers. They courteously explained that they were not going to ask deliverance of any money or valuables that might belong to either ladies or hardworking farmers. The robbers seemed to relish taking money and jewelry from the more affluent passengers as they enjoyed acting out their Robin Hood impersonation. The dramatization continued. A middle-aged man either made a remark to the robbers or for some reason caused them to suspect that he might possibly be a Pinkerton. He was taken to a private compartment and strip-searched. Two apparently wealthy women were also asked to contribute their jewelry. Two other well-dressed gentlemen were directed to step down from their passenger car and instructed to strip down to their underwear. The robbers declared that these two gentlemen looked to them as if they might be either bank or railroad officials. Unbeknownst to them at the time, their assumptions were correct. One of the men was John F. Lincoln, the superintendent of the St. Paul & Sioux City Railroad. Lincoln's companion was

John L. Merriam, the founder of the Merchant's Bank of St. Paul.
The robbers were happy to appropriate $200 from Mr. Lincoln.
Mr. Merriam relinquished his watch plus $75.[13] Another of the
passengers was J. H. Morley, chief engineer of the Cairo & Ful-
ton Railroad. When Morley started to give the robbers a hard
time, he was told to be quiet. Morley, however, does not appear
to have been robbed. Conductor Alford was one of those who
was ordered to turn over his money. Alford informed the outlaws
that the watch they were taking was of great sentimental value
to him. He was allowed to keep it. The robbers continued to
delight in the reactions of the passengers. One of them asked
Reverend T. A. Hagbrit to pray for them. Another of them exchanged hats with one of the passengers. The group of men who
robbed the Iron Mountain Railroad that night were likely Jesse,
his brother Frank, and Cole, John, and Bob Younger. The outlaws had no way of knowing then that their public humiliation
of two of the passengers, Kennedy and Merriam, would have
dire future consequences for three of them.[14]

One of the robbers handed a piece of paper to engineer Wetton
as they mounted their horses. Wetton was instructed to get the
note to Silas Huchings at the *St. Louis Dispatch*. The robbers
shook hands with Wetton. They cleverly advised him to "always
stop when you see a red flag."[15] Wetton then watched the men
disappear into the night. When he looked down at the paper, he
saw that it was a written account of the robbery that had just
taken place. Wetton held in his hand a press release. It read:

The most daring robbery on record. The southbound train on the
Iron Mountain Railroad was robbed here this evening by five heavily armed men, and robbed of ——— dollars. The robbers arrived
at the station a few minutes before the arrival of the train, and
arrested the Agent, put him under guard, and then threw the train
on the switch. The robbers are all large men, none of them under
six feet tall. They were all masked, and started in a southerly
direction after they had robbed the train, all mounted on fine
blooded horses. There is a hell of excitement in this part of the
country.[16]

Only the amount of money taken during the robbery needed
to be filled in to make the account complete. The outlaws wanted

the newspaper coverage to be as complete and accurate as possible if the event was to be reported.

When the train reached Piedmont, some seven miles down the line, a posse was formed. By that time, the outlaws had disappeared. The owners of the Iron Mountain Railroad surmised immediately that this robbery was likely not a one-shot confrontation by a group of boys out for an evening's escapade. This was a carefully executed plot against them that without a doubt would be repeated in the future. The United States Post Office called in the Pinkertons to investigate the crime when it was realized that registered mail packages had been taken.

The members of the gang stopped for a meal at the farmhouse of a widow named Cork near Carpentersville. It was believed from there they rode off in the direction of Arkansas.[17] Apparently they eventually returned once again to their friends and relatives in western Missouri. Cole, John, and Bob Younger stopped off in St. Clair County to visit with their brother Jim. Shortly afterward, Cole and Bob left for Hot Springs, Arkansas. John Younger claimed he wasn't feeling well. He promised to join his brothers in Hot Springs in a few days.[18] This trip by the Youngers to Arkansas seems to lend further credence to the theory that they were not part of the group who robbed the Malverne-Hot Springs stagecoach. It would not have been wise or safe to return to that area so soon after the event. The Youngers were very observant and cautious.

The *St. Louis Dispatch* ran a report on the robbery at Gad's Hill on June 7, while John Newman Edwards was visiting the state capitol on a business trip. The article contained a straightforward accusation of the James and Younger brothers having been the perpetrators of the crime. A detailed list of all of the robberies that had occurred since the event at Liberty strongly suggested Jesse and Frank James together with Cole Younger had been involved. An anonymous St. Louis policeman was quoted as having been in Richmond on the day of that robbery. He identified Jesse and Frank James and Budd and Cal Younger as the robbers. The fact that a person who felt he could positively identify "Budd" and "Cal" Younger but did not know that they were one and the same seemed to be either overlooked or ignored. Edwards was infuriated by the slant of the article. He immediately wired his editor to publish nothing further about the incident at Gad's Hill.

The newspapers were aflutter with accusations and details of the pattern of Midwest robberies. A grassroots movement was started in an effort to put an end to the outlawry. The Pinkertons underestimated the cunning and intelligence of the members of the James-Younger Gang. Pinkerton made claims that his officers should have no trouble succeeding where local law enforcement had failed in capturing the outlaws. The agency launched an aggressive campaign to locate the James and Younger brothers. They did not appear concerned that the men they sought had been involved in some of the fiercest fighting the United States had ever encountered. They would soon change their minds.

ELEVEN

༄

Married and Pursued

"Of course Jesse did not participate in all of these affairs, but they all affected him. It can be safely stated that he alone participated in the honeymoon."

—Homer Croy, *Jesse James Was My Neighbor*

THE YEAR 1874 would turn out to be an extraordinarily significant one for Jesse, his family, and his friends. Things had been going rather well. Jesse no doubt felt that his chosen means of revenge had been successful. He had, after all, declared rather loudly to the country at large that there remained Confederate sympathizers who were not yet agreeable to abandoning their cause. The only fly in the ointment seemed to be the appearance of the Pinkertons on the scene. The boys of the James-Younger Gang probably doubted that these professionals would have any more luck finding and arresting the gang than all of the posses that had been inspired by their own personal losses. The administration of the gang would continue to carefully select the railroads and banks that would be their targets. The odds were high that meticulous planning would ensure the outfit's continued success. Jesse, Frank, and Cole Younger did not know at the be-

111

ginning of the year that the Pinkertons had made the decision
that they would do everything within their power to eliminate
the outlaw gang. They had made implicit plans to locate and
capture or exterminate the pesky miscreants before they could
strike again. The plan was to infiltrate their personal domain.
The Pinkertons intended to bring them to justice once and for
all. Pinkerton himself fully believed that such a plan could succeed without too much trouble and in a minimal period of time.
The agency's motto was "The Eye that Never Sleeps." Unfortunately for them, the Pinkertons gravely and seriously underestimated the intellect, shrewdness, and fidelity of the members
of the James-Younger Gang.

On March 10, 1874, a twenty-six-year-old Pinkerton detective
named James W. Whicher arrived in Liberty. He met with former
sheriff O. P. Moss and Commercial Bank President D. J. Adkins.[1] During the meeting, Whicher informed the two Clay
County representatives that he planned to make an appearance
at the James-Samuel farm. He would not reveal his true identity,
but rather would request work as a farm hand. Whicher felt his
offers of help would no doubt be appreciated by the Samuels.
He would then quickly and efficiently ingratiate himself into
their lives. He believed he would soon gain intimate knowledge
of the comings and goings of Jesse and Frank James. Whicher
felt it was a surefire plan that would enable him to eventually
arrest the outlaw brothers without their suspicions being raised.
Moss and Adkins were likely stunned at the naïveté of Whicher's
plan. They quickly informed Whicher that it was preposterous
for him to think that Zerelda Samuel would welcome a stranger
to the farm without serious suspicion. The egotistical Whicher
informed Adkins and Moss that his strategy had been carefully
planned. He would proceed as he had indicated. He would not
need the blessing of local law enforcement. He had, after all, the
full confidence of the Pinkerton Detective Agency.

Whicher boarded a train bound for Kearney at 5:15 the afternoon of March 10. He arrived at the Kearney station about dusk
and almost immediately began his four-mile trek to the James-
Samuel farm. The detective should have listened to Moss and
Adkins. Whicher's body was found the next morning lying at
the side of the road at the intersection of the Liberty, Indepen-

dence, and Lexington Roads. The crossroads was located just a few miles east of Independence in Jackson County. He had been shot in the temple, through the neck, and in the shoulder. The bullets were fired at such close range that there were burn marks on Whicher's neck. Whicher would obviously not be hiring on at the James place.[2]

Deputy Sheriff John Thomason questioned the Blue Mills Ferry operator. Operator John Brickley told Thomason he had been approached by three men on horseback at about 3:00 in the morning. He had then been directed to take the ferry across the river. The men had a fourth man with them who was bound to the horse. This man had his arms tied behind him, his hat tied on with a handkerchief, and was gagged. It was explained to Brickley that the man was a captured horse thief. The ferry operator assumed the men to be peace officers when they advised him that they needed to cross the river in order to continue their pursuit of the thief's partner. The prisoner was allowed to get down from his horse while the men spoke to Brickley. Brickley later recalled that the man stomped his feet as if to warm himself and did not appear nervous or threatened. The man in charge threatened to set the boat adrift if Brickley did not cooperate after the ferry operator hesitated to make the crossing at such an hour. Thomason asked the operator for a description of the four men. Thomason considered that description and concluded that the men had been Jesse James, Arthur McCoy, and Bloody Bill Anderson's brother Jim. The bound man was James Whicher, on his way to his own execution.[3]

The murder of Whicher gave the newspapers something new to write. Some public opinion reflected the belief that the James boys had been alerted to the imminent arrival of Detective Whicher by someone of authority in Clay County, namely Sheriff George Patton. The newspapers that had been critical of most efforts to capture the outlaws jumped on the bandwagon. Sheriff Patton in turn filed libel suits against the *St. Louis Republican and Globe* for what he considered "maliciously false" statements about him. Though the suit went no farther, the *Republican* publicly recanted by stating that Patton was a "fearless and honest officer who has not flinched from performance of his duty as sheriff."[4]

Two other Pinkerton detectives arrived in the Youngers' home area of St. Clair County at the same time Whicher arrived in Clay County. One of them was a twenty-nine-year-old former Union Army soldier from Illinois named Louis J. Lull. Lull had been serving as a captain on the Chicago police force when he accepted an assignment from the Pinkerton Detective Agency to locate and arrest Cole and John Younger. The other detective was a former Confederate soldier from St. Louis named James Wright. Lull used the alias W. J. Allen, and Wright posed as a man named Boyle. The two men checked into the Commercial Hotel in Osceola where they met with a third Pinkerton operative named Ed Daniels. Daniels was a constable of Osceola Township who had been recruited by the Pinkertons to act as a local scout.[5]

John and Jim Younger attended a dance at the Monagaw Hotel on the night of March 16, 1874. They rose late the next morning in time to travel the short distance to the small settlement of Roscoe. They had been invited to dinner by their close friend, Theodrick Snuffer. The trio heard the sound of approaching horses shortly after they sat down for their meal. The Youngers were always on the alert. They immediately took to the attic and watched as Snuffer ambled outside to greet the riders. Lull and Daniels approached the house. Wright was visible to Snuffer, but he remained in the road. Lull asked Snuffer if he knew where they might find a widow named Sims. He explained that the three men were cattle buyers. They had been told that Mrs. Sims might have some cattle for sale. Snuffer gave them directions to the Sims place, then watched as they rode off in the opposite direction from that which he had told them. The Youngers descended from the attic to talk with Snuffer. John Younger immediately voiced the opinion that the three men were too well armed to be cattle buyers. He felt that the younger of the two (Daniels) looked nervous. John proposed that he and Jim follow the men to see what they were up to. The older, less impetuous Jim suggested that the brothers return to their meal. They could deal with the men later if the need arose. John insisted the men be followed. Jim reluctantly agreed to accompany him.[6]

Three-quarters of a mile up the road from the Snuffer place, Wright joined Lull and Daniels as they walked their horses. The men discussed their plan of action should they locate the

Younger boys. They turned when they heard hoofbeats behind them. They stopped in their tracks when they saw two young men approaching with guns drawn. Wright wasted no time, although he may or may not have known the identity of the two men. He gave his horse the spurs and headed in the direction of Osceola. Jim called to Wright to wait up, but the detective continued his flight through the fields. Jim aimed his revolver in Wright's direction and fired. Wright's hat flew from his head. The detective didn't even slow down. He was soon out of sight.

The Youngers turned their attention back to Lull and Daniels. John trained his double-barreled shotgun on the two men. He ordered them to drop their guns to the ground. Jim picked the guns up and examined Lull's English-made .43 caliber Trantor. He thanked Lull for the present. John Younger then asked the two men to identify themselves. Lull responded that they were from Osceola. Jim asked what they were doing in Roscoe. Lull replied that they were "just rambling around." John emphasized the presence of his shotgun and asked Lull and Daniels point-blank if they were detectives. Lull answered that they were not. Jim asked them why they were so heavily armed. Lull insolently answered that they had the right. Amused at Lull's attitude, John lowered his gun to Daniels's chest. He asked if Daniels also had something to say. Lull reached under his coat while the Youngers' attention was on Daniels. He withdrew a small No. 2 Smith & Wesson pistol. He promptly shot John Younger through the neck. John returned the fire and hit Lull in the shoulder and arm.[7]

Jim Younger fired at the detective as Lull's horse bolted down the road. His bullet found no target. Daniels spurred his horse in the direction that Lull had taken. Jim turned his gun immediately on Daniels and fired. Daniels fell to the ground. He had been shot through the neck. John Younger was not yet willing to give up the fight. He took off after Lull and chased him through a grove of trees. Lull was suddenly knocked from his horse by a low-hanging branch. John fired his revolver at the detective as he lay on the ground. Younger's bullet missed its mark, but the mortally wounded outlaw swayed in his saddle and fired again. This time the bullet hit Lull squarely in the chest. John rode back toward where his brother crouched, examining Daniels's dead body. John looked at his brother when Jim called his name. He then fell from his horse and landed on the far side of the nearby fence. John Younger was dead at the age of twenty-four.

Detective Wright had returned to Osceola where he informed Deputy Simpson Beckley of the incident. Beckley quickly organized a posse, but Wright disappeared while the posse was gathering. He was never seen in St. Clair County again. Allan Pinkerton would later declare him a coward.[8]

Younger's friends guarded John's body throughout the night. The following morning, the young man was buried in a shallow grave in Snuffer's yard as directed by Jim. The body was moved that night to the Yeater Cemetery that was a few miles southeast of Snuffer's farm. It was laid at an angle with John's head to the northwest and his feet to the southeast. This was done to insure that John Younger's grave would be apparent only to those who knew how to find it. A coroner's jury was called on March 18. It was determined that John Younger had been killed by W. J. Allen and that Ed Daniels had been killed by James Younger. The local doctors who attended him were at first optimistic that Lull would survive his injuries. Then his condition inexplicably took a turn for the worse. Lull's mother and wife arrived in the company of Pinkerton official Robert J. Linden. The detective's care was then transferred to Dr. D. C. McNeill. Ironically, Dr. McNeill was the father of Jim Younger's fiancée, Cora. Even the respected Dr. McNeill apparently could not save Louis Lull. Linden proclaimed Lull dead within a few days. Lull's body was placed in a wagon, put on a train in Clinton, and returned to his home state of Illinois.

Many people in St. Clair did not believe that Lull was dead. There existed the possibility that Lull's death had been faked by the Pinkertons. This would have enabled him to leave western Missouri before the Youngers arrived in St. Clair County to finish him off and avenge the death of their brother. Cora McNeill gave credence to this theory years later. She claimed that whenever her father was asked about the incident, he would not come out and deny that Lull had indeed been dead at the time he left St. Clair County. Dr. McNeill would always say the same thing: "You must learn to keep the game in your lead."[9] If Lull was not dead at the time he left Missouri, he did die sometime shortly thereafter. Lull was given an impressive funeral attended by hundreds of Chicago police officers and was buried in Rose Hill Cemetery in Chicago. The date on Lull's tombstone reads May 6, 1874.

Shortly after the deaths of Whicher, Lull, and Daniels, the Pinkertons began a word-of-mouth campaign against the friends of the James boys. They accused the people of Clay County of harboring outlaws and supporting their illegal activities. The matter soon began to be debated in the national press. The people of Missouri were accused of allowing a handful of lawless bullies to run their state and terrorize anyone who passed through it. Missouri Governor Silas Woodson suggested to the General Assembly of Missouri that a military unit with secret agents be organized. Woodson believed that the unit should be funded by the state to address the problem of outlawry.[10] In 1874, the Missouri House and Senate voted to appropriate $10,000 to hire secret agents to find and capture the outlaws. One-third of the House refrained from voting at all. A bill calling for a fund to be established for the widows and orphans of those killed attempting to arrest the James and Younger brothers was tabled. John Newman Edwards and other friends of the outlaws were offering motives and excuses for the actions of the James-Younger Gang. At the same time, the citizens of Missouri were being called upon to take a stand against their lawlessness. Editorials ran rampant as the issue was debated. Lines of either support or disapproval were drawn. The question of whether or not the murderous outlaws of Missouri were being somehow allowed to continue their vile and wanton acts was far-reaching. The *New York Herald* proposed that the brigands remained alive only because of the ''unpardonable cowardice of the whole community.'' This would not be the first or the last time the efforts, influence, and effectiveness of the gang would be argued.

Zee Mimms probably did not approve of Jesse's chosen profession as a bank and train robber, yet she was deeply in love with her cousin. She remained devoted to him throughout the nine years after Jesse had first arrived at her parents' house knocking at death's door. Zee's mother and father definitely did not approve of Jesse's outlaw activities, although they could not help liking their affable nephew. Mr. and Mrs. Mimms strongly discouraged the romance. So deep was her love that Zee uncharacteristically chose to ignore her mother's protests. When Jesse finally proposed that they be married, she readily agreed. Only Jesse would know if his decision to marry Zee was prompted by his desire for the couple to finally be man and wife. It may have been another of his schemes to promote his image. There seems little doubt, however, that Jesse was as deeply devoted to Zee as she was to him. Zee threatened to simply elope with Jesse when John Mimms declined to give the union of his daughter and the outlaw his blessing. The young woman was determined to marry the man she loved. Mrs. Mimms reluctantly agreed to the marriage only after the death of Zee's father.[11]

The wedding was held at the Kearney home of Zee's sister, Lucy Mimms Browder, on South Jefferson Street. The happy day was April 24, 1874. An elated Jesse boldly rode his horse down the main street of the town on the morning of the ceremony. He greeted friends and announced that he and his Zee were going to be married. Jesse was dressed in a new suit with a new pair of boots. Zee had hired a carriage from John H. Pemberton. Pemberton owned the Sheridan Hotel on Fifth Street in Kansas City, a site where Zee's father had also once been the proprietor of a hotel. She and her uncle William James left Kansas City bound for Kearney before sunup.

When Jesse arrived at the Browders' house that evening about 9:00, he was greeted by his Uncle Billy James. Uncle Billy was a Methodist minister whom Zee had asked to perform the ceremony. Reverend James voiced his concern to Jesse that life as an outlaw's wife was not something to which he could readily commit one of his favorite nieces. Jesse assured his uncle that he was not the evil antagonist portrayed in the newspapers. The reverend eventually submitted to Jesse's charm and determination to marry the girl he loved. Word was received that two detectives had been spotted riding toward Kearney from Liberty just as the ceremony was about to begin. Jesse saw no place other than the huge feather bed to hide his bride-to-be. He carefully placed Zee between the feather bed and the mattress. Then he left by the back door to retrieve his saddled horse. Jesse watched the detectives enter Lucy's house, then rode his horse by the front of the house, making as much noise as he could.

Zerelda Amanda ''Zee'' Mimms, Jesse's wife. *The Jesse James Farm*

The detectives ran out the door and took off in pursuit of the mysterious rider. Jesse sneaked back inside the house when they were well on their way back to Liberty. He fetched Zee from the bed, and Reverend James conducted the wedding ceremony.[12]

Jesse and Zee boarded a buggy that took them to the James-Samuel farm after they were pronounced man and wife. Jesse

remained with his new wife for a short time while they visited
with his mother and stepfather. Zee stayed on an additional couple of weeks as Jesse prepared a honeymoon for his bride. Ever
cautious, Jesse knew it would be safer for Zee to travel separately
from him until they were out of Missouri. On May 11, Zee
boarded a train bound for Sherman, Texas.[13] Zee was met there
by her new sister-in-law, Susan, and Susan's husband Allen
Parmer. Jesse reunited with Zee shortly thereafter. The couple
visited with the Parmers for a while, then spent time in Galveston
and Dallas. They eventually returned to Kansas City. A reporter
from the *St. Louis Dispatch* claimed to have run into the couple
on their travels. He said that Jesse told him all about his new
wife and marriage. Jesse was quoted as saying, "On the 23rd of
April, 1874, I was married to Miss Zee Mimms, of Kansas City,
and at the house of a friend there. About fifty of our mutual
friends were present on the occasion, and quite a noted Methodist
minister performed the ceremonies. We had been engaged for
nine years, and through good and evil report, and not withstand-
ing the lies that had been told upon me and the crimes laid at
my door, her devotion to me has never wavered for a moment.
You can say that both of us married for love, and that there
cannot be any sort of doubt about our marriage being a happy
one."[14] Rather than simply a comment, this testimony reads as
if it were another of Jesse's prepared, written statements. Here
Jesse claims to have been married in Kansas City rather than in
Kearney. He may have been trying to safeguard his new sister-
in-law's identity. The date of the wedding is also incorrect by
one day. Jesse mentions here that fifty people attended the ceremony. A party of fifty people would have been difficult to deny
if we are to believe the story about the wedding night detective
visit. Jesse's future daughter-in-law, Stella, later claimed that
there were no guests at the wedding.[15] One also has to wonder
why there has been no public acknowledgment of Jesse's mother
having attended her son's wedding.

Frank James may have been inspired by Jesse finally committing to family life. Frank eloped with Anna Reynolds Ralston
on June 6, 1874. Annie's father was Samuel Ralston of Jackson
County. Ralston was a prominent citizen of Independence. His
intelligent, demure, and attractive daughter was quite a catch for

Jesse James wedding portrait, c. 1875. Insert: Jesse in death, 1882.
The Jesse James Farm

the farm boy from Kearney. Although Ralston had lost a great deal of his property during the war, he had managed to hold on to some of his wealth. Annie had graduated from the Independence Female College with a bachelor of arts degree in science and literature on June 21, 1872. She taught school in Little Santa Fe, Missouri. Annie was known as a pretty, fun-loving young lady who liked to have a good time. She enjoyed picnics with her friends, boating and fishing, pistol shooting, and horseback riding.[16] It is not clear how Frank James and Annie Ralston came to be involved. Samuel Ralston was a Confederate sympathizer whose home had been used as a safe haven for the guerrillas during the war. It seems likely that one of the boys who found shelter there was Frank James. Even though both Ralston and Frank had championed the same cause during the War between the States, the outlaw activities of the James brothers were not met with approval by the Ralston family. Annie well knew that news of her involvement with the now-notorious Frank James would not be well received by her parents. She never told them that the two had fallen in love. Annie made the decision to withhold the news of her engagement from the Ralstons. She suggested to Frank that they elope. Samuel Ralston would not know who it was his daughter had married until well after the fact.

Annie told her parents that she was going to visit her sister and brother-in-law, the Hickmans, in Kansas City. Annie said that she wanted to continue a visit with a friend who was still aboard the train when Ezra Hickman met her at the train station. She told him she would take a buggy and meet him at his home in an hour or so. Annie met Frank after Hickman's departure. Annie had left a note at home for her mother that was discovered after she had left the state. The note read, "Dear Mother, I am married and going west."[17] Frank and Annie traveled northwest by train. They were married shortly after their arrival in Omaha, Nebraska. The Ralstons could only guess who it was their daughter married. They were informed only after an uncle of Frank James's encountered one of Annie's brothers in Kansas City weeks later and informed him of the identity of his new brother-in-law. Frank and Annie were honeymooning in Texas with Jesse and Zee by that time. Two years later, Frank visited the Ralston home for the first time since his marriage to their daughter. Frank claimed that he was calling on the Ralstons to let Annie's parents know that their daughter was well. The visit did not go well. Frank refused to tell Ralston the whereabouts of his daughter. The two men had a violent argument. Ralston later related to the *Kansas City Times* that Frank "talked about Annie a good deal and said she was well, and wanted to know if I 'had forgiven him.' I told him he was a damned rascal and had stolen my daughter and I wanted her to come back." The argument ended with Frank hotly shouting, "By God, she shan't come back and you shan't see her." Frank abruptly left the Ralston home.[18] So much for promoting amiable relations with the in-laws.

The spring was a quiet, reflective time for the Youngers as well. Bob Younger returned to Texas after the death of his brother John. He heard that Jesse James was honeymooning with his new bride at the Texas home of his sister Susan. Bob decided to visit the couple to offer his congratulations. That visit was to be the beginning of a close relationship between the two men. Jim Younger in the meantime was settling into the life of a rancher in Santa Margarita. He had taken a job with Jesse and Frank's uncle Drury James on his La Panza ranch.[19] Cole Younger continued to wander the countryside with his cattle. He was probably giving a great deal of thought to the next great escapade of the James-Younger Gang.

TWELVE

⌖

Death of an Innocent

"There is no crime, however dastardly, which merits a retribution as savage and fiendish as the one which these men acting under the semblance of law have perpetrated."
—*Kansas City Times*, January 28, 1875

THE EVER-CHANGING LIVES of Jesse and Frank James could have meant a new start as family men for both of them. Yet the fact that Jesse and Frank had both become husbands did not stop the periodic robbing of banks and trains. The people of Missouri were still fair game, regardless of whether or not Jesse was involved in the next noted criminal activity. On the Sunday afternoon of August 30, 1874, an interesting pair of events took place in Lafayette County. A trio of men wearing masks jumped in front of the Waverly-Carrollton omnibus that morning. They leveled their revolvers at the passengers and demanded whatever money was available. A few hours later, a second omnibus was ordered to stop in its tracks on the opposite side of the Missouri River near Lexington. The passengers were ordered to surrender their money and jewelry as well. Three armed men on horseback had been seen earlier that day boarding the ferry that took the

124

omnibus across the river to North Lexington. Many families and couples were out enjoying a Sunday stroll along the high road that ran alongside the river. They watched in stunned silence as the three men later emerged from behind a house and approached the omnibus. The men casually pointed their guns at the passengers on board and politely asked them to step down from the coach. The alarmed passengers complied and were asked to surrender their money and jewelry. A woman named Mollie Newbold stopped to watch the incident. She ran down to the ferry to alert the driver and those on board once she had determined what was happening. The ferry pilot quickly crossed the river toward the scene of the robbery. The bandits, however, had ridden off by the time they could be approached.[1]

Professor J. L. Allen was one of the passengers who had been aboard the bus. He later told a newspaper reporter that he was pleased to have been robbed by men of such national reputation as that of the James-Younger Gang.[2] There seems a fair amount of doubt, however, that the robbers were the members of the James-Younger Gang. Mattie Hamlett of Lexington told the newspapers after the robbery that she was well acquainted with the James and Younger families. She said she recognized the robbers to be Frank and Jesse James and Will Younger. Miss Hamlett claimed that she asked the men how they could stoop so low as to rob their Lafayette County neighbors—innocents who were only out for an afternoon of relaxation on an omnibus ride. She professed that after the men recognized her, they admitted that the deed was "a bit small" for them.[3] Indeed, had the robbers been the real James-Younger Gang, the stunt would have been small. The city of Lexington is close to the Clay County home of the Jameses. The Youngers had relatives who had lived in the town for years. Their brother Dick as well as other members of their mother's family had attended college there. If someone as casually acquainted as Mattie Hamlett, who had misidentified Cole Younger as Will, could recognize them, they certainly ran the risk of encountering family and friends. The unchivalrous act of drawing a gun on someone they might be friendly with doesn't seem to be something either the James or Younger boys would do. When Miss Hamlett was later asked to sign an affidavit stating that the men had been Jesse, Frank,

Archie Peyton Samuel, Jesse's eight-year-old half-brother. *The Jesse James Farm*

and Cole Younger, she refused.[4] A letter Miss Hamlett wrote to Zerelda Samuel was published on September 15 in the *New York Times*. It read:

My Dear Madam: Your letter of September 1 was received on the 2nd. After a hasty consideration of its contents, I have the privilege of replying as follows: I was accidentally in North Lexington on Sunday evening at the time of the robbery of the bus, the subject matter of the article in the Kansas City Times referred to by you. The statement does not correspond with my recollection of the circumstances; but that is not material to the letter. When called upon, with my escort, to return to the bus, I thought I recognized in the person who gave the order William Younger, and I hastily gave impression to the belief. On arriving at the bus I thought I recognized in one of the two persons who had it in possession Frank James, and on the impulse of the moment addressed him by name. The recognition (real or imagined) was acknowledged and from this circumstance it was repeated, on my authority, that the James brothers were the perpetrators of the deed.

After mature reflection on the subject I am prepared to doubt the accuracy of my recognition sufficiently to warrant me in refusing to make formal affidavit to the fact.[5]

There is a good chance that this was another of the copycat robberies that were taking place in various towns throughout the Midwest.

A St. Louis Police Department detective named Flourney Yancey was assigned the responsibility of investigating the robbery on behalf of the state of Missouri. Yancey questioned at least a dozen people but came up against a dead end. He claimed people who might otherwise have information about the robbers were silenced by their fear of retribution from the James and Younger brothers. There was no substantial evidence that pointed to the James-Younger Gang as being the perpetrators. Yancey evidently wanted to believe that the James and Younger brothers had been involved not only in the Waverly and Lexington robberies but several other small illegal encounters throughout western Missouri in the days following the robberies of the omnibuses. He claimed that they moved too quickly for him to form any kind of posse. He said that they were "mounted on the fleetest horses in the country and thoroughly versed in its geography."[6] Yancey claimed that he had squared off with Jesse James and Jim Younger in the brush near the Clay-Ray County line at one point during his investigation. Jesse may have returned from Texas by this time, but Jim Younger was still living in California. Additionally, Jim Younger wrote years later that he had never liked Jesse James and the two were never friends.[7] It does not seem likely that Jesse and Jim Younger would have been roaming the countryside together.

Detective Yancey's final report corroborated Governor Silas Woodson's claim that he did not have enough evidence to secure an affidavit with which to formally charge the James and Younger brothers with the crime. The *Lexington Register* sought to help him: ''The editor of this paper has this day forwarded to His Excellency an account of this robbery, and an offer to furnish, when and where demanded, the proper affidavit making the formal charge. The Governor can have a chance to show his zeal in the matter if he desires to do so.''

The gang's friends at the *Kansas City Times* countered on September 9 by claiming to have reliable information. They placed the Youngers in St. Clair County at the time of the robbery. They said that Frank James was laid up in bed. Jesse and Zee were on their honeymoon. Zerelda Samuel herself decided to visit Lexington in person to disclaim the rumors about her sons' involvement. She gave an interview to the *Lexington Caucasian* in which she informed everyone that ''No mother ever had better sons, more affectionate, obedient, and dutiful.''[8]

Cole Younger later wrote a letter to his brother-in-law, Lycurgus Jones, explaining his role in the events of the past few years. In a letter dated November 15, 1874, with a return address of Cass County, Younger wrote:

> You may use this letter in your own way. I will give you this outline and sketch of my whereabouts and actions at the time of certain robberies with which I am charged. At the time of the Gallatin bank robbery I was gathering cattle in Ellis County, Texas; cattle that I bought from Pleas Taylor and Rector. This can be proved by both of them; also by Sheriff Barkley and fifty other respectable men of that county. I brought the cattle to Kansas that fall and remained in St. Clair County until February. I then went to Arkansas and returned to St. Clair county about the first of May. I went to Kansas, where our cattle were, in Woodson county, at Col. Ridge's. During the summer I was either in St. Clair, Jackson or Kansas, but as there was no robbery committed that summer it makes no difference where I was.

This is no doubt an accurate alibi. Younger was not believed to have participated in the Gallatin robbery and was likely not there at the time Captain Sheets was killed. There is no doubt that the good folks of Ellis County would be absolutely truthful if they were to attest to Younger's presence there on that day. Younger continued with another pat alibi for another robbery he likely didn't commit.

The gate at the fair grounds was robbed that fall. I was in Jackson county at the time. I left R. P. Rose's that morning, went down the Independence road, stopped at Dr. Noland's, and got some pills. Brother John was with me. I went through Independence and from there to Ace Webb's. There I took dinner and then went to Dr. L. W. Twyman's. Stayed there until after supper, then went to Silas Hudspeth's and stayed all night. This was the day the gate was robbed at Kansas City. Next day John and I went to Kansas City. We crossed the river at Blue Mills and went up the other side. Our business was to see E. P. West. He was not at home, but the family will remember that we were there. We crossed on the bridge, stayed in the city all night and the next morning we rode through the city. I met several of my friends. Among them was Bob Hudspeth. We then returned to the Six-Mile country by the way of Independence. At Big Blue we met Jas. Chiles and had a long talk with him. I saw several friends that were standing at or near the gate, and they all said that they didn't know any of the party that did the robbing. Neither John nor myself was accused of the crime until several days after.

Younger was not at all pleased that Jesse had taken it upon himself to offer a denial that Younger was involved in the fair-ground robbery:

My name would never had been used in connection with the affair had not Jesse W. James, for some reason best known to himself, published in the Kansas City Times a letter stating that John, he and myself were accused of the robbery. Where he got his authority I don't know, but one thing I do know, he had none from me. We were not on good terms at the time, nor have we been for several years. From that time on mine and John's names have been connected with the James brothers.

Clearing his own name was an iffy proposition at best. Younger at least wanted to make an attempt to clear his brother's:

John hadn't seen either of them for eighteen months before his death. And as for A. C. McCoy, John never saw him in his life. I knew A. C. McCoy during the war, but have never seen him since, notwithstanding the Appleton City paper says he has been with us in that county for two years.

Younger's letter was clearly intended for newspaper publication. From there on out, it started to sound almost identical to the letters written by Jesse. It is likely that John Newman Edwards helped Younger compose his letter as well.

Now if any respectable man in that county will say he ever saw A. C. McCoy with me or John I will say no more; or if any reliable man will say that he ever saw any one with us who suited the description of A. C. McCoy then I will be silent and never more plead innocence.

Poor John, he has been hunted down and shot like a wild beast, and never was a boy more innocent. But there is a day coming when the secrets of all hearts will be laid open before that All-seeing Eye, and every act of our lives will be scrutinized; then will his skirts be white as the driven snow, while those of his accusers will be doubly dark.

Younger had a lot of friends in St. Clair County. It wasn't a stretch for him to come up with additional alibis:

I will come now to the Ste. Genevieve robbery. At that time I was in St. Clair county, Mo. I do not remember the date, but Mr. Murphy, one of our neighbors, was sick about that time, and I sat up with him regularly, where I met with some of his neighbors every day. Dr. L. Lewis was his physician.

As to the Iowa train robbery, I have forgotten the day, I was also in St. Clair county, Mo., at that time, and had the pleasure of attending preaching the evening previous to the robbery at Monegaw Springs. There were fifty or a hundred persons there who will testify to any court that John and I were there. I will give you the names of some of them; Simeon C. Bruce, John S. Wilson,

James Van Allen, Rev. Mr. Smith and lady. Helvin Fickle and wife of Greenton Valley were attending the springs at that time, and either of them will testify to the above, for John and I sat in front of Mr. Smith while he was preaching and was in his company for a few moments, together with his wife and Mr. and Mrs. Fickle, after service. They live in Greenton Valley, Lafayette county, Mo., and their evidence would be taken in the court of heaven.

Younger and his brother probably did attend religious services. While they were living in Texas they even sang in the church choir. But Younger's inability to recall the date of either the robbery or the services he attended make his alibi a little shaky. Mr. and Mrs. Fickle could probably go no further than to state that they had seen Younger at the service sometime during the month in question. Younger closed with:

As there was no other robbery committed until January, I will come to that time. About the last of December, 1873, I arrived in Carroll parish, Louisiana. I stayed there until the 8th of February, 1874. Brother and I stayed at Wm. Dickerson's, near Floyd. During the time the Shreveport stage and the Hot Springs stage were robbed; also the Gad's Hill robbery.[9]

On December 7, the Tishimingo Savings Bank of Corinth, Mississippi, was robbed of $5,000. Two knife-wielding strangers entered the bank and demanded money while two others waited outside. The cashier was slashed across the forehead during the robbery. One of the men was later identified by use of a photograph as having looked like Cole Younger.[10] It seems plausible that the robbery in Corinth was another copycat. The James-Younger Gang had never attempted a robbery using knives. Few people in Mississippi, leastwise those who would talk, knew what Cole Younger looked like. It is dubious that law enforcement would have an actual photograph of Cole Younger to show in the first place.

On December 8, 1874, the day after the robbery in Corinth, a robbery of the Kansas Pacific Railroad took place near Muncie, Kansas. This time it seems reasonable to assume that Jesse and his friends were involved. Five men ordered the section hands to pile ties on the track. They were then bound and gagged inside a shed while the robbers flagged down the train. The crewman was ordered to uncouple the baggage and express cars when the train stopped. At least $30,000 was removed from the two cars by the robbers.[11]

This robbery has been the subject of controversy in the years following its occurrence. The operation points to the method employed by the James-Younger Gang, yet several other names have been mentioned in popular histories. If the robbers were the James-Younger Gang, those in attendance were probably Jesse, Frank, Cole and Bob Younger, and Clell Miller. The story becomes complicated when one considers the other theories presented. One James family member believes that the James-Younger Gang was present, but he claims that they only interrupted a robbery already in progress by Bud McDaniels and Bill Ryan.[12] Ed Miller, brother of Clell, has been mentioned as having possibly been one of the bandits as well as former guerrilla Jim Cummins. A mystery man named Billy Judson participated according to Jesse's great-grandson.[13] Jesse added to the confusion of the accounting of the robbery when he later wrote: "Clell Miller, Tom McDannial, Wm. McDannial, Jack Kene and Sol Reed are the five men who robed the Muncie Kan R R train the 8th of Dec 1874. . . . When those scondrals robed the train at Muncie they took a horse and rode it to Clay county and turned it out to leave the impression that it was the James boys."[14]

The railroad officials were furious. They immediately offered a $5,000 reward. Additionally, they asked that the governor of Kansas match that amount with state funds. Kansas certainly did not want to gain Missouri's reputation as an outlaw state. The governor agreed to the railroad's request. He also offered another $1,000 of state funds for any information leading to the capture of the robbers. John Younger's friend Tom McDaniel's brother Bud was arrested in Kansas City a few days after the robbery. McDaniel was placed in jail for public drunkenness. He had over $1,000 and several pieces of jewelry in his pockets when he was searched by the sheriff. The sheriff was immediately suspicious that the jewelry in McDaniel's possession was some of that which had been taken from the safe aboard the Kansas Pacific train when it had been robbed at Muncie. McDaniel was charged as having been one of the robbers, but he escaped from jail before he could be brought to trial. McDaniel was tracked by a posse that quickly located the former Confederate. McDaniel was shot and killed when he attempted to run through a field to elude a farmer who was pursuing him. McDaniel never voiced whether or not he was guilty or who his accomplices might have been during the course of his brief incarceration.[15]

The various railroads who found themselves the victims of a robbery wasted no time in consulting with professional law enforcement agencies. They decided to take quick action against the outlaws involved. Posses were formed and generous rewards offered for information. The Pinkerton Detective Agency was technically still on the case. They had, to date, realized little results other than the death of John Younger, although they had made the claim that they were the best in their field. Younger had only been mentioned as a possible suspect in the Kansas City Fairground robbery. He had not been named a suspect in the Gad's Hill robbery for which investigation the agency had been hired. The Pinkerton hierarchy became desperate for results when it was recalled that three of their operatives had been lost with so little effect. Allan Pinkerton decided to call off all bets. He would now involve as many people and agencies as it took to carry out his most reckless and extreme plan to date. Pinkerton's men would confront the outlaws in their own homes. They would be quickly and effectively eliminated.

The Pinkertons' plan was set into motion when agent Jack Ladd was somehow able to become employed by a farmer named Daniel Askew. Askew was the next-door neighbor of the James-Samuel family. A special train supplied by the Hannibal and St. Joseph and the St. Louis, Kansas City, and Northern railroads delivered a specialized team of Pinkerton detectives and operatives to a station near Kearney, Missouri, some time during the night of January 26, 1875. Zerelda James Samuel and her family were awakened by the sound of their kitchen window breaking during the dark hours of this ominous night. Reuben Samuel was immediately alerted to danger. He leaped from his bed and ran into the kitchen. Zerelda realized that the noise she heard had come from that room. She ran outside so that she could go around to enter since the door of the kitchen was bolted from the inside.

Zerelda saw that the west side of the house was in flames. Her eight-year-old son Archie took in the terrifying sight just a few steps behind his mother. On the floor in front of her husband burned a huge wad of material. Reuben grabbed a shovel and tried desperately to push the sinister device into the fireplace. The room exploded in flames before the object reached the hearth. The entire house pitched and rolled with the sound of a terrible eruption that could be heard three miles away. Large fragments of the object flew about the room. Little Archie did not have time to get out of the kitchen and away from jeopardy. He was struck in the side by a jagged section of the explosive. Zerelda was hit herself before she could react to her son's disastrous injury. Part of her right hand and right arm were blown away. The fire raged within the kitchen of the small farmhouse. Reuben Samuel could do little but beat at the flames. The children of the James-Samuel family screamed in terror and confusion. The men who had lurked outside the house and thrown the fiery missile inside the home of an innocent, unsuspecting family escaped into the night.

Reuben finally managed to put out the fire. He then turned to stare in horror at his wife and small son. Reuben Samuel was a doctor. He knew that the hole in Archie's side was beyond repair. The little boy died within the hour. James A. Hall was a neighbor and friend of the Samuel family who arrived at the home shortly after the explosion. Hall rode to Kearney to get help. He returned with Dr. James V. Scruggs. Hall put Dr. Scruggs's horse in the barn and left the family to deal with their grief. Zerelda's anguish at the loss of her youngest son was interrupted only by the amputation at the elbow of her own ravaged arm.[16]

It has never been determined whether or not Jesse, Frank, or both brothers were at their mother's farm that night. There seems to be only one clue that points to the possibility that they may have been there. James Hall reported that Zerelda asked to be left alone shortly after he returned to the Samuel farmhouse with Dr. Scruggs. Hall believed that she said good-bye to someone. Hall further reported that Dr. Scruggs's horse disappeared from

Zerelda Elizabeth Cole James Simms Samuel, Jesse's mother. (Note missing right arm, blown off in the Pinkerton raid.) *The Jesse James Farm*

the Samuels' barn that night. It was found three miles away two days later.[17]

A pistol bearing the initials PGG (Pinkerton Government Guard) was later found near the fence.[18] This discovery allowed Jesse and Frank to further substantiate their solid belief that the men who had pledged to locate and annihilate them had become so desperate that they had attacked an unsuspecting woman and her children. History would confirm the James boys' instincts. Allan Pinkerton wrote a lengthy letter detailing the plan to destroy the James home in correspondence revealed almost a hundred and twenty years later. Pinkerton wrote to his Clay County operative Samuel Hardwick. He was very definite about what he wanted done: "Above every thing destroy the house . . . to . . . the fringe of the earth. . . . Let the men take no risk, burn the house down."[19]

It wasn't just the Pinkertons who were in on the planning of the attack. Allan Pinkerton had friends in high places. He was more than ready to ask their assistance. The Pinkertons had been getting nowhere with the James-Younger Gang. The deaths of Whicher, Lull, and Daniels had embarrassed and enraged Pinkerton. It was time to call in the United States Army. Dated December 30, 1874, an entry in the Rock Island Arsenal registry of letters posts a note from Lieutenant General Philip Sheridan in which he introduces Robert J. Linden: ". . . one of Pinkerton's Detective Police, who wishes to obtain certain materials from Rock Island Arsenal, to aid him in arresting certain railroad robbers."[20]

The bomb was later determined to be a shell filled with Levi Short's solidified coal tar and powder concoction. The cloth in which the shell was wrapped was soaked in Alfred Berney's "liquid fire."[21] There can be no mistake that this was a bomb meant to do some serious damage. The public outcry against the men who would do anything to achieve their goal was resoundingly in favor of the James boys. The vile act was considered contemptible, regardless of who it was the detectives had been seeking to destroy. Of course, John Newman Edwards at the *St. Louis Dispatch* had his say: "Such a species of warfare is worse than any ever yet painted of savage vengeance or atrocity. It showed the nature of the dastardly dogs who were hunting human flesh for hire, and who although the men sought were only two even if they had been at home, dared not meet them six to one and kill them in open fight or bring them in as prisoners for a mob to hang or a fanatical public opinion to condemn and execute without a trial."[22] The *Kansas City Times* proclaimed, "There is no crime, however dastardly, which merits a retribution as savage and fiendish as the one which these men acting under the semblence of law have perpetrated." Other newspapers, many of them avowed enemies of the Jameses and the executors of the crimes within Missouri, wrote equally scathing editorials against the methods used by the Pinkertons. The *Richmond Conservator* made the point that "the James boys never fired a dwelling at midnight."

Within days after the bombing, the Missouri legislature authorized investigation into the matter. Governor Charles H. Hardin appointed Adjutant General George Caleb Bingham to lead the investigation. Bingham filed this report, addressed to Governor Hardin, as it appeared in the *Jefferson City Peoples Tribune* on February 10, 1875:

Dear Sir: In pursuance of instructions received from you on Friday last, I proceeded without delay to Clay County to ascertain, as far as possible, the facts relating to the recent outrages, perpetrated in said county upon said family of, the step-father of the notorious James brothers, and to cooperate with the authorities there in any proper effort to bring the perpetrators to justice.

Having no power to compel witnesses to testify under oath, I have been able to obtain little information beyond which has already been given to the public by the press.

Mr. Samuels resides about 2½ miles east of Kearney, a small town 9 miles north of Liberty, and located on a branch of the H. & St. Jo R.R. running from Kansas City to Cameron. On the night of January 16th between 12:00 and 2:00 o'clock, the residence of Mrs. Samuels was approached by a party of men, the precise number of them is [sic] not known. A portion of the men stationed themselves behind an ice house on the eat side of the house and in front of the dwelling, about fifty or sixty yards therefrom. Another portion went in the rear of the building, the same being in the form of the letter "l" containing two rooms; the one farthest from the main building serving as a kitchen and sleeping room for negro servants. The entire building is a weather boarded wood structure, somewhat dilapidated by time. The party which approached the rear and west portion of the building set fire to the weather boarding of the kitchen in three or four places, and threw into the window a hand grenade.

This instrument was composed of cast and wrought iron or malleable iron, strongly secured together and covered with a wrapping saturated with turpentine or oil. As it passed through the window and as it lay upon the floor, it made a very brilliant light, alarming the family who supposed the kitchen to be on fire and rushed in to extinguish the flames. Mr. Samuels, seeing the burning instrument upon the floor, mistook it for a turpentine ball and attempted to kick it into the fireplace. Failing in this on account of its weight, he seized a poker and a pair of iron tongs, by means of which, he succeeded in getting it into the fireplace. It then immediately exploded with a report that was heard a distance of two or three miles. The part composed of cast iron broke into fragments and flew out with great force. One of the fragments shattered the right arm below the elbow of Mrs. Samuels the mother of the James brothers, to an extent which made amputation necessary. Another entered the body of her little son, Archie, wounding him mortally and causing his death in a few hours.

Mr. Samuels succeeded in putting out the fire in the weatherboarding, and arousing the surrounding neighbors with a cry of "Murder" which he continued to repeat until he was exhausted. Four pistol reports were heard by the neighbors as they came toward the dwelling, but when they reached it, the parties perpetrating the outrage had disappeared.

Who were these parties? This is a question which yet finds no answer, except in circumstances which do not seem sufficient for a complete solution of the mystery. On Monday, January 26, about half past seven o'clock in the evening, an engine with only a caboose attached came down the road from the north of Kearney. Several unknown men got out of the caboose, which then continued south in the direction of Kansas City. About two or three o'clock in the morning, Tuesday, the same or similar engine and caboose came from the direction of Kansas City and stopped for a considerable time at the place where the unknown men had been left after dark on the previous evening. The tracks of persons who were stationed behind the house and of those who set fire to and threw the grenade into the kitchen, and which were found on the path of their retreat, are made of boots of superior quality, quite different from those usually worn by farmers and farm hands in the surrounding country. In following the trail of the party on their retreat, a pistol was found which is now in my possession. The pistols has marks upon it which would scarcely be seen unless sought for, and which, I have been credibly informed, are identically such as to be known to be on the pistols of a well known band of detectives.

The bullet holes found on the fence on the east side of the dwelling, of which frequent mention had been made, do not indicate a conflict. If discharged from the direction of the ice house the Samuel dwelling would have been out of their range, and it cannot be supposed that the James brothers, had they really been home, would have left the dwelling to expose themselves openly to a superior force under cover. There are seven of these holes, and all within a space of 18 inches or two feet. The neighbors who came to the house immediately after the alarm was given all concur in the statement that but five reports were heard, one very loud and the other four subsequent thereto and such as might be caused by the discharge of pistols. Their impression is that this firing was for the purpose of keeping them at a distance until the assailants could make good their retreat. These bullet holes may be the result of some previous target shooting with pistols.

A little blood was found in several places on the snow in the path of the assailants as they retreated from the dwelling, but not more than might be caused by an accidental scratch on the hand or by bleeding at the nose. The parties who perpetrated the outrage doubtless approached the house under the belief that the James brothers were there, and set fire to it and threw in the grenade for the purpose of forcing them out and then shooting or capturing them; and on discovering that they had murdered an innocent lad and mutilated his mother, they deemed it prudent to retire and leave as little evidence by which they could be traced and identified.

I could not learn from any reliable source that either of the James boys had been in the area since last April. If they were in the house at the time they could have escaped through the cowardice of those attempting their capture. I had correspondence of some length with Mrs. Samuel their mother. She has had the advantage of an early education, and seems to be endowed with a vigorous intellect and masculine will; but she could give no information bearing upon the object of my visit.

I am satisfied that nothing short of the inquisitorial power of a

Grand Jury is likely to elicit such evidence as will lead to the identification of the parties engaged in a transaction the nature of which naturally permits them to resort to every possible method of concealment.

In the foregoing statement I have omitted the names of the citizens from whom I obtained such information as it contains, believing it best for the ends of justice that they should not be given to the public. I am convinced that the people of Clay County would feel greatly relieved if the James brothers could be captured and brought to justice. Their notoriety as desperadoes and the impunity which has accompanied their reckless doings are regarded as a most serious injury both to the character and material interests of their County, charged as it has been with affording them cover and protection.

Respectfully,
G. C. Bingham
Adjutant-General

The Pinkerton Detective Agency itself was not named as the perpetrator of the crime. The Clay County grand jury indicted Robert J. King, Allan Pinkerton, Jack Ladd, and five other unknown participants for the murder of Archie Samuel.[23] The case never came to trial, but was continued generally on September 13, 1877. This was practically the same thing as dismissing it.

Jesse must have been frantic with the need to publicly denounce those who killed his half-brother and maimed his mother. A letter was received by the editor of the *Nashville Banner* soon after this appalling event. Jesse asked the help of that newspaper in allowing him to state his views on the incident in a cover letter that was obviously written without the assistance of John Newman Edwards:

I will be under many obligations to you to publish the inclosed article. Publish it just as I have written it, though I wrote in great hast pleas correct all bad spelling in the article. I have gave you nothing but the truth. They is no doubt about Pinkerton's force committing the crime & it is the duty of the press to denounce him. The St. Louis Times & Dispatch, and many other Democrat papers in Mo. have stood up faithfully for us and last winter when the Amnesty bill was before the Legislature every ex-confederate in the Legislature voted for our pardon, among the number were

Gen. Shield, Gen. Jones who forwarded the bill & Col. Stichan Huchins Editor of the St. Louis Times, and it is against reason to suppose we are guilty of murder and robbery, the best men in Mo are our friends, and it is only a question of time about us being granted a full amnesty our friends will forward the Amnesty bill again this winter in the 29th assembly of the Mo Legislature, as soon as I get time I will write you a sketch of the lives of the James & Youngers. Major Jno. N. Edwards of the St. Louis Dispatch is at the present time writing the history of Quantrill and his men, which gives the history of the lives of the James & Youngers. Pinkerton has gained great notariety as a Detective, but we have so easily baffled him & he has got his best men killed by sending them after us, & he is fast loosing his Laurels & he wants to poison the minds of all Democrats against us. He would rejoice at our extermination. Pleas send one copy of the Banner to Mrs Samuel, Kearney, Clay co., Mo., so I will get the article I wish to publish. If Pinkerton has any cards published also send them to my mother, burn this note, Yours, Jesse W. James.

The article bore the return address of Kansas City and was dated August 4, 1875. It read:

My attention has just been called to an article published in the Banner of date July the 28th, in which W. A. Pinkerton denounces my statement to the Banner as a pack of falsehoods. It does not become me to reply to an article written by Pinkerton, but as the present opportunity gives me the opportunity to show the true character of Pinkerton & his force I will reply, also I consider it the greatest stains ever thrown on my character to notice an article written by him.

Pinkerton sed my statement to the Banner was false. If any honest man will investigate my statement to the banner and say I misrepresented anything, I will acknolledge my guilt to the world. If Mr. Tom Marshal, Proprietor of the Hotel at Chaplin, Nelson Co., Ky., will say I was not at home March the 20th 1868 the day of the Russellville, Ky, Bank robbery I will acknolledge I was in the Russelville robbery, and if D. B. Blackburn, ex Sheriff of San Louis Obispo co Cal. will say Frank James was not at work on Mr. Thompson Ranch on that day in Cal. I will say Frank James is guilty, and if the officers in Mo. that I sed I had been corresponding with will say that my statement is false, I will say Pinkerton has told the truth. As to Pinkerton proveing he was in

Chicago at the time he committed the outrage at mothers I do not
doubt as far as that is concerned. Pinkerton can prove in Chicago
that Black is white and white is Blac. So can Gen Wm T Sherman
prove in Chicago that Jeff Davisse had Lincoln assassinated &
that the brave Gen Wade Hampton burnt Columbia, S.C. all this
can be proven in Chicago, if people in the South didn't know that
Chicago was the home of Phil Sheridan and filled with Sherman
Bummers it might have some effect for Pinkerton to say what he
can prove in Chicago. There is hardly a child in Mo but known
it was Pinkertons force that committed the crime at Mothers & today Gov. C H Hardin has a Remington navy pistol in his possession that was found at mothers the morning after the Tragedy,
branded P.G.G. which stands for Pinkertons Government Guards
& it is a well-known fact that Pinkertons force and no other force
has pistols branded in that manner. Pinkertons men did commit
the crime and it is absurd for them to deny it.

Jesse knew the score. It was obvious that many of the details
of that night had been provided to him:

Pinkertons force chartered a special train on the H. & St. Joe R.R.
and com in to Clay Co. at night & crept three miles through the
woods to mothers residence and fired it in seven places & hurled
incendiary balls in to the house to kil & criple the entire family
& then gives them over to the mercy of the flames. But Providence
saved the house from being burnt altho it was saturated with Turpentine & fiered with combustable materials and the shell did not
do fatal work and they fled away to the special train that was
waiting to carry them beon the reach of outraged justice.

Jesse explained how he felt that justice was this time on his
side:

This is the work of Pinkerton the man that sed in his card he just
wished to set himself right in the eyes of the world. He may
vindicate himself with some, but he better never dare show his
Scottish face again in Western Mo., and let him know he is here,
or he will meet the fate of his comrades, Capt. Lull & Witcher,
meet, & I would advise him to stay in New York but let him go
where he may, his sins will find him out. He can cross the Atlantic,
but every wave & white cap he sees at sea will remind him of the

innocent boy murdered and the one armed mother robed of her child (and idol). Justice is slow but sure, and they is a just God that will bring all to justice. Pinkerton, I hope and pray that our Heavenly Father may deliver you into my hands, & I believe he will, for his merciful and protecting arm has ever been with me, and Shielded me, and during all my persecution he has watched over me & protected me from workers of blood money who are trying to seak my life, and I have hope and faith in him & believe he will ever protect me as long as I serve him. Oh, Pinkerton (if you have got a heart or conscience), I know the spirit of my poor little innocent brother hovers around your pillow, and that you, never close your eyes, but you will see his poor delicated & childish form around you & him holding his shattered arm over you and you looking at the great wound in his side and seeing his life blood ebb away. You may vindicate yourself with some people, but God knows if you did not do the deed it was by your force. The public press of Missouri has time and again charged this to you, and you have never denied it until your card to the Banner.

And in case Pinkerton needed to be reminded:

Joe Witchers came to Clay county, Mo., March 9 1874, and went to the honorable sheriff of Clay county with ten thousand lies, and that night he was kidnaped and got his just deserts; and it was in revenge for him that the Pinkerton force tried to destroy an innocent, helpless family. And a man by the name of Angle went to Chicago and filled the Northern press with his stories, charging the officials in Missouri with being in with the outlaws and that said Sheriff Patton, of Clay county, betrayed Witchers into the outlaw's hands. George E. Patton, sheriff of Clay county, is a relative of Gen Frank Cheatham, of Tennessee, and a one-armed Confederate, and one of the noblest and bravest officers that ever was in Missouri. It was this honorable Sheriff that Pinkerton's forces denounced to the world as being in with the outlaws, and Pinkerton's forces have also tried to injure John S. Groom, the present Sheriff of Clay County, and a more conscientious, braver and honorable oficer never lived than Captain Groom.

With that Jesse closed:

I have made these statements because they can't be disputed. I defy man to prove one word of my statements to be false. Pinkerton's force, Bly of Kentucky, and Jim Tracy, of St. Louis, are the men who have filled the world with stories about the James and Youngers. I could fill pages with Detective Tracy's doings, but from the papers it is not necessary from me to tell the Nashville anything about Tracy. Pinkerton, let me hear from you again.[24]

The wave of public sentiment in favor of Jesse and the gang continued. On March 8, an editorial appeared in the *St. Louis Dispatch* suggesting the James and Younger brothers be granted amnesty. Edwards wrote in part:

How much better it would be to amnesty those unfortunate men, to whom are attributed all crimes bold and startling in their daring, and so far are astounding for their impunity, which have for the past two years been committed from Iowa to Texas, and from Tennessee to Kansas. Give them the opportunity to come home and be honest and peaceful citizens, instead of being hunted like wolves by detectives, who are willing to sell their blood for the gold of a paltry reward. Relieve them from apprehensions of caprious arrest, and their families from danger of assassination by hand granades and infernal machines. Let them be assured that arson, murder and assassination shall not be employed against them and their innocent ones, and it is more than probable they will make at least as good citizens as Pinkerton's midnight spies and house burners. We speak of all citizens who like the James and Younger brothers have been educated to desperation by cruelties perpetrated on them and their families during and since the war, and who are only hunted upon suspicion. For so far as we have been able to learn there is neither warrant nor requisition for them in the hands of any officer of the law in this State.

Their supporters had believed in the past that the members of the James-Younger Gang had been driven to their crimes through persecution. Now evidence of such harassment and molestation was clearly evident. A resolution reflecting that theme was submitted to the Missouri House by representative Jefferson Jones of Callaway County. It was dated March 17, the first anniversary of the death of John Younger. A full pardon for the gang's wartime activities was proposed. A certain amnesty would guarantee a fair trial for any of the crimes for which they had been charged since that time. The phrasing was clearly that of John Newman Edwards, although Jefferson Jones delivered the legal content of the document. Those who opposed the bill argued that citizens who had been placed in similar positions to that of the James and Youngers during the war had somehow been able to lead productive, nonviolent lives since the end of the war.[25] Jones's bill failed to receive the two-thirds vote necessary to pass it. General James Shield then filed a proposal on behalf of the Commission on Federal Relations. He suggested that the outlaws be allowed a fair trial during which they would be promised protection. This bill also failed by a slim margin.

On April 12, all of the headway the members of the gang had made with the legislators through the outpouring of sympathy over the bombing deteriorated. Daniel Askew, the neighbor who had employed and apparently harbored Jack Ladd during the planning of the raid on the James-Samuel household, was alone at his well one night. He was shot three times in the head. A letter discovered years later seems to confirm Askew's knowledge of the true identity of Ladd and his own involvement in the conspiracy. Allan Pinkerton wrote to Askew's widow Adaline: "... when you first heard the shot which told of your husband's death, you sent your daughters out of the room and destroyed the letters of mine, it showed careful forethought when it occured to you that none other should know what your husband held in life, in death proof died with him. ..."[26]

The immediate suspect in Askew's murder was Jesse James. A letter written to someone named "Jim" dated June 10, 1875, and addressed from Commanche, Texas, surfaced years later. It has been speculated that it was authored by Jesse:

> I hear that they are making a great fuss about old Dan askew, and say the James Boys done the killing. It's one of old Pink's lies, circulated by his sneaks. I can prove I was in Texas, at Dallas, on the 12th of May, when the killing was done. Several persons of the highest respectability know that I could not have been in Clay county, Missouri, at that time. I might name a number who could swear to this, whose word would be taken anywhere. It's my opinion Askew was killed by Jack Ladd and some Pinkerton men. But no meanness is ever done now but the James Boys must bear the

blame for it. This is like the balance of lies they tell about me and my brother. I wish you would correct the lies the Kansas City papers have printed about the shooting of Askew, and oblige. Yours faithfully, Jesse.[27]

Some people verbalized the belief that since the murdering of Jesse's innocent little brother had garnered so much positive publicity for Jesse and the gang, maybe it was the Pinkertons who killed Askew in an effort to turn the sympathetic tide. The *Chicago Times*, the Pinkertons' hometown newspaper, speculated that when Askew had threatened to reveal the details of the conspiracy and the role he played in the drama, he had been silenced.[28] Clay County's Sheriff John Groom, once a supporter of Jesse James, evidently was more inclined to agree with those who knew that certain enemies of Jesse often wound up dead. Groom asked new Missouri Governor Charles H. Hardin to ensure the James boys a fair trial in the hope that they would turn themselves in and the bloodletting would end.

THIRTEEN

~~~~~

Fatherhood and Robberies

"The other three entered the house and had the coffin opened. Said he did not look like he did before. One of them was crying. They asked for me and then went into the cornfield. I was at the house about five minutes after they left. I look for a desperate attack today."

—*Louisville Courier-Journal*, September 25, 1875

JESSE WAS ENJOYING his new life as a family man, but Missouri law enforcement was not making it easy for him. He must have felt that it would be safer for Zee if he were to take her away from the scrutiny of his enemies for the time being. Zee was pregnant with the couple's first child. She certainly didn't need the daily anxiety that living in Missouri no doubt caused her. Jesse took his family responsibilities very seriously. He decided to relocate to Tennessee. Few people actually knew him there. He could lie low until after the birth of the baby. This small concession would enable Jesse to fulfill his desire to support his pregnant wife. Jesse rented a small house at 606 Boscobel Street in Edgefield, Tennessee.[1] Edgefield was across the Cumberland River from Nashville. Jesse had traveled to Nash-

147

ville after the war and had been treated by physician Dr. Paul
Eve. He had been satisfied with Dr. Eve's treatment of his lung
wound and had found the city attractive.[2] Jesse could move
freely there without the constant worry of being recognized and
confronted. Not only would he and Zee be safer, but Jesse could
enjoy a respite from the tension that he had been under in Missouri. So Edgefield it was.

Jesse had always enjoyed his mobility. Just because he was
now living in Tennessee it is unlikely that he felt tied to adventure within that one state. Jesse traveled whenever he liked and
wherever he saw fit to go. An interesting event occurred in Clinton, Missouri, shortly after Jesse moved to the Nashville area. It
suggested that Jesse may have reunited with his brother and two
of the Youngers for more of the same that caused him to relocate
to another state in the first place. On May 13, 1875, the dry
goods store of D. B. Lambert was the scene of encounter between eight young people playing croquet on the lawn beside
the store and four well-dressed gentlemen on horseback. The
strangers approached the group of young men and women with
their guns drawn and asked them to move inside the store. Jewelry was taken from the women along with some of Lambert's
firearms. All in all, the take from the robbery was a mere $300.[3]

The identities of the robbers were not known or even suggested until after Clinton farmer Matthew Dorman made a statement. Dorman remarked that he had spoken with two of the
Youngers and two of their friends as they passed through Clinton
a few days before the robbery had taken place.[4] Dorman's having
seen them in the area did not necessarily tie the group to the
crimes. The Youngers passed through the area often. No formal
warrants were issued. The paltry robbery may have been the
work of two of the Youngers and unnamed friends of theirs. It
could have been the work of Jesse and Frank with the Youngers.
It may have been nothing more than a robbery by highwaymen
who were simply passing through the railroad town.

Jesse himself is the one who made the Clinton robbery particularly significant to the history of the James-Younger Gang.
For whatever reasons, Jesse may have felt it necessary to not
only deny his own participation in the event but to offer his own
suspects. A letter addressed to "My Dear Friend" was written

after the Muncie and Clinton affairs but was not published until after Jesse's death. The author provided details pertaining to those incidents. The details were, however, likely fictitious paragraphs designed to completely question the credibility of any of those who felt they had any knowledge whatsoever on the makeup or comings and goings of the James-Younger Gang. The letter is apparently addressed to a lawman, possibly Sheriff John Groom of Clay County. The author was said to be Jesse James. He wrote:

> Your welcome letter of date the 21st reached Mrs. [deleted by the newspaper] yesterday morning, and was forwarded to me immediately, and as I have an opportunity to send a letter to Kansas City to be mailed I will write to you in haste. You said you was greatly surprised, you suposed I was in Texas or Mexico. I am generaly where people least expect me to be. You asked me if I was innocent why I did not give my self up. [name deleted by newspaper] you are a man of reason but I ask you to reflect for a moment. I believe Gov. Hardin would give me an impartial trial if it was in his power, but don't you know that I have ben lied on and persecuted so long that the public prejudice is so great against me that it would take one hundred thousand dolars to defend me of all the charges that would be brought against me, and I am a very poor man and have not got the money it would require to defend me, although I am innocent, and besides that a requisition would be issued for me from Iowa and how long do you supose I would be spared a MOB in that radical State.

The author claimed he was innocent of any crime and asked to be believed:

> You say I should leave the country. If I was guilty I would flee the U.S. and never return, but I am innocent and this is the land that gave me birth and right here I intend to stay and contend for my rights, and have my character vindicated or die in the attempt.
>
> So, reflect for one moment and give my case a rational thought, and then I am sure you will say that I am right. The slanderous newspapers have published ten thousands lies on me which you know, but I have a clear conscience and believe I will yet be vindicated of all the slanderous charges against me. There are men in Mo. who have ben robing on the James & Younger credit and

my object is to have those parts aprehended and then that will
rectify the charges against us and lift the dark stain from our character and then we can easily prove our innocence to the world. I
am now in correspondence with Gov. Hardin (This I tell you con-
fidentially) and I believe I wil succeed in having those scondrels
captured.

For one month I have had a corps of detectives at work, not
Chicago detectives, true and honest Missourians, feriting out the
robbers who have been disgraceing Mo. in the name of the James
& Youngers, and I have ferited them out and now the thing is to
catch them. You will be surprised but it is true. I will make it true
to you.

The author's next few paragraphs are not only surprising but
incredible when one considers that the men he names had served
as guerrillas, all been a part of the James-Younger Gang at one
point in time or would work again with Jesse in the future. The
guerrilla network had served Jesse well. It doesn't seem practical
or likely that Jesse would incur the wrath of that network by
implicating his fellow guerrillas in crime. If the author were indeed Jesse, whether he had a temporary falling out with these
men or was working with smoke and mirrors is not known. He
stated:

Clell Miller, Tom McDannial, Wm. McDannial, Jack Kene and
Sol Reed are the five men who robed the Muncie Kan R R train
the 8th of Dec 1874. Wm McDannial is in custody, Clell Miller,
Tom McD, Jack Kene and Sol Reed are the four men who robbed
the store in Henry co Mo a few days ago, they cannot be a doubt
of this for I have had a true determined man on their trail, they
can all be identified as the store robers and they is no trouble
about convicting they of the Muncie robbery which they is a reward of $3500 for each one of the party. But it is not this reward
I seak. I wish to vindicate the persecuted.

The author even went so far as to provide a short criminal
history of the comrades he accused:

I will now give you the history of Reed and Kene. Reed is a
brother to the celebrated robber Jim Reed, who was killed in La-
mar county, Texas, August 6 1874, by John T. Moriss, and Sol

Reed is a noted horse-thief and robber. Jack Kene is a brother-in-law to Reed and was outlawed several years ago for robbing an old man in Pettis county, Mo. He then fled to Texas and was with Jim Reed and Cal Carter one year ago when they robed the El paso stage between Austin and San Antonio Tex. Kene was then going by the name of Rogers. They is a reward of $2250 for Kene from Texas for this stage robbery. After Jim Reed was killed Kene fled to Clay co Mo, his object was to come to Clay co and steal and rob in the Jameses names which he has successfully done. Last winter he lived near Fielden Kendlys on Mr. Arnolds farm and went by the name of Tom Brock. Sol Reed married a daughter of Arch Deness and lived on Illmore Rileys farm.

He claimed to have even more current information:

When those scrondrels robed the train at Muncie they took a horse and rode it to Clay county and turned it out leave the impression that it was the James boys. A few months ago Reed and Kene left Clay county very secretly but after a thorough search I have located them. They have got a house rented in the north-east portion of St. Joseph, Mo., near the tan yard, and Reed is going by the name of Tom Brockman, and I believe that is where all the stolen horses go to from Clay county. I believe that is headquarters for Miller and MacDannial and I believe all four of these men are in St. Joe at present. From the description of Strawther Gaine horse I believe Jack Kene was riding in the store robbery in Henry co. and no doubt but the horse is in St Joe at this time. I have positive proof those men crossed the Mo. river Saturday evening May the 15th going north, and I have information Dr. Yates of Kearney lost a fine horse that night which I believe they got.

There is no doubt but they are fixing to rob a bank or R.R. I will show them how it is to rob on my credit. I am having them hunted with vengence. Gov. Hardin is fully posted and is working to get them. I have just received a letter from the Gov. If Reed and Kene are not very cautious they will be captured in a few days, also Miller and McDannial. Miller and McDannial may be in Clay co. at present. If they are they can be easily killed or captured, but I want Miller taken alive. If he is I believe he will tell all he knows about the robbing and stealing, for he has been in with the McDannials for a long time. If they are in Clay co. you can get them if you will do as I say.

With that he presented a plan:

Take 10 or fifteen good men with Shot guns and surround Mose
Miller and Mrs Foxes houses some morning at daylight and also
search the strip of woods betwen Moses Millers and Mrs Arnolds
house. You are more liable to find them in that skirt of the woods.
Also search Kendleys house. This may surprise you. Kendley has
put on a bold front and hunted I and Frank and at the same time
had horse thieves harbored.

I know this to be true, but if you desire to capture those thieves
don't let Kendley know that you are after them, if you do he will
give them a warning. You had better get up your party in Liberty
and Kearney and let nobody but those you have with you know
your business, and be certain you know who you have with you.
My plan would be if was you to send reliable men out to watch
Mrs. Foxes, Mose Milers and Kendleys houses and when they go
into their dinners or breakfasts close in on them with shot Guns.
I want them caught and will do all I can to have it done for I
cannot stand to have men rob on my credit always.

I have positive proof Clell Miller was riding his fathers iron
Gray mare in the henry co store robbery, and if you can find the
mare about Mr. Millers it is good proof Clell is at home or been
there. Clell or this mare can be identified as being in the store
robbery. The mare is blind in the right eye. Find out if this mare
is at home and if she is inform the sheriff of henry co, and tell
him to send up some one to recognize the mare, and if that is
done a warrant should be put in your hands for Clell. You get
Clell and you are good for $3500.

You had better go to Kansas City and see Fred Mitchell, attorney for Wells, Fargo & Co. and have the proper papers fixed up
for Miller and McD, and then if you can get them you are sure
of the reward. But dont tell Mitchell you heard from me. Dont tell
anyone but Gov. Hardin that I am posting you. I dont cair for your
telling him, but dont breathe it to any one else.

The friends of bill McDaniel have tried to implicate I and James
O hinde in the Muncie robbery is why I am determined to have
those parties captured. You remember the paper spoke of a little
man in the Muncie also a little man in the store robbery. That is
Sol Reed.

Once again an attempt to prove the author's credibility was
offered:

Now, [name deleted by the newspaper] a word with you. Did you know [name deleted by the newspaper] had made the detectives believe you are in league with the robbers? He has. I have a few good friends on the detective force who keep me fuly posted, so I know every move that is made, altho my enemys are not aware of this tho Pinkerton is suspicious of every one. He believes I have got in with some of his men and they tell me all, which is true, but no one will ever know from me.

My best friends pretend to be my worst enemys in order to carry out my points. So you see I can be traped. If I was disposed I could tell you many things that would surprise you. One night a party of six men met at Walter Arnold's to watch Branders for me. A dog started to follow them and went one hundred yards with the party and they drove it back. I am even better posted than that, so you see I find out all. If you believe me guilty I honor you for hunting me. It is your duty to put down crime, but I solemnly assure you Clay co. is no danger from the James boys, and as soon as four men I write of are captured the most of the crime in Mo. will ceased.

I have wrote long and fully to you and I bind you to secrecy to all but Gov. Hardin. Burn this letter. I will try to keep you posted. I cannot be traped by letters, for all letters I get go through several hands before I get them. Please write immediately and let me know what you think about what I have written. [Name deleted by the newspaper] the dirty dog is writing all those lying newspaper reports about Clay county and the James boys.

He fears us and he is telling all the lies he can to get us killed but he will get his just dues in times. Write in haste. Address as before to Mrs. Hannie McBride, Tracy Avenue, Kansas City, Mo. Mrs. McBride will forward to me in haste. May you and your live long and prosper in the prayer of your sincere friend.

P.S. As fast as I get news from those men I will post you and don't you make a strike for Miller until you can make a sure one. After the way you acted after the tragedy at mother's I was very mad at you, but after I reflected on I could not blame you and now have no harsh feelings at you.[5]

This letter, if really written by Jesse, is fascinating. If he was tired of people "robbing on" his "credit," why didn't he stop them himself? Especially since he had so much information. Jesse would have had all the information he needed as to the whereabouts of former guerrilla comrades through his use of the guerrilla network. He would have had no use for hiring or using detectives. Did Jesse James befriend and use Pinkerton detectives? Doubtful. Yet the writer of this letter has some very intricate and personal knowledge of the men he accuses and their habits. Additionally, the style, punctuation, and spelling are very similar to the letter Jesse had published that was not edited by John Newman Edwards. It is certainly possible that the writer of this letter was not Jesse at all. Perhaps the Pinkertons are responsible for this letter. It may have been an effort to smoke out Sheriff Groom's, or whoever's, affiliation and support of Jesse and his gang. Information the detectives may have gathered themselves in regard to the activities of Jesse's friends and gang members may have been incorporated to make it sound as if this was all new information. Jesse's letter-writing style could have been easily duplicated by an educated man. The use of Mrs. Hannie McBride's name as a contact is interesting also. Mrs. McBride was Zee's sister. It does not seem likely that Jesse would involve an in-law in so nefarious a plot as to rat out his gang members. It would be easy for a Pinkerton detective to watch Mrs. McBride's mail closely and intercept any letter that would be in answer to this epistle. If the Pinkertons were able to prove that Sheriff Groom was indeed in cahoots with the James brothers, they would have something big to take to Governor Charles H. Hardin. They would have been able to vindicate themselves as to any charges that they were not doing their jobs well enough. Perhaps this was a plan approved by the governor. That may be the reason it is asked in the letter that the governor be the only one informed of the letter's existence. There doesn't seem to be any evidence that Jesse wrote to any Missouri governor other than through the newspaper. Correspondence from a governor to Jesse has never surfaced, either. We may never know either the writer of this letter or its authenticity.

Regardless of whether or not Jesse was in Clinton, Missouri, on May 13, he was in Nashville with Zee when on August 31, 1875, she gave birth to Jesse's first son.[6] Jesse Edwards James was named after his father and John Newman Edwards. Jesse's son entered the world with little fanfare but with the deep love and affection of his parents.

Frank and Cole Younger were extending their expertise in

bank robbery while Jesse was learning how to be a father. The pair of former guerrillas probably welcomed an opportunity to embark on their own adventure without the presence of their younger brothers. Perhaps their next move was purely impulsive and improvisational. It seems fairly evident that Frank and Cole were present at the 1875 robbery of the bank in Huntington, West Virginia, regardless of the degree of planning that may or may not have gone into the adventure.

Frank and Cole needed someone they could trust to accompany them. They recruited John Younger's friend, Tom McDaniels. McDaniels was still wanted in Texas for his part in the death of Deputy Nichols, but he had since returned to Missouri. Since McDaniels had not revealed Younger's whereabouts before John's death, it was determined that he could be trusted. Former guerrilla Tom Webb was also invited to participate. Webb had been present at Lawrence and had supported Cole Younger's retreat from the burning city. Evidently, the actions of these two men in the past had earned the respect of Cole and Frank.

One of the men posed as J. C. Johnson when he stayed at the Huntington House a few days before the planned robbery. The others stayed at the farm of Isaac Crump outside town near Barboursville. The four men arrived midmorning in Huntington on September 5, the day of the proposed robbery. One of the men pretended to be a customer at Sanburn's Blacksmith while another posted himself close to their horses. A third man entered the store of P. A. Powell. This afforded him a good view of the front of the bank. Powell immediately suspected that the bank was about to be robbed, but there was little he could do. The stranger in front of him positioned him with his back to the back entrance of the store. The only way Powell would have been able to leave the premises would have been to push his way past the large, heavily armed man in front of him. Two of the outlaws quietly entered the bank while all of this was going on.

The pair walked up to Cashier Robert T. Oney and lowered their revolvers. They demanded Oney open the vault. Oney claimed that he had no idea where the key to the inner safe was kept. He left it to the robbers to find it for themselves. The outlaws successfully located the key and removed at least $9,000 from the vault. They grabbed another $1,000 from the counter. Then something out of the norm of the usual bank robbery occurred. Oney was asked by one of the bandits whether any of the money in the bank was his own personal funds. The cashier replied that his account balance was about $7. The robber handed him that amount while explaining that it wasn't necessary that the robbery should cost any employee his own money. At this point, a bank messenger named Jim entered the room. Jim was immediately taken hostage. The robbers put their revolvers to the backs of Oney and Jim's heads. They walked behind the two men as they left the bank through the front door. Then they quickly crossed the street. They paused only long enough to grab the reins of their horses as they were proffered by their accomplices. The two men were allowed to go free as the four bandits took off down the street and out of town. Bank president John H. Russell was returning from lunch with the town druggist when Oney hollered to him that the bank had been robbed. There was little for Russell to do by that time except join the posse that was immediately called into action. Men from the town of Huntington scampered to find clues that might lead them to the outlaws.[7]

The first clue that the posse was on the right track was when they came upon a sack containing $32 in nickels that had been tossed aside. By afternoon, the posse encountered a man named Barbour who informed them that he had been forced at gunpoint to guide the robbers through the countryside several miles outside of Huntington. Barbour explained that he traveled with them for nearly an hour and then was allowed to go free.[8] Posses were formed from the various small towns in the area but the increase in size did not increase the effectiveness of the posse. The West Virginia posse followed the trail of the outlaws to the state of Kentucky. Detective Yankee Bligh was once again called in to scour the countryside in search of clues to the bandits' whereabouts. Descriptions of the robbers were made public:

No. 1: Heavy-set man, at least six feet high, weight two hundred pounds, tolerably dark hair, with reddish whiskers and mustache, red complexion, black hat, long linen duster and blue overalls, gold ring on left little finger. [Cole Younger?]

No. 2: Tall, slim man, about six feet, one hundred and fifty pounds, delicate looking, light hair and sandy whiskers, high forehead, long nose, gold buttons in shirt, left little finger had a ring, long duster and blue overalls. [Frank James?]

No. 3: Tall, slim man, about six feet high, weight one hundred and sixty-five pounds, short, black whiskers and black hair, slim face, black hat, long duster, blue overalls, suit of black twilled cloth with stripes, fine boots, two gold rings on left little finger, had two collars washed with "London" printed on the bands. [Tom Webb?]

No. 4: Heavy-set man, about five feet ten inches high, weight one hundred and eight pounds, very stout, square-looking man, brown hair, round red face, patches of red whiskers on his chin, light-colored hat, linen duster, gray striped coat and vest, pants similar, but not like coat and vest, red drilling overalls, fine boots, broad gold ring with flowers cut in it on his left little finger.[Tom McDaniels?][9]

The bandits were spotted a day or so later by a posse lead by a Captain Littrell. Shots were exchanged, then the outlaws disappeared into a thicket. Word was received from Pine Hill, Kentucky, that the outlaws had been seen at Livingston Station. Farmer William Dillon noticed a group of strangers approaching his farm that was not far from that location. The men shot at Dillon when he called to them asking the nature of their business. Dillon was not one to take any guff. He wasted no time in returning the fire. Dillon's sure shot seriously wounded one of the outlaws. The bandit called out to his companions: "I can't get away. Take my pistol and go."[10] The fugitives attempted to camouflage their wounded colleague in a cornfield, then quickly continued their retreat. Very soon the posse led by Yankee Bligh approached Dillon's farm. Dillon told them what had happened and how he thought that one of the outlaws had been left in the cornfield. Bligh and his men found the wounded robber who by now was somewhat delirious. He had been shot in the chest and appeared to be close to death. Bligh asked his name and the outlaw answered "Hutchinson." Then he changed his reply to "Charley Chance." Bligh was not fooled and said so. A rumor spread among the posse that the wounded man had to be Jesse James when the outlaw refused to identify himself further. The

Frank James with horse Dan and dog. *The Jesse James Farm*

robber was in fact Tom McDaniel. As McDaniel lay dying, he asked, "Did they get Bud, my partner?" No one would know if he was calling his dead brother Bud or Cole Younger, who was often called Bud by his friends. Bligh went through McDaniel's pockets after the outlaw breathed his last breath. He found maps of Kentucky and Tennessee, a gold watch, a charm of an eagle's head, a letter addressed to "Dear Brother" from "Anna," and a compass. Also in the dead man's pocket was a photograph of Bob Rickets of Kansas City. When Rickets was later identified as being a neighbor of Thompson McDaniels, he claimed that McDaniels was the only one who had his photograph. Cashier Oney quickly recognized the dead man as having been one of those who was involved in the robbery.[11]

The other three outlaws continued their flight toward Tennessee after they left McDaniel dying in a cornfield. Three miles away from Dillon's place, a watchman guarding a locomotive at a coal mine talked briefly with the robbers, then they disappeared. Farmer Dillon later told authorities that the men who had been with McDaniel at the time of his death returned to see the body of their fallen comrade. The visit made Dillon extremely uncomfortable.

The posse kept a vigilant eye and was able to continue their close pursuit. One of the outlaws' horses threw a shoe as they approached Fentess County, Tennessee. The rider was forced to dismount. The bandit was immediately surrounded by the members of the posse. His comrades spurred their horses forward and disappeared into the countryside. This time, Bligh wasted no time in searching the man's pockets for identification and/or booty. The outlaw told them his name was Jack Keene as nearly $4,500 of the bank's money was removed from his pocket. Keene offered to give the posse the money in exchange for his freedom. His offer was denied. Bligh at first believed he had captured Cole Younger as he believed Younger had been the "money man" in previous robberies. "Keene," however, was somehow revealed to be Tom Webb. Was Webb posing as the real-life robber Keene whom Jesse had accused of the Clinton robbery, or was Keene a fictitious personality all along?[12] Webb was promptly arrested and returned in irons to West Virginia. He was tried for the Huntington robbery shortly thereafter. Webb was easily and promptly convicted. His sentence was twelve years in the state's prison.

The other two robbers, likely Frank James and Cole Younger, escaped the posse altogether. Jesse later decided to defend Cole Younger against any claims that Younger had been involved in the robbery in an effort to discredit Yankee Bligh. Jesse wrote a letter dated September 21, 1875, to the editor of the *Nashville American*. His return address was St. Louis:

In a previous communication I spoke of how the Jameses and the Youngers had been lied on by Bligh, the incompetent detective of Louisville, Kentucky. I will take the present opportunity to inform you that Bligh's present Statement about the Jameses and Youngers robbing the Huntington, West Virginia, bank is a fake. Instead of my being shot and captured, I am in St. Louis with friends, well, and feeling much better than I have for years. I can't see what motive any one can have in reporting such malicious lies as

Detective Bligh is certainly doing. I know that Jarrette and the Youngers had no hand in the robbery, and if the wounded man is ever recognised, it will be seen that he is unworthy of the title of detective. He has never captured but one man, and he slipped on the blind side of him. As for shooting, he doesn't know what that means. I am thankful that at least one robber has been got who was published everywhere by Bligh as first being Cole Younger and afterwards Jesse James. The world can now see that neither one of the Jameses and Youngers are the man shot and captured. Every bold robbery in this country is laid on us, but after a few of the robbers have been caught, and when it is seen two or three times that other people are robbing banks, maybe we will get a fair play from the newspapers. In a few days it will be seen how the Jameses and Youngers have been lied on by such men as Pinkerton and Bligh. I and Cole Younger are not friends, but I know he is innocent of the Huntington robbery and I feel it is my duty to defend him and his innocent and persecuted brothers from the false and slanderous reports circulated about them. I think the public will justify me in denouncing Bligh, and I now do, as an unnecessary liar, a scondrel and a poltroon.[13]

No mention had been made about Frank James. In April 1876, another rumor circulated that Frank had been captured and was currently incarcerated in the Missouri Penitentiary under another name.[14] The state authorities soon squelched the story by denying that they had Frank in custody. The gang was not heard from until at least the following summer. A bank robbery took place in Baxter Springs, Kansas, on April 19, but it doesn't appear that the culprits were members of the James-Younger Gang. At least they weren't then. The men who robbed the Kansas bank may have been two fellows named Charlie Pitts and Bill Chadwell. In May, Jesse and Frank were accused of being involved in several stagecoach robberies that occurred in Texas that month. Once again, there was no evidence to tie them to the crimes.

FOURTEEN

༄཰

Preparing for the Big Adventure

"Every daylight robbery in any part of the country, from the Al-
leghenies to the Rockies, was laid at our doors; we could not go
out without a pair of pistols to protect ourselves from the attack
of we knew not whom; and finally, after one of the young ruffians
who had helped in the robbery of the Missouri Pacific express
car at Otterville 'confessed' that we were with the robbers we
decided to make one haul, and with our share of the proceeds
start life anew in Cuba, South America, or Australia."
—Cole Younger, *Cole Younger by Himself*

THE FRIENDSHIPS BETWEEN certain members of the
gang allowed them to at least pretend they were living normal
lives. Bob Younger had enjoyed visiting with Jesse while Jesse
and Zee had been honeymooning in Texas. The two men had
quickly become good friends. Jesse seemed to enjoy taking an
almost paternal interest in the young man. Bob allowed Jesse's
patronization as he missed the guidance and advice of his brothers, Jim and John. Bob never had cared for the domineering
nature of his brother Cole. The twenty-two-year-old Bob was
impressed by Jesse's quick wit and insidious accomplishments.

In 1876, Bob looked to Jesse to help him solve a problem that had been weighing on his mind. Bob Younger had become engaged to a young woman named Maggie in the time since his brother John's death at the hands of the Pinkertons. He wanted to settle down on a farm, yet he didn't have enough money to accomplish his goal.[1] According to a later account by Zee James, Jesse and his family moved to Baltimore, Maryland, during the winter of 1875–76.[2] They evidently had returned to Missouri by spring, as Jesse visited Bob in St. Clair County some time during those months. Bob listened closely as Jesse proposed how he might help the younger man come up with the money needed to underwrite his farm. It wasn't as if Bob Younger had never participated in a robbery. Bob explained to his mentor that he would invest the money in his farm and retire from outlawry if he could make enough money from the robbery that Jesse had in mind. Jesse supported Bob's objective. He told Bob that he would contact him when he could work out a plan.[3]

Jesse soon sent word asking Bob to meet him in a Kansas City hotel within the week. Jesse finally had a plan, but it was an idea that surprised Bob Younger. Jesse suggested that they gather the members of the James-Younger Gang, recruit a couple of new associates, and target a bank in the far-removed state of Minnesota. Bob was puzzled as to how the gang would find their way around such unfamiliar territory. Jesse informed Bob that a man who had been born in Minnesota and who had been active in other outlaw activity had offered to be their guide. The man's name was Bill Chadwell. Charlie Pitts would also be asked to go along. The strategy of the proposal took Bob Younger aback. He explained to Jesse that he would have to confer with his brother Cole before he could commit to the plan. The idea was simply too overwhelming to enable him to make such a decision on his own.[4]

Jesse and Bob made plans to meet in Monagaw Springs the following week. Jesse said he would bring Clell Miller with him. He asked that Bob locate Cole and have him present at the meeting as well. No mention was made of Frank James at the time. Cole Younger was in Texas when Jesse and Bob first met. Bob addressed a letter to his brother there asking Cole to meet him at Monagaw. Bob had yet to hear from Cole by the time the day of the meeting with Jesse arrived. He didn't even know if his brother had received the letter. Bob delayed committing to Jesse and asked that Jesse give him more time to try to get together with Cole. Jesse told Bob to contact him when he had some information. Bob returned to Jackson County to decide how he might best get in touch with his nomadic brother.[5]

Bob heard that Cole had shown up in Monagaw shortly after he returned home to Jackson County. Bob immediately returned to St. Clair County. He met with his brother and recapitulated Jesse's idea. Cole was infuriated that Jesse had solicited the involvement of his brother without first consulting him. Cole immediately suspected that Jesse knew that his plan was extremely risky and had approached Bob first as an incentive for Cole's involvement. Jesse knew that Bob prided himself on his independence from Cole. He also knew that Bob would likely bristle at Cole's resistance to a plan that Bob brought to him. It was not a surprise when the two brothers argued over the feasibility of Jesse's plan. Bob had been made to believe that his position in the gang was equal with Cole's. He felt that he should have a say in the future endeavors of the enterprise. It didn't take Cole long to realize that Jesse's influence on his youngest brother was far greater than his own. Bob told Cole that Bill Chadwell would serve as guide to the gang once they were in Minnesota. Cole responded by saying that he hardly knew Chadwell. He reminded Bob that Chadwell was a friend of Jesse's, not the Youngers. Cole argued that it was irresponsible to rely on one man for their safe passage within the state. Minnesota was quite a distance from Missouri. Bob refused to be swayed from his commitment to Jesse by any of Cole's common sense as he grappled with his need to assert his autonomy and credibility. Bob told his brother that he was over twenty-one and would accompany Jesse on the trip north whether or not Cole was involved. Cole considered his brother's determination and requested that Bob give him some time to think over the proposal. Cole agreed in the meantime that he would at least meet with Bob and Jesse at the end of the month as long as Bob would guarantee that Frank James would be at the meeting.[6]

Cole secretly sent a wire to Jim Younger in California after he committed to hearing more about Jesse's irrational plan. The wire simply stated, "Come home. Bob needs you." No further explanation was given. Cole hoped that the level-headed Jim would be able to exert his influence over the impulsive Bob where Cole himself had failed. Jim left La Panza immediately. Jim Younger could always be counted on to respond to his family's needs. He would certainly be available if Bob had such a serious problem that Cole had felt it necessary to summon Jim from California.[7]

Jim, too, was amazed by the scenario Jesse put forth when the three Youngers met with Jesse and Frank in Kansas City at the end of June. The Youngers left the James brothers to talk among themselves. It wasn't long before Cole and Jim were embroiled in an argument with their younger brother about the irresponsibility of Jesse's strategy. Cole grew increasingly frustrated as Bob continued to voice his stance that he would go with Jesse with or without his brother. Cole threw out as a deterrent the only thing he believed would change his stubborn brother's mind when he realized that Bob's desire to commit to Jesse could not be swayed. Cole notified Bob that both he and Jim would have no choice but to accompany their brother if he was set on going to Minnesota. Cole hoped that Bob would relent if Jim was to be included. Bob knew Jim was happy and settled in California. Bob made it clear to Jim that there was no need for him to go to Minnesota and participate in an act he abhorred. He told Jim that he did not want him to go to Minnesota. Jim quickly picked up on Cole's motive for involving him. He told Bob that he would have no choice but to go to look out for Bob's best interests if Bob insisted on participating. Bob was sorry that Jim felt that way, but he informed his brothers that he had already decided to throw in his lot with Jesse. He apologized to Jim for hurting him by his willfulness but explained to his brother that it was important to make his own decisions. Jim later wrote that he was infuriated that Jesse would involve Bob in such a foolhardy and dangerous scheme. The decision had been made.[8] Jesse and Frank James together with Cole, Jim, and Bob Younger would be going to Minnesota. Before they could embark on that adventure, they would need to pull off another robbery to finance the escapade.

The details of a plan for a robbery close to home that would result in the money needed to finance their trip north were worked out with the involvement of Jesse, Frank, Cole, and Bob. It was felt by Jesse, Frank, and Cole that the gang participating in the robbery that would be scheduled to finance the Minnesota sojourn should consist of the same men who would be taking part in the Minnesota caper. Jim evidently notified his brothers and the James boys that he still detested their illegal activities, even though he had agreed to go to Minnesota. Jim would not participate in a robbery that would take place in his home state of Missouri. Someone then suggested that a man named Hobbs Kerry stand in for Jim as the eighth member of the gang. Kerry was an associate of the Youngers' cousin, Bruce Younger. The boys selected a site for their unscrupulous deed and their plan was quickly set into motion.

The Missouri Pacific Railroad was designated the gang's next target. They had learned that a railroad bridge was being erected over the Lamine River near Otterville, Missouri. Trains along this line had to pass through a dangerous gash called Rocky Cut on their way through the area under construction. The boys considered it an ideal spot to conduct their business. Trains would automatically slow down as they traversed the track through the construction area. It was at Rocky Cut that Jesse and the boys congregated on the night of July 7, 1876. Members of the gang apprehended the night guard as he waited near the unfinished bridge to assist the engineer of the oncoming train to navigate the cut. The guard's red lantern was confiscated and handed off to one of the boys as the train was signaled to a stop. The outlaws jumped aboard. They held the passengers and crew at gunpoint while they unloaded over $15,000 from two safes. During the robbery, a preacher on board the train led the startled passengers in the singing of hymns as he prayed loudly for their souls. The gang posed no real threat to the safety of the passengers. Once the outlaws finished their job, they jumped on their horses and disappeared.[9]

A former state militia officer named Bacon Montgomery was able to gather together a small posse. The outlaws were, as usual, long gone by the time anything could be done. Missouri Governor Charles Hardin posted a reward of $300 each for any of the men who participated in the Otterville robbery. St. Louis

Police Chief James McDonough was called upon to help with the investigation this time. McDonough was about to get very lucky.

The gang made a huge mistake by including the untried and inexperienced Hobbs Kerry in the robbery. Kerry either had not been properly instructed on how to keep his mouth shut about his activities or was simply ignorant about the consequences of revealing anything unusual to his daily routine. Kerry separated from the others after their business was conducted. He soon appeared in a small town named Granby. He made virtually no attempt to conceal the fact that he had come into some money. Kerry wrote to Bruce Younger while in Granby. Younger was at this time involved in breeding and trading horses. Kerry likely asked Younger about the availability of a thoroughbred horse that he might purchase. One of McDonough's men soon learned of Kerry's boasting as well as his correspondence with one of the Younger family. Detectives were promptly dispatched to the area to investigate him.[10]

The investigation quickly reached western Missouri. A farmer who claimed that Kerry was one of a group of strangers who ate a meal at his farm just before the robbery was interviewed.[11] A warrant was drafted for the arrest of Bruce Younger. Hobbs Kerry was arrested in the meantime and charged with having been one of the Otterville robbers. Kerry panicked and almost immediately confessed. When authorities spoke to Bruce Younger in St. Clair County, they had to admit that there was no evidence linking Younger with the crime. Kerry apparently was not savvy enough to realize the consequences of turning over on his pals. While admitting his own involvement, he wasted no time in volunteering that his accomplices were Jesse and Frank James, Cole and Bob Younger, Bill Chadwell, and Charlie Pitts.[12] Those men were out of the area on their way to Minnesota before they could be located, let alone interviewed and arrested.

Jesse was not able to resist rising to his own defense. He was able to quickly compose one of his famous letters to the newspaper before he left for Minnesota. The *Kansas City Times* reported that a friend of Jesse's had delivered the epistle to a *Times* reporter who had been on the street in front of the newspaper

office. In a second letter Jesse wrote on August 23, he reported
he had heard that Bacon Montgomery headed the gang that
robbed the Missouri Pacific Railroad. Montgomery responded in
the *Kansas City Times* on August 25 that he would be happy to
participate in any investigation of his involvement if Jesse would
agree to the same and present himself in Sedalia. Nothing else
was heard from Jesse on the matter. Zerelda Samuel offered her
two cents as to the involvement of her sons in the crime. Mrs.
Samuel once again denied that Jesse and Frank had anything at
all to do with it.

The *Kansas City Times* claimed to have evidence that Jesse
was living in Kansas using an alias. They said that both Jesse
and his brother Frank had been seen in Kansas City the week
before the robbery. The paper did, however, claim that Jesse "is
not generally such an object of popular detestation that he cannot
secure a fair trial in our courts." The newspaper suggested that
Jesse prove his innocence by turning himself in and take his
chances within the judicial system. On August 11, Frank James's
father-in-law, Samuel Ralston, was visited by a group of detectives. The Ralston home was searched at dawn in an attempt to
locate Frank or Jesse. Evidently, the law didn't realize that Frank
and his wife's family were not on good terms. The detective's
next lead was that Frank and his brother were holed up in Pomeroy, Kansas, at the home of E. E. Wells. Ralston's neighbor,
Joseph Connelly, was taken by train to Pomeroy to identify
Frank James, should he be captured there. Connelly was released
to go home when the James brothers were not located.[13]

Jesse was clearly offended at Kerry's confession. The letter
he wrote to the *Kansas City Times* was dated August 14, 1876,
with a return address of Oak Grove, Kansas. This time Jesse
almost certainly enlisted the help of John Newman Edwards:

Dear Sir: You have published Hobb Kerry's confession, which
makes it appear that the Jameses and Youngers were the Rocky
Cut robbers. If there was only one side to be told, it would probably be believed by a good many people that Kerry has told the
truth. But this so-called confession is a well-built pack of lies from
beginning to end. I never heard of Hobbs Kerry, Charlie Pitts and
William Chadwell until Kerry's arrest. I can prove my innocence

by eight good, well-known men of Jackson County, and show conclusively that I was not at the train robbery. But at present I will give only the names of two of these gentlemen to whom I will refer for proof.

Early on the morning after the train robbery east of Sedalia, I saw the Hon. D. Gregg of Jackson County, and talked with him for thirty or forty minutes. I also saw and talked to Thomas Pitcher of Jackson County, the morning after the robbery. Those two men's oaths cannot be impeached, so I refer the grand jury of Cooper County, Mo., and Gov. Hardin to those men before they act so rashly on the oath of a liar, thief and robber.

Kerry knows that the Jameses and Youngers can't be taken alive, and that is why he has put it on us. I have refered to Messrs. Pitcher and Gregg because they are prominent men, and they know I am innocent, and their word can't be disputed. I will write a long article to you for the Times, and send it to you in a few days, showing fully how Hobbs Kerry has lied. Hoping the Times will give me a chance for a fair hearing and to vindicate myself through its columns, I will close.[14]

On August 18, the *Times* published the letter Jesse promised. This time the letter was said to have been sent from somewhere designated "Safe Retreat":

Dear Sir: I have written a great many letters vindicating myself of the false charges that have been brought against me. But last fall, after I proved to the world that the Jameses and Youngers had nothing to do with the West Virginia robbery, and branded old Detective Bligh as one of the biggest liars and poltroons that ever lived, I thought I would let the public press say what it would, and I would treat it with silent contempt. Detectives have been trying for years to get positive proof against me for some criminal offence, so that they could get a large reward offered for me, dead or alive; and the same of Frank James and the Younger boys, but they have been foiled on every turn, and they are fully convinced that we will never be taken alive, and now they have fell on the deep-laid scheme to get Hobbs Kerry to tell a pack of base lies. But, thank God, I am yet a free man, and have got the power to defend myself against the charge brought against me by Kerry, a notorious liar and poltroon. I will give a full statement and prove his confession false.

Thus Jesse began his defense:

Lie No. 1. He said a plot was laid by the Jameses and Youngers to rob the Granby bank. I am reliably informed that there never was a bank at Granby.

Lie No. 2. He said he met with Cole Younger and me at Mr. Tyler's. If there is a man in Jackson County by that name, I am sure that I am not acquainted with him.

Lie No. 3. He said Frank James was at Mr. Butler's, in Cass County. I and Frank don't know any man in Cass County by that name. I can prove my innocence by eight good citizens of Jackson County, Mo., but I do not propose to give all their names at present. If I did, those cut-throat detectives would find out some of my friends that they think are my enemies. I think the names I give in my article of the 14th are sufficient at present.

Will the Times please correct one mistake they made in my other statement. I saw Mr. Gregg and talked to him; but I only met Mr Pitcher in the road, and we passed the compliment of the day and rode on.

Jesse then offered his own opinion about the perpetrators of the robbery. He vented some wartime animosity and advised as to how authorities might proceed:

My opinion is that Bacon Montgomery, the scoundrel who murdered Capt. A. J. Clements, December 13, 1866, is the instigator of all this Missouri Pacific affair. I believe he planed the robbery and got his share of the money, and when he went out to look for the robbers he led the pursurers off the robber's trail. But one thing I know he did do when he was in command of Tom Fletcher's cut-throat militia. He had Arch Clements, one of the noblest boys, and the most promising military boy, of his age, murdered in cold blood; and if poor Clements was living to-day, he would be worth more to this country than old Tom Fletcher and all the militia that ever were in Missouri. I would like for the Times to send a reporter to Lexington and Dover, and ask the good citizens about Montgomery and his thieves, that were there in 1866. If the truth were half told about Montgomery, it would make the world believe that Montgomery has no equal, only the Bender family and the midnight assassins who murdered my poor, helpless and innocent eight-year-old brother, and shot my mother's arm off; and I am of the opinion he had a hand in that dirty cowardly work. Montgomery, roll in your special trains, and break down doors, and arrest quiet citizens and put them in irons. Everywhere you turn makes friends for me.

Jesse did have good words in regard to Missouri's current governor, however:

Now a word to Mr. Garrison. Ain't you fraid those special trains will injure the Missouri Pacific Railroad? You are liable to have trouble if you don't stop such weak brain work. I can't believe that Gov. Hardin had any hand in this special train work. I give him too much credit for that. Gov. Hardin is a man of too much brains to act in a manner that would kill him in the eyes of the majority of the people who have elected him, and thinks he is the best Governor Missouri has had since the war.

But back to the issue at hand:

But I can't vouch for Mr. Bingham's innocence. I[f] we had been granted full amnesty, I am sure we would have been at work, trying to be good, law-abiding citizens. If we have a wise Congress this winter, which I believe we will have, I am sure they will grant us a full pardon. I will not say pardon, for we have done nothing to be pardoned for. But they can pass a law having all those bogus warrants that are out for us destroyed, and let us go home and live in peace. What sense is there in spending so much money in trying to have us arrested? I am sure we have thousands of friends which can't be bought, although the Detectives think they are playing things very fine. Poor fools they are.

Robin Hood James rode to the front:

If the Express Company wants to do a good act they had better give the money they are letting thieving detectives beat them out of to the poor. Now take my advice, express companies, and give your extra money to the suffering poor, and don't let thieving detectives beat you out of it.

Back to detectives and Bacon Montgomery:

The detectives are a brave lot of boys—charge houses, break down doors and make the gray hairs stand up on the heads of unarmed citizens. Why don't President Grant have the soldiers called in and send the detectives out on special trains after the hostile Indians? Arm Pinkerton's force, with hand-granades, and they will kill all the women and children, and as soon as the women and children are killed it will stop the breed and the warriors will die out in a few years. But if Montgomery gets in with the Indians as he be with the Otterville boys, he would be a bad man on the trail. If Montgomery gets offended at this and comes on a scout, I hope he and his party won't get drunk, as they did on a previous occasion, and shoot and yell as they did at Brownington, on Grand River, and scare women and children as they did there. A few words to Mr. Oll Garrison, son of Mr. Garrison—Missouri Pacific Railroad officer—have you forgot the time when you was paymaster on the Sedalia and Lexington Railroad? Yes, well do you remember how you proposed to get someone to rob you and give you half; and you failed to get your job put up? I got this from a friend of yours that gets drunk, but he was not drunk when he told me. But probably the old man don't know what a rascal you are, or he would send up special trains after you. I believe the railroad robbers will yet be sifted down on someone at St. Louis or Sedalia puting up the job and then trying to have it put on innocent men, as Kerry has done.

Hoping the Times will publish just as I have written, I will close.[15]

Recent research has suggested that Jesse's "Safe Retreat" was Nemaha County, Nebraska. Jesse and Frank had many relatives there and this was the place where their mother had brought her family in a safe retreat during the final days of the war. Zerelda's brother Jesse Cole lived in Rulo. Many of the Cole relatives were well-respected citizens in that county and several adjacent counties.[16] Jesse seemed to enjoy visiting Nebraska City. At one time, he had his photograph taken there. Jesse did spend some time in this area and it may well have been his Safe Retreat. One of the members of the James family, however, believes that Jesse's Safe Retreat was in Texas on a ranch that he and Frank had bought many years before. Jesse also likely spent some time in Texas. Many of the former guerrillas and their families relocated there after the war. Jesse must have found safe retreat there as well.[17]

Cole Younger later wrote that since he and his brothers had been innocent of any wrongdoing in the state of Missouri up to that point, they decided to make a stand. If they were going to be accused by people such as Hobbs Kerry, and the law was going to take an admitted train robber's word, they might as well "make one haul, and with our share of the proceeds start life anew in Cuba, South America or Australia."[18] Kerry's actions, according to Younger, forced him into participating in the Minnesota scheme.

The boys now had the financing for their northern adventure. Jesse and Frank said good-bye to their mother at her home in Clay County, then hid themselves under a tarp in the back of a wagon that was probably driven by Bill Chadwell. They united with Cole, Bob and Jim Younger, and Charlie Pitts north of Clay County. Eight horses had been secured and the group continued on horseback to Council Bluffs, Iowa. There the horses were sold as the gang divided into small groups and boarded trains bound for Minnesota.[19]

FIFTEEN

⌒⌒⌒⌒

Northfield, Minnesota

"When the robber is the only or the principal actor in the scene, and his prowess or brutality the only feature worth mentioning, the less said of it the better. But when a great crime is the occasion of great heroism, courage, fidelity, intrepid resistance, and the triumph of virtue over violence, then there is a story worth telling, and a lesson worth learning."
—George Huntington, *Robber and Hero*

PLANNING A ROBBERY smack-dab in the middle of Minnesota must have been a scary thought for some members of the gang. But for the most part it was all one big adventure. Jesse and the gang arrived in Minneapolis sometime on the 15th or 16th of August 1876.[1] They thought it would not be wise to be seen together, so they divided into three smaller groups. They kept close tabs on one another as they moved quietly about the city. The men from Missouri attempted to appear no more out of place than any other traveling businessmen. Several months later it was reported in the *St. Paul Pioneer Press* by one of the residents of Minneapolis that Bob Younger and Charlie Pitts had been seen sleeping on the bank near Sibley and Fifth Street that night.

The boys traveled in separate groups and arrived in St. Paul the next day. Staying in the red light district allowed the outlaws an opportunity to blend in with the transitory nature of the neighborhood. The boys gambled and made the acquaintance of several of the other patrons at the Nicolette House. They very carefully gleaned information about Minnesota, its people and its banks. One of the more popular girls, Kitty Traverse, later claimed that she noticed that one of the men appeared ill and never left his room.[2] This was probably Jim Younger. Not only was he uncomfortable around Jesse, but he preferred to be by himself away from the activities of the others.

Jesse, Frank, Miller, and Jim Younger departed by train for Red Wing on August 26. The "cattlemen" registered at the National Hotel under the aliases of Ed Everhard, A. L. West, Chas. Wetherby, and J. C. Hortor upon their arrival. After dinner the first evening, a couple of them visited J. A. Anderberg's Livery where Frank bought a dun horse.[3] Two additional horses were soon purchased from a man by the name of A. Seebeek. A fourth horse was obtained from someone somewhere within the city. Cole Younger and Pitts took the train to St. Peter while the Jameses and their companions were in Red Wing. Younger and Pitts bought two horses from a man named Hodge, then registered at the American House as J. C. King and J. Ward.[4]

Jesse and Frank briefly parted company with Jim Younger and Miller. By August 28, they were in the area known as Brush Prairie. Here they posed as prospective land buyers interested in the farm of John Mulligan. Through their conversations with Mulligan they were able to gather quite a bit of information about the bustling city of Northfield just a few miles away. After the two brothers negotiated a price with Mulligan, they informed the farmer that their money was in a bank in Red Wing. Mulligan was told that his buyers would return to buy the property after they withdrew their money from the bank.[5]

The town of Northfield had been settled by immigrants from New England after its establishment by John W. North, a prominent Republican and businessman who was appointed surveyor general of the Nevada Territory by Abraham Lincoln. North built a good-sized mill and a beautiful hotel. Soon the establishment of Carleton College and St. Olaf College drew many people into the town. Northfield grew as a wealthy, prosperous community.

Arriving in Northfield for their first visit, Jesse and Frank ate at Jeft's Restaurant and walked freely around town as they posed as the potential buyers of Mulligan's farm. They chatted briefly with a man named Trussel. Trussel gave them valuable information about the roads in the area.[6] Jesse and Frank also checked out the First National Bank of Minnesota.

Having missed their train, Bob Younger and Chadwell joined Cole Younger and Pitts in St. Peter a day later than had been agreed. They registered as G. H. King and B. T. Cooper at the local hotel. Cole Younger and Pitts left for Madelia. They arrived on August 30 and once again posed as cattleman. They registered as guests of the Flanders Hotel and enjoyed a long dinner conversation with proprietor Thomas L. Vought.[7]

The eight members of the James-Younger Gang reunited in Mankato on September 1. Two of the outlaws stayed at the Gates House while two others were guests of the Clifton House. A local resident named John Jay Lemon later stated that two of the men visited Jack O'Neil's saloon that evening.[8]

On September 2, 1876, two of the men walked through the door of the First National Bank of Mankato. They approached the counter and asked the teller to change a $50 bill. They had a good opportunity to look over the operation of the bank while they waited. They went back outside to join two of their colleagues after they gathered their visual information. The others sat on their horses a short distance away and watched for a signal. There were many people in town that day as there was a meeting of the board of trade. Additionally, groups of farmers, businessmen, and children stood around observing the construction of a new building next to the bank. The initial plan had been to reenter the bank and rob it. The fact that there were too many people in the street seems to have served as a deterrent. Jesse signaled to the others and both groups quickly left town. Jesse was asked by Cole Younger what the problem had been when the gang met up outside Mankato. Jesse told the gang that he thought he had been recognized by a man he believed to be someone named Charles Robinson.[9] Jesse didn't think it was wise to conduct their business in Mankato. Cole voiced the opinion that it was only Jesse's vanity that lead him to believe that someone so far away from Missouri had recognized him.

Jesse and Frank told the others what they had seen in Northfield as they pondered their next step. Jesse suggested the bank in that town become their target. Bill Chadwell was in immediate agreement. He was familiar with Northfield and gave his associates some very interesting information. Chadwell informed them that Adelbert Ames and Benjamin Butler were prominent citizens of the town. These two men were no doubt recognized by Frank and Cole as two of the foremost carpetbaggers who took advantage of the people of the South after the war. Ames had been elected governor of Mississippi several years before but had been impeached by that state's legislature earlier in the year. Ames left the state with a cloud over his head although he had been cleared of all charges. He eventually showed up in Northfield to join his father and brother. Ames bought a major interest in the Northfield mill operations with money said by those sympathetic to the South to have been obtained from his carpetbagging activities. Ben Butler also had carpetbagging interests in Mississippi and relocated to Northfield. There was no love lost between Butler and the Confederates. The Southerners had nicknamed him Spoons as a reflection of their opinion that he would steal even his grandmother's silverware. Chadwell told Jesse and the others that he had heard that both of these men kept their money in the First National Bank of Northfield. The thought of robbing two representatives of the carpetbagging community must have delighted the members of the gang. Cole Younger, in fact, later wrote, "Butler's treatment of the Southerners during the war was not such as to commend him to our regard, and we felt little compunction, under the circumstances, about raiding him or his."[10] The boys once again split into two groups and headed east to Northfield.

By September 4, Jesse, Frank, Bob Younger, and Pitts had traveled as far as Janesville. Tongues planted firmly in cheeks, they posed as railroad engineers. They registered at the Johnson House under the names of Dave Smith, George Pryor, Jno. Jones, and James Johnson. Cole and Jim Younger and Miller and Chadwell stayed nearby in Le Sueur County that night. They likely stayed at the Adams Hotel in Cleveland. Jesse's group made it to Waterville by September 5. It was later reported that someone answering Jesse's description had been seen arguing with another fellow as to whether or not Jesse was someone the man recognized. No mention was made of Jesse James, however.

On the night of September 5, Cole and Jim Younger and Miller and Chadwell registered at the Dampier House in Cordova. The hotel was overbooked, and two of the boys were asked to share a room with W. W. Barlow of Wisconsin. Barlow later identified one of his roommates as Bill Chadwell. He claimed that both of the guests had been friendly and polite. He had been pleased to have been in their company.[11]

Jesse, Frank, Pitts, and Bob Younger stayed at the farm of C. C. Stetson five miles outside Northfield on the Faribault Road the following night.[12] It was here that the plans for the next day were finalized. Cole and Jim Younger and Chadwell and Miller put up at the Cushman Hotel in Millersburgh. It was later reported that one of the men claimed he was ill and stayed in his room during dinner. Again, this was likely a very nervous and unhappy Jim Younger.

The gang met up west of Northfield outside the town of Dundas on the morning of September 7. It had been decided that Jesse and Bob Younger would go into the bank as they were the organizers of the adventure. They would be joined by Frank. The three men would cross the street from Jeft's Restaurant and approach the bank. Cole Younger and Miller were to watch the proceedings from the bridge just outside town. Jim Younger, Pitts, and Chadwell would wait about a quarter mile away. The men in the street would enter the bank when they saw Younger and Miller cross the bridge. Miller and Younger would take positions close to the door once Jesse and the others were in the bank. Chadwell and his group would take position on the bridge as Cole Younger and Miller moved forward. All would watch the bank closely. They would be ready to become actively involved if they were needed. The others would divert attention and cause confusion if the robbery was detected before Jesse, Frank, and Bob Younger could get to their horses. They would holler their loudest Rebel yell and fire their revolvers into the air. No civilians were to be allowed to interfere with the robbery nor were they to be shot. The gang would take whatever they could from the bank and exit the town as quickly as possible with Chadwell leading the way. The plan was ready to be put into motion.

Jesse, Frank, and Bob Younger rode into Northfield about 1:00 P.M., September 7, 1876. They ate lunch at Jeft's Restaurant, then casually walked the short distance to Lee & Hitchcock's Dry Goods. They sat on some packing crates that were stacked in front as they awaited the designated time to spring into action. The three men entered the First National Bank of Minnesota at exactly 2:00. Cole Younger later expressed the fact that he was amazed that the trio actually went through with the robbery. It had been agreed that if too many people were seen strolling around the town, as had been the case in Mankato, the outlaws would wait for a better opportunity. Younger remarked to Miller that he believed there was a good chance of trouble since there were several merchants and shoppers going about their business. The two men would back up their colleagues, however. They crossed the bridge and slowly entered the town as planned. They passed Adelbert Ames walking with his father and his son, Mayor J. T. Ames, as they rode down Division Street. Younger was surprised to actually see his enemy and said to Miller, "Look, it's the governor himself." Ames overheard Younger's remark and watched as the two strangers rode down the street. He expressed concern to his companions by stating, "Those are Southerners. Nobody up here calls me Governor."[13]

Younger and Miller arrived at their position in front of the bank. They quickly noticed that the door had been left ajar after their comrades had entered the bank. Younger nonchalantly got down from his horse and adjusted his saddle girth. Miller followed suit and walked over to close the door. Hardware merchant J. S. Allen approached the bank. Miller put his hand out to stop him. Allen assessed the interference quickly. He turned away from Miller and ran down the street yelling, "Get your guns! They're robbing the bank!" Medical student Henry Wheeler had been watching the two strangers in front of the bank from the sidewalk in front of his father's drugstore. Wheeler saw Miller grab Allen's arm and shouted, "Robbery!" Younger and Miller jumped up on their horses. Jim Younger, Pitts, and Chadwell charged down the street to join them. The gang kicked up dust, spurring their horses up and down the street as they fired their revolvers into the air.

The boys in the bank were oblivious to the excitement in the street. They had quietly entered through the front door. They saw no customers as they drew their guns. Jesse ordered book-keeper Alonzo E. Bunker to throw up his hands. Bob and Frank trained their revolvers on cashier Joseph Lee Heywood and clerk Frank J. Wilcox. Jesse wasted no time in informing his captives what was about to happen. He yelled, "We're going to rob this bank. Don't any of you holler. We've got forty men outside."[14] The robbers climbed over the counter and asked Heywood if he was the cashier. The outlaws refused to believe him when he responded that he was not. Heywood was telling the truth. He technically was only acting cashier. His boss, G. M. Phillips, was in Philadelphia attending the Centennial Exposition. Hey-wood was then ordered to open the door "damn quick" lest his head be blown off. The directive was imparted to the two other employees when Heywood replied that he could not open the safe. Each denied knowing the combination of the safe's lock. Frank James walked over to examine the safe more closely. Hey-wood broke away from the others and attempted to push Frank into the vault and close the door. The irate outlaw quickly pulled away from the cashier. As Heywood tried to slam the door, Frank's arm and hand were nearly crushed.[15] Heywood was roughly thrown to the floor by Bob Younger, and Bunker was told to get on the floor as well. Jesse stood over him with a knife at his throat. Once again, the cashier was ordered to open the safe. Jesse drew a knife out of his pocket and said to Bob and Frank, "Let's cut his damn throat."[16] Heywood again refused. He informed Jesse that his throat would have to be cut. He was not able to open the safe due to a recently installed chronometer lock that could only be opened at a predetermined time. Bunker silently rose to his feet as he contemplated making an escape. His movement caught Bob's attention. Bob looked at him and demanded to know where the rest of the money was being kept. Then he grabbed Bunker and once again threw him to the floor, put the muzzle of his gun against Bunker's temple, and ordered the bookkeeper, "Show me where the money is, you son of a bitch, or I'll kill you!" Bunker said nothing. Bob's attention

shifted away from Bunker as he listened to Heywood's explanation of the time lock. Bunker broke away and ran toward the
back door of the bank. Bob shot at Bunker. The bookkeeper was
hit in the shoulder. Bunker staggered out the door yelling
"They're robbing the bank! Help!"

By this time, the scene outside on the street was rapidly de-
veloping into bedlam. Cole Younger ran to the door of the bank.
He hollered in, "Hurry up! They've given the alarm!"[17] The
people of Northfield did not intend to allow their bank to be
robbed by hooligans like the ones in the street. They quickly
responded by running to get their revolvers, rifles, and shotguns.
Even though the outlaws fired into the air and posed no threat
to the citizens in the street the same "courtesy" was not afforded
the robbers. The five strangers were fired at with whatever weapons the good folks of Northfield had been able to procure. Cole
Younger commanded the townspeople to get off the street. Most
of them quickly followed Younger's directive. An immigrant
named Nicholas Gustavson remained in the line of fire. Younger
glanced at the man in disbelief. He yelled again, "Get off the
damn street!"[18] Younger's order was too late. The non-English-
speaking Gustavson was mortally wounded by one of the bullets
whizzing around him.

The Dampier Hotel stood across the street from the bank.
Wheeler had by this time appeared in the second-story window,
armed with an old Army carbine. All the outlaws except those
in the bank were now on their horses dodging bullets. Miller had
dismounted in an attempt to make his way to the bank to call to
the men inside. His face was peppered with shot from the fowl-
ing piece of Elias Stacy as he attempted to jump back up on his
horse. Hardware store owner Anselm Manning had armed himself with a breech-loading rifle. As he stealthily inched closer to
the outlaws from his initial location at the corner, he observed
the horses of the robbers inside the bank tethered to a nearby
rail. Manning took careful aim. He shot Bob Younger's horse
dead as Cole Younger once again ran to the door of the bank.
Manning quickly reloaded. He shot at Younger but missed. Bill
Chadwell had been busy spurring his horse up and down the
street and was not aware of Manning's activities. Manning fired
at Chadwell from seventy yards. His bullet pierced the outlaw's

heart. Chadwell fell into the street, dead. Wheeler continued shooting from the second-story window. Jim Younger was hit in the shoulder. Wheeler reloaded, then fired again. This time his bullet severed Clell Miller's subclavian artery. Manning fired again as Cole Younger ran to the aid of his friend. Younger was hit in the thigh. Younger quickly assessed that Miller was dead. He limped to the bank door yelling, "They're killing our men! Get out here!"[19]

The men inside the bank were determined to get to the money. Jesse dragged Heywood over to the vault and once again demanded that the cashier open the lock. Heywood again refused to comply with Jesse's demand. The frustrated Jesse fired a shot into the floor. Bob saw Cole at the door and left the fruitless mission to help his comrades in the street. Jesse heard the gunfire outside. He scooped up what little money was sitting out on the counter and followed Bob out the door. Frank James watched his brother and Younger leave, yet he remained inside. He was angry over Heywood's attempt to lock him in the vault and the injury to his hand was painful. Frank glared at Heywood. He then pointed his revolver at the cashier and fired. The shot missed as Heywood fell into his chair. According to an account Wilcox gave later, ". . . as the robber made over the desk railing he turned and placing his revolver to Heywood's head, fired." Frank James then nonchalantly left the bank and joined the others in the street.[20]

Bob Younger had emerged from the bank to see that his horse had been killed and Miller and Chadwell lay dead in the street. Bob attempted to rein in one of the dead men's horses as he ran through a deluge of bullets. Younger ran down the sidewalk, exchanging fire with the determined Manning. At one point, he ducked under a staircase near the corner of Division Street. Wheeler watched from his roost across the street. He took aim and fired when he saw Younger reach out his arm to fire at Manning. The bullet struck Younger in the arm, breaking it at the elbow. The ambidextrous Bob Younger calmly shifted his gun to his other hand and resumed firing. Cole observed the gunplay and rode over to rescue his brother from the assault. Bob staggered toward Cole. Cole grabbed his brother by the belt and pulled him up behind him.

Jesse and Frank had been able to mount their horses. Cole's saddle horn was ripped loose by a bullet as Jesse gave the signal to retreat from the town. Cole held on to the mane of his horse as his brother grasped his waist. Cole swayed as bullets tore into his side and thigh. Pitts had so far avoided injury. Now he, too, was struck as he waited to make sure that Cole and Bob would be able to get out of town. Other reports, both at the time and years later in popular histories, mentioned one of the two other men being hit in the thigh.[21] The outlaws withdrew from North- field concealed in the heavy cloud of dust and gunfire.[22]

The controversies surrounding the Northfield robbery continue to this day. The identities of the men who entered the bank have been confused over time by various inaccurate reports and spec- ulations. Bob Younger later freely admitted that he had been one of the robbers who had been inside, but he refused to identify his accomplices. Charlie Pitts was identified as being in the bank only after his death and when Cole Younger later lied and con- firmed that fact.[23] Younger's claim was likely made because his friend Frank James was still alive.

The identity of the man who killed Heywood is contingent on the identities of the men inside the bank. Bob Younger was never believed to have been guilty of the murder of Heywood. There had been, after all, eyewitnesses. It was assumed by many that it was the vicious Jesse James who committed the deed once it was determined that Jesse was likely one of the Northfield rob- bers. Having had his hand slammed in the vault door gave Frank James motive. Frank having been the last one out the door gave him opportunity. Considering this, Wilcox's statement supports the theory that Frank James was the killer of Heywood. Cole Younger later wrote in his autobiography that Pitts had been the man guilty of Heywood's murder. Yet as Younger lay dying, he revealed the identity of the killer to Harry Hoffman and Jesse Edwards James. He swore the two men to secrecy as he revealed the guilty party to have been the rider of the dun horse.[24] Hoff- man was later able to get around his pledge not to reveal that information by not denying that it was Frank James who pur- chased the dun horse in Red Wing. Most contemporary members of the James family accept that it was Frank who killed Hey- wood, although they claim the shooting was in self-defense.[25]

One of the more convoluted controversies began only after Cole Younger voiced his side of the story in regard to the Northfield robbery. Younger attempted to save grace in the evidence of his defeat. He claimed in letters written to friends while in prison that the disaster at Northfield was precipitated by the drinking of whiskey by the men who entered the bank. Cole claimed that he never had any confidence in a man who drank.[26] It is likely that Frank James shared this sentiment as both he and Younger had been educated to the importance of reliability during combat. It is unlikely that Frank would drink before the onset of an event by which he was knowingly placing his life and the lives of his brother and friends in jeopardy. Jesse James drank on occasion but certainly had no need for alcohol to ensure his nerve. Bob Younger was apprehensive about the robbery, but he had likely been well trained by his brothers and the James boys as to abstinence and clarity of thought before embarking on such a dangerous event. Younger claimed that it was originally decided that Bob would stay at the door of the bank in an account Cole Younger later gave to Harry Hoffman. Younger claimed that plan was abandoned when it was determined that Bob had been drinking. Cole said he then changed the blueprint and sent his brother into the bank.[27] This statement contradicts two of Cole's earlier statements regarding the robbery. Younger had previously stated that he was on the bridge with Miller when he saw the three men enter the bank. If that were so, he did not have any direct contact with Bob prior to Bob's entering the bank. Secondly, Younger wrote in his autobiography that he was not aware of any drinking before the Northfield raid, and if he had been, he would not have gone into the town.[28] Younger did not develop the whiskey defense until after Bob Younger was dead. The idea of any of the members of the James-Younger Gang jeopardizing themselves and their comrades in such a manner is totally out of character. It seems Cole Younger invented such a defense to save face for his part in the fiasco.

SIXTEEN

∾∾∾

The Largest Manhunt

"Of course by that time the gang was several miles away."
—"L. M. Demarary Recalls Story of Narrow Escape
by T. J. Dunning and of Raid on Mathews
Flock of Chickens," Minnesota newspaper article

THERE WAS NO way to tell in advance if a James-Younger Gang robbery would be successful. Sometimes great amounts of money had been realized. Other times the pickings had been slim. The gang had enjoyed themselves at times, yet other times they had met with unexpected, unplanned tragedies. Nothing yet though had occurred that would put an end to the gang.

Northfield would be different from anything they had yet encountered. Jesse and the gang had carefully planned their retreat after the robbery. The first thing that they planned on doing was to cut the telegraph wires just outside town. This would buy them time once the people of Northfield had been alerted that their bank had been robbed. Bill Chadwell would then lead them through a maze of alternate routes so that they would be able to elude any posse that might be quickly thrown together to chase after them. But Bill Chadwell lay dead back in the street. The plan of retreat was by necessity immediately discarded. There had been no time to cut the wires as the gang was made to run for their lives west out of Northfield. A few men did pursue the robbers, although it was the message immediately transmitted down the wire that would cause the gang the greatest problem. Soon everyone within a hundred-mile radius would know that the Northfield bank had been robbed and that three men were dead. Mayor J. T. Ames immediately telegraphed the state capital asking for assistance in coordinating a massive hunt for the robbers. Minnesota did not intend to cater to the outlaw trade. Every effort would be made to locate the men who had been so brazen as to violate one of its towns.

The outlaws retraced their steps through Dundas. They paused briefly at the Cannon River to cleanse their wounds. The various routes and roads they had traversed the past couple of days were quickly reviewed. Retreat would be slow. The boys were a bloody mess. Bob Younger had been hurt the worst. His arm hung limp at his side. Cole Younger had been shot three times. They didn't even have enough horses. A farmer named Philip Empey appeared on the road above the band as they grouped together to decide which way to continue their flight. Empey led a horse that pulled a cart loaded down with rails. A couple of the men scrambled up the bank of the river and commanded Empey to hand over his horse. Bob's mount lay dead back in Northfield. The young man was in no condition to walk. Empey looked nervously down the barrels of several revolvers. He quickly complied with the order.[1]

The gang was able to pass through Millersburgh without incident, although two men later reported that they had seen the outlaws confront Empey. These two fellows were quick to recognize that challenging the strangers would not be a good idea. They stayed hidden in the brush until the outlaws moved on. They were not seen and were able to briefly follow the strangers. Cole decided to stop at the farm of a man named Robert Donaldson to get some clean water to cleanse Bob's injury. Donaldson asked how the young man had come to injure himself so badly as he provided the strangers with a bucket of water. Donaldson was informed that there had been a fight with a ''black-leg'' back in Northfield. Bob had been shot and the ''blackleg''

killed. The farmer asked the name of the "blackleg." He was
told "Stiles."[2] The boys resumed their retreat after Cole
wrapped Bob's arm in a shredded shirt. Bob had lost so much
blood that it was difficult for him to stay in his saddle. Cole led
Bob's horse by the rein as Bob attempted to stay on top of his
mount.

The outlaws stopped again near Shieldsville to water their
overheated horses. They watched a group of several men leave
their guns outside while they entered a house. The gang quietly
availed itself of the well after the men were inside. The men
came outside as the outlaws watered their horses. They were
curious to know who the strangers were and what they were
doing there. The outlaws drew their guns and directed the others
to leave their guns where they were. The gang was several miles
away by the time the Minnesotans were able to gather their
weapons and pursue the strangers. The small posse got close
enough to the robbers to exchange fire about four miles out, but
the outlaws were soon once again out of sight.[3]

An event of nature that would prove to be both a blessing and
a curse to the gang would soon commence. A torrential rain
began to fall as the boys made their way into an area known as
the Big Woods. The rain would persist for the next two weeks.
The outlaws continued to make their way through the murk and
mire of the unfamiliar terrain. They knew they were in serious
trouble. For starters, they were unsure of their position. Several
of their wounds were about to cause serious setbacks in the time
needed to make their escape. Bob Younger's arm was dreadful.
Jim's shoulder was really in bad shape. Cole's thigh was so
painful that he had been forced to wrap it as tightly as he could
stand to enable him to walk with the assistance of a makeshift
cane. The others suffered shell shock but were able to do what
was necessary to encourage the Youngers in their retreat.

Over 200 men had answered the call for a posse by the time
of the encounter in Shieldsville. The number grew to at least 500
by the next day. Professional sheriffs and their deputies attempted to supervise scores of untrained men. Many, if not most,
of the inexperienced volunteers had been attracted to the manhunt by the $1,500 reward being offered by Minnesota Governor
J. S. Pillsbury. Others were in it for the thrill of the adventure.

George Huntington of Northfield later wrote, "Their failure at critical moments and places to do what they had been depended on to do made them more than useless, worse than enemies."[4] Yet many law enforcement officers and former Civil War veterans were trained and organized enough to direct the actions of some of those who had offered their help. Picket lines were erected at every possible route of escape. Even so, the severe weather gave the advantage to the outlaws. The rain made tracing them almost impossible. Additionally, the men involved in the hunt had no way of knowing what the robbers actually looked like. This also served the gang well. Several times when they had unintentionally crossed paths with small groups of men, they had identified themselves as posse and been believed. Reports of sightings were many, but information received only a short time before contradicted that which was offered, more often than not.

The gang attempted to cross the Cannon River, but the water was too high. They were forced to remain on one side. The wife of farmer George James was approached on September 8 by two scraggly men who inquired if she had seen two mules in the area. They were afraid that the animals might have become engulfed in the marsh. They wondered if Mrs. James might tell them a little about the nearby terrain.[5] The boys decided to remain on the Cordova Road until they could somehow gain a better knowledge of the river. Two of them posed as posse and rode up to a group of road workers to ask where they might cross the Cannon. The men were directed to a bridge. They were forced to duck under cover to elude a bona fide posse before they had the chance to cross over. They circled Tetonka Lake only to encounter a posse led by a war veteran named Captain Rodgers. Shots were exchanged, but the outlaws were able to cross the lake and disappear into the woods once again.

By midafternoon, two of the horses went lame and were replaced by horses belonging to farmer John Laney. Two others were soon stolen from Ludwig Rosenau. Rosenau's son Wilhelm was ordered to guide the group across the river. Wilhelm was allowed to go back home after his hosts arrived on the other side of the river. The gang advanced toward Janesville. Two additional horses were obtained after a brief visit to the Rosenhall farm. Two young men working in the field were ordered to un-hitch their plow horses. The boys were then employed to escort the gang up the Elysian Road. The original two horses were left at the Kohn farm near Waterville. Two of the outlaws were able to obtain a meal there by posing as posse. They somehow were able to bring food back to share with the others.

The gang hid on an island off Lake Elysian during the evening of September 10. They were suddenly surrounded by over 200 posse. In the morning they let three of the horses go free in the hopes that the horses would serve as a diversion. The other three horses were tied to a tree and left behind. The men waded through the marshy area on foot. They stopped to redress their wounds about one mile west of the lake. Bloody rags were found at the scene several days later. The outlaws were exhausted and hungry. They holed up in a deserted farmhouse ten miles north-east of Mankato the next day. They remained until the following day. They were simply too tired to continue. They were unaware that on this day Nicholas Gustavson had succumbed to his injury and died back in Northfield. No witnesses had come forward to identify who it was who fired the bullet that killed him. Gustavson's death was marked an unfortunate incident within the larger event.

The gang unintentionally encountered a farm hand named Jeff Dunning on September 12. Killing men in cold blood was not a common practice of the boys in the James-Younger Gang. The boys had thus far released everyone with whom they came in contact but that had been while they were on the road and not so tired. They were moving slower now. If Dunning was to be allowed to go free, he might quickly reveal their location. They had a brief heart-to-heart with the frightened man. Dunning was warned that he should tell no one of having seen them. The farm hand was then allowed to go home. Dunning held his silence for three hours before he told employer L. M. Demarary that he had met the Northfield robbers. Demarary later reported that by the time Dunning told him of his encounter, the gang was miles away. Not as far as Demarary might have thought, however. The next day, the outlaws stole chickens from Demarary's neighbor, Mr. Mathews, and enjoyed their first meal in a long time. They eventually crossed the Blue Earth River at a railroad bridge.

They were able to follow the tracks around Mankato without running into a posse.

By September 14, Bob Younger's arm injury and the infection in Jim Younger's shoulder made it necessary for a decision to be made. The two men had tried with all they had in them to stay focused upon keeping up with the others. They could only do so much. The seriousness of their injuries caused the group to lose time and distance every day. Bob suggested to the others that he be left behind in order to ensure their escape. His unselfish offer was refused, but it was agreed to split up in order to confuse the posse. Those who could move faster would likely be followed. The group that needed to take more time would possibly be left undetected. It has often been written in popular histories that Jesse suggested shooting Bob so that the gang could make its escape. Cole and Jim Younger both completely denied this bit of folklore years later. Cole addressed the issue with Harry Hoffman: "No, Jesse James nor any person ever made that request or suggestion."[6] Cole explained to Hoffman that Jesse and Frank went in search of horses the night before the decision to divide into two groups was made but could only steal two. Jesse suggested that Bob take one of the horses. Cole later stated, "During this night Bob's arm had taken a turn for the worse and he was suffering great pain and I told Jesse and Frank to take the horses and go. And this they did. Their acts and treatment of us were honorable and loyal."[7]

The James brothers were as loyal to the Youngers as the Youngers would prove to be loyal to the Jameses. Charlie Pitts had decided to stay with his friend Cole Younger. The four men gave Jesse and Frank most of their personal items as they parted company with them. Frank and Jesse continued to follow the Blue Earth River. Later that evening, they approached Lake Crystal. They saw a small group of men asleep on the bridge. The two outlaws were spotted as they attempted to sneak past. A shot was fired at them. The outlaws disappeared into the night before the others could come to their senses. Jesse and Frank stole two fresh horses that night. They had to ride bareback since they were without gear. They reached South Dakota after forty-eight hours of hard riding. They stole two more horses on September 17. They probably had a good laugh later over the fact that one horse was blind in one eye while the other was blind in both.[8] The impaired horses were soon replaced as the brothers headed toward Sioux Falls.

The ruse had worked for the Youngers and Pitts. The posse followed the trail of the James boys as the slower group continued to follow the railroad tracks. They stopped along the Crystal Road near Linden. Here they were able to find and prepare corn, watermelon, chickens, and a small turkey. Voices were heard on the bank above them before they could eat. The outlaws scrambled up the bank and ran toward the woods. A posse chased them before they disappeared somewhere near the top of Pigeon Hill. The posse returned to the area where they had first seen the gang. There they found two leather bridles, a small piece of carpet, a blood-soaked handkerchief, a shirt with the initials G. S. O, a ripped, backless shirt, and two of Bob Youngers' coats; a blue gossamer and a new brown linen duster.[9]

The Youngers and Pitts would continue their arduous trek many miles before eventually encountering farm boy Oscar Soble on September 21. The next time they saw Soble they would be surrounded by the posse that would bring them down at a godforsaken place called Hanska Slough.

Dr. Sidney Mosher of Sioux City, Iowa, was accosted by two men on a bridge on September 25. Mosher was driving his buggy toward the town of Kingsley to treat a patient. The strangers on horseback accused the good doctor of being an agent of the St. Paul police. He steadfastly denied any such thing. Mosher insisted that he was a doctor and invited the pair to search him. They found only a small box with a scalpel. Dr. Mosher then told the men that if they doubted his identity, they should ask the people who lived in the next farmhouse to describe Dr. Mosher of Sioux City. The outlaws took Dr. Mosher hostage and continued on their way. The group came upon a farm a few hours later. One of the men, later identified as having looked like Jesse James, walked up to the farmhouse. He told the farmer that Dr. Mosher of Sioux City had a breakdown with his buggy. Since the doctor needed to borrow a saddle, would the farmer mind lending them one? Once they had the saddle in their possession, it was placed on Frank's horse.[10]

A light was seen radiating from another farmhouse sometime

after dark. The doctor was then ordered to climb down from his buggy and remove his clothes. Mosher was handed Frank's clothes to wear as Frank donned Mosher's pants and coat. The doctor was then allowed to go free. The outlaws continued on their way. The identification that Dr. Mosher gave of his captors fit Jesse and Frank James perfectly. This incident appears to have been the last sighting of the James brothers for quite some time. In a detailed, though questionable, account published by G. W. Hunt of the *Sioux City Democrat*, the author writes about having seen these two men the day after Dr. Mosher was released. Hunt claimed to have told the outlaws that he had no desire to apprehend them. He simply wanted to hear their account of the Northfield raid. Hunt maintained that he was then provided with an in-depth account of the events of September 7.[11]

Charlie Pitts never made it out of Hanska Slough. A posse of seven surrounded Pitts and the Youngers there on September 21. After a blazing gun battle which left the Youngers bullet-ridden and Pitts dead, the Youngers surrendered. The Youngers were then taken to the Flanders House in Madelia where they were treated for exposure and a multitude of bullet wounds. Cole suffered twelve bullets while Jim Younger held out against five. Bob had both the elbow wound and a bullet wound in his lung that he had obtained upon his surrender. The folks in Medalia were most eager to know the identities of the Youngers' accomplices at Northfield. The gang had agreed during the planning stages of the robbery not to reveal the names of their comrades either alive, dead, or absent. Police Chief James McDonough of St. Louis had already been to Northfield. There he had concluded that the two robbers killed in that city were Clell Miller and William Chadwell. His identification was based on the descriptions provided by Hobbs Kerry. McDonaugh was very sure that the outlaws who had been able to leave Northfield included Jesse and Frank James and Cole and Bob Younger. McDonough had been shown the body retrieved from the slough. He was able to identify Charlie Pitts. Bob and Cole freely admitted who they were, but Jim was unable to talk due to a serious injury to his mouth and jaw. McDonaugh had trouble naming this eighth man as Kerry had provided identifications only for the men who participated in the Rocky Cut robbery. A rumor naming this outlaw as the famous Texas brigand Cal Carter persisted, even though Jim Younger shook his head in denial. Jim was finally able to state his name. Even so, he was not believed to be who he said he was until sometime later when his sister arrived from Missouri to identify him.

Cole and Bob kept their silence. They adamantly denied ever having anything to do with the James brothers when they were questioned as to whether or not Jesse and Frank James had been with them at Northfield. The press was allowed in to talk to the prisoners the next day. Bob informed them that he had been one of those inside the bank during the robbery. But he once again refused to name the men with him or disclose who it was that had shot cashier Heywood. Bob revealed only that the murder of Heywood was "an act of impulse" on behalf of the man who shot him. Younger said that the murder was something that the entire group had regretted.[12] When Cole was questioned by Sheriff Ira Glispin, he was again asked who his accomplices had been. Younger informed the sheriff that he would have a statement on the matter by the next morning. The following day, Sheriff Glispin was handed a note written by Cole: "Stay by your friends even if heaven falls."[13] The authorities realized that there was no way that any of the Youngers were going to reveal who was with them that day at Northfield. Cole, Jim, and Bob Younger were then moved to the Rice County seat of Faribault. They were arraigned and pled guilty to robbing the First National Bank of Northfield, Minnesota, attacking A. E. Bunker with the intent to do bodily harm and accessory to the murder of J. L. Heywood. Cole Younger was charged as principal and Bob and Jim Younger as his accessories in regard to the murder of Nicholas Gustavson. They were all sentenced to life in prison.

The bodies of Pitts, Miller, and Chadwell were being disposed of elsewhere in Minnesota. Pitts's body was sold to a doctor named Murphy for use as a skeleton. Chadwell's body somehow ended up in the possession of Henry Wheeler. Miller's corpse was embalmed and displayed at various statewide events months after the robbery. Miller's family was eventually able to obtain a court order to retrieve his body for burial in the Muddy Fork Cemetery in Clay County.[14]

The Youngers were visited by John F. Lincoln, the superintendent of the St. Paul & Sioux City Railroad after they had taken up their temporary residence in the Faribault jail. Lincoln brought with him State Legislator John L. Merriam. The two men wanted to talk to the outlaws about the Gad's Hill robbery. Both had been passengers aboard the train that had been robbed there. Cole asked the visitor if they had not met somewhere before being introduced to Merriam by name. The older man looked familiar to him. Merriam smiled and informed Cole that he had been on the Little Rock Express the night of the robbery. Cole backed off and denied having had anything to do with the robbery. He assured Merriam that both he and his brother Bob had been in St. Clair County on that night. Bob Younger, in the meantime, was telling John Lincoln that he and Cole had been in Arkansas at the time of the robbery.[15]

Mayor John Ames of Northfield soon called on the Youngers to inform them of the death of Gustavson. Ames accused Cole Younger of firing the shot that killed the immigrant. Younger adamantly denied it. The two men argued until Younger asked to have Ames removed from his cell. Ames did not reveal to Younger that a Northfield coroner's jury had already found that the death of Nicholas Gustavson had been caused by "a stray bullet that had been fired by an unknown party." Other visitors were eager to talk to the Younger boys about other crimes of which they had been suspected. Yankee Bligh attempted to get Cole Younger to admit he had been involved in the Huntington robbery. Younger denied any knowledge of any such claims of his being involved in any robbery apart from the one at North-field.

Chief McDonough was not through with his attempt to bring all of the Northfield robbers to justice. He arranged in October to have Sergeant Morgan Boland and his men from St. Louis make an unannounced visit to the home of Dr. William W. No-land of Independence. He had received a report that the Jameses had returned to the Jackson/Clay County area. Dr. Noland was an admitted Confederate sympathizer. He was treating a man named John Goodin for a wound received several months before at the time of Boland's visit. Despite protests from Dr. Noland and Goodin, the sergeant believed that the patient's true identity was Frank James. McDonough believed that Frank or Jesse had been wounded in the leg during the Northfield escape and Goodin fit the profile. McDonough and Boland surmised that since Goodin was being treated for a leg wound, there was a good chance that he was in reality Frank James. Goodin was released only after he was taken to St. Louis where doctors confirmed the fact that the man's wound was several months old.[16] It was likely that by this time Jesse and Frank had crossed the Missouri River near Council Bluffs and headed to Nebraska City where they could be sheltered by family and friends.

Cole, Jim, and Bob Younger were beginning their new lives behind bars at the Minnesota State Penitentiary at Stillwater. Jesse and Frank may well have been regrouping from the Northfield fiasco in either Nebraska, Kentucky, or Texas. They had family in all those states who could and would have helped them keep a low profile until things calmed down in the Midwest. Jesse's exact location for the next nine months can only be surmised. McDonough continued to believe that at some point the James brothers had returned to their mother's home in Kearney. McDonough also presumed that Jesse and Frank would never be caught in Clay County. He felt their friends and neighbors would do everything within their power to safeguard them. The newspapers argued this point through the use of editorials. Letters to the editors reminded the public that not all of the people of western Missouri supported the actions of the James-Younger Gang. The fact was, however, that quite a few of them still did. McDonough was absolutely right in his assumption.

SEVENTEEN

~~~~~

Nashville

"I told Jesse that if that was the way he was going to conduct himself that I would not stay with any of them, and that I would not board at a house with Bill Ryan, as he was always getting drunk."

—Jim Cummins, *Jim Cummins' Book*

THE INDIVIDUAL FATES of the Northfield robbers were quite different from one another. Three of them were dead. The Youngers were assigned the task of making tubs and buckets in the Stillwater Penitentiary. On the other hand, Jesse and Frank were enjoying their lives with very little consequence for having participated in the Northfield robbery. The ears of the public went up when they first heard rumors that the James brothers had been in partnership with the Youngers at Northfield. Missouri's law enforcement agents impatiently looked for signs that Jesse and Frank had returned home to the western region of the state. Zerelda Samuel had just returned to Missouri after having announced a month earlier that she was going to take up permanent residence in Texas. She proclaimed that she didn't want to cause trouble for her neighbors by her family's presence in

195

the area.[1] Clay County's Sheriff Groom had heard reports that the brothers were visiting their mother at her farm. He surrounded Zerelda's home with a posse on November 22. Someone approached one of the posse as they waited. The unidentified young man was ordered to halt. The young man instead fired a pistol into the air and ran into the woods. The posse fired at the fleeing suspect to no avail. Groom stated that he strongly believed that the man was either Jesse or Frank James, but no further pursuit was made at that time.[2]

The *St. Louis Republican* claimed on August 6, 1878, that they had been given credible information that Jesse James had been living in Callaway County during the months after the Northfield robbery. Folklore perpetuated there has Jesse living in the homes of Washington Kidwell and Allen Womack. He was said to have passed his time preaching sermons in the local church and teaching voice lessons, of all things. It appears as though a stranger with many talents may well have visited Callaway County, but it is doubtful that this engaging gentleman was Jesse James.[3] Jesse and Frank had taken up residence in Humphreys County, Tennessee, by the summer of 1877. It was a good idea for the two of them to stay away from their known stomping grounds of Missouri and lay low somewhere else. Jesse fetched Zee and their small son from their short-term residence in Kansas City. He took them to a house on a small farm that he rented from W. H. Link near Box's Station.[4] The last time that Jesse had been in Tennessee he had masqueraded as a grain speculator. Jesse now told Link that his name was John Davis Howard. He was a farmer without much capital but with the desire to take care of his small family the best he could. Dave Howard's persona was that of a milquetoast. He went out of his way to avoid interacting with others. Jesse demonstrated just how faint of heart Dave Howard could be one day when he ran into some drunks near the Nolan Hotel in Waverley. Howard called on some passersby to please help him when he was hassled by the inebriated revelers.[5] Jesse's love of dramatics was legendary among those who knew him. He no doubt enjoyed the charade.

The days passed fairly quietly for Jesse and Zee. Zee was pregnant again and was having a hard time. Jesse was greatly concerned about Zee and the baby. He was at his wife's side when she gave birth to twins in February 1878. Two doctors were called in to assist with the birth when the babies were born prematurely. Jesse named the twin boys Gould and Montgomery in honor of the doctors who attempted to save the lives of his tiny sons. Their efforts were to no avail. The babies died within days of their birth.[6] Jesse was devastated.

Frank James also attempted to put his past behind him. He and Annie went to live on the Josiah Walton farm off the Clarkesville Pike near Nashville. Frank was known as Ben J. Woodson and Annie was his wife Fannie.[7] Annie Ralston James gave birth to a child of her own about the time of the birth of Jesse and Zee's twins. Robert Franklin James was born on February 6, 1878. A story Robert told years later provides evidence of the closeness of the families of Jesse and Frank. Robert claimed that his own mother could not produce enough milk to adequately feed her new son. Annie enlisted the help of the babyless Zee James to nurse the baby during his infancy. Frank's friend John Phillips later summed up the relationship between Frank and Annie James: ''One of the most beautiful things connected with the life of this man [Frank] was the deep, unaffected affection between him and the gentle woman who sits at my left [Annie]. Throughout the days and nights of their early wedded life, when the tempests and storms beat so hard upon him, like a good angel she rode and walked by his side, whispering in his ear of peace and hope.''[8] The noble Annie was prepared to stand by her man at all cost.

Jesse grew more despondent when he was stricken with malaria shortly after he lost his sons. He was ill for several months and was unable to work or earn money. Jesse's inability to financially care for his family must have been personally discouraging. He prided himself on always finding ways to provide for his extended family even when he felt that he was being denied adequate opportunities to do so. Jesse had entered into a business arrangement regarding a crop of corn shortly after his arrival in the Nashville area. The venture involved borrowing $1,000 from a man named Steve Johnson. Now that Jesse was out of work due to his illness, he was unable to repay the loan. Johnson felt that he had no choice but to sue Dave Howard. Jesse responded by countersuing Johnson. Jesse claimed that

Zee James and friend. *The Armand De Gregoris Collection*

Johnson had kept all of the profits from the corn and cheated him out of $56. Jesse wrote a series of letters to his attorney, John P. Helms. Jesse claimed Johnson had damaged his credit rating. The next letter Helms received informed him that Jesse would be willing to drop his suit if Johnson would agree to pay him the money that was due him. Shortly after that, another letter was received by Helms from J. D. Howard. Jesse cited his problems at home. He claimed that his wife needed him and that he would like Helms to bring the case to trial as soon as possible. Jesse also claimed that Mr. B. J. Woodson of Davidson County would be present at the trial to bear witness for him.[9] Neither Jesse nor Mr. Woodson showed up when the case was set to be heard. Jesse bought a small herd of cattle from a farmer named Ennis Cooley while all of this was going on. He closed the deal with an unfunded check. Cooley eventually sued Dave Howard himself. By that time, Jesse had already sold the cattle at the Wade and Kessler stockyard using the alias Mr. Young. He may have paid off Steve Johnson with the money from the sale as Johnson's suit against him was dismissed on September 11, 1878. Cooley never did get his money back.[10]

Later in the year, Jesse and Zee moved to Nashville. Frank and Annie had been living there on the Felix Smith farm since the birth of Robert.[11] Jesse was overwhelmed by his debts and was unable to fully recover from his bout of malaria. He had to be treated for that illness again on March 17, 1879. Dr. W. A. Hamilton was called to the house.[12] Frank no doubt felt sorry for his brother and allowed Jesse, Zee, and little Jesse to move in with his family. There was later a report in a Nashville newspaper that Jesse may have been teaching Sunday school during this time at the Tulip Street Methodist Church.[13]

Frank James was involved with racehorses while he lived in Nashville. Jesse also played the ponies. Frank told a reporter years later, ''I took the prize for exhibiting the Poland China hogs at the Nashville and Jackson fairs and entered my horse 'Jewel Maxey' for the gents stakes at Nashville two years in succession, winning the first prize the first time and second money the second time.''[14] Frank had become friendly with a local breeder named William Berry Cheatham. Cheatham introduced Frank to blacksmith Jonas Taylor. Frank must have introduced Taylor to Jesse, for soon Jesse and Taylor bought two horses together. The horses were named Col. Hull and Jim Scott.[15] Jesse also owned a horse named Red Fox at this time. Sometimes Jesse's horses would run well. Sometimes they wouldn't.

Zee James recovered from her difficult delivery of the twins and soon became pregnant again. She gave birth to a healthy daughter on July 17, 1879. The little girl was named Mary Susan after her maternal grandmother and paternal aunt. Jesse needed money to take care of his responsibilities more than ever. He knew only one way to quickly get what he needed. Jesse returned to Missouri alone shortly after his daughter's birth. The only real difficulty in pulling off another successful robbery in his home state was recruiting some boys he could trust to accompany him. Jesse was unable now to call on the Youngers. He would have to think of others on whom he might be able to rely. The trustworthy Cole Younger had come out of Jesse and Frank's past by virtue of his being one of their former Confederate comrades. That pool of prospects seemed a likely place to start looking. Jesse had kept tabs on most of the guerrillas, even if he had not seen or spoken to many of them over the years. Still, putting together a new gang would not be easy. He realized that many of the men who might have been agreeable to participating in the gang's activities in the beginning had left Missouri for Texas, Oklahoma, or the West. Others were now family men who wouldn't be interested in being involved in any illegal activities he might propose. Jesse was desperate. He didn't have much time to give the issue a lot of thought. Jesse asked his cousin Wood Hite if he would like to engage in a little business with him. The same proposal was made to former Quantrillian Dick Liddil and Clell Miller's younger brother Ed. Tucker Bassham was asked to ride along as he had brothers who had served as guerrillas. Bill Ryan was a man whose reputation for drinking was better known than any past accomplishments he may have enjoyed. Jesse completed his merry band by recruiting Ryan. Jesse wasted no time. His new gang promptly robbed the express car and the passengers aboard the Chicago & Alton railroad of approximately $6,000 near the Glendale, Missouri, station on October 8, 1879.

Immediately after dark on that night, a group of men rode up to the Glendale village store in Jackson County. A handful of farmers were sitting around chatting with the owner of the store. They soon found themselves under guard as the armed strangers ordered them to lead them to the nearby train station. Friends of the outlaws were already busy in the depot as these events were unfolding. The telegraph equipment was destroyed and the station agent was directed to lower the green signal and stop the next train. The conscientious employee refused. He changed his mind when a gun barrel was shoved into his mouth and the request was repeated. Rocks were placed on the track that would ensure that the train would be stopped one way or another.

Everything was in place by 8:00. The outlaws and their hostages watched as a train slowed down outside the station and came to a halt. Intimidating shots were fired into the air by the robbers so as to warn away anyone from within the train who might think of becoming involved. Two of the outlaws then forced the express agent to open the door of the express car. The agent made a foolish mistake. He complied with the demand to deliver the contents of the safe by cramming all the money he could into a valise. He then held onto the bag and tried to jump through the open door of the car. He went flying when one of the robbers stopped his attempt to save the money in his charge by savagely slamming the butt of his revolver against the head of the misguided agent. The train was then released, the hostages let go, and the outlaws quickly and quietly left the scene.[16] Between $6,000 and $50,000 had been taken. As expected, Jesse and Frank James were immediately named as suspects. And, as usual, Jesse probably was guilty.

Jesse returned to Nashville right after his visit to Jackson County. He brought Ed Miller back with him.[17] Jesse and Miller decided to buy a successful racehorse named Jim Malone with some of their robbery money after they arrived in Tennessee. Frank later observed, "Jess was a great patron and lover of the race track, and spent much time there. He had several fine horses, among them the great Jim Malone, which won a big race not too long ago in St. Louis, a four-mile race in Louisville and a big Cup in Atlanta, Georgia. Jesse moved with perfect freedom down there."[18] Jesse and Ed Miller were delighted when Jim

Jesse on his horse, c. 1880. *The Jesse James Farm*

Malone won a few more races at tracks throughout Tennessee, Kentucky, Ohio, and Illinois. The horse had done so well that Jesse decided to enter him in another important race taking place in Atlanta. Jim Malone evidently didn't feel up to the challenge that day. Jesse and Miller lost everything they had with them.

They had to sell the horse in order to finance their trip back to Tennessee. Jim Cummins later wrote that Jesse and Miller were only able to get $300 for Jim Malone when they sold him in Atlanta although his purchase price had been $800.[19]

Sometime during the time that Jesse was visiting the racetracks with Jim Malone, an article appeared in a newspaper. The paper claimed Jesse had been killed by his friend and former confederate George Shepard. An involved, convoluted story emerged during the following couple of days. Shepard was said to have been in cahoots with Marshall James Liggett to engineer the capture of Jesse James. Shepard had recently finished serving ten years in the Missouri penitentiary for his involvement in the Russellville robbery. Liggett confirmed that a plan had been developed whereby Shepard would attempt to gain entry into Jesse's current gang. The story becomes a tall one from there. Liggett said Shepard claimed that he rode out to the Samuel farm. He was then blindfolded and taken to Jesse. Jesse was camping out in the woods with Ed Miller, Jim Cummins, a man named Sam Kaufman, and someone named Taylor. Shepard said that Jesse told him during this meeting that his brother Frank had died from consumption. Jesse agreed that Shepard could be included in Jesse's next robbery. The target was to be a bank in Short Creek, Missouri. Shepard told Liggett and Liggett in turn posted a guard. Jesse spotted the guard while making his final casing of the bank. The plan was called off. Shepard claimed to have at this point decided to kill Jesse. Shepard got his chance one day near Galena, Kansas, while he rode with Jesse, Cummins, and Miller. Shepard wasted no time in seizing the opportunity to eliminate his former friend. He shot the outlaw behind the ear and killed him. Cummins chased Shepard while Miller tended to Jesse. It was Shepard's plan to lead the rest of the gang to a position where they could be ambushed by Liggett and his officers. A running gun battle ensued. Shepard was hit in the calf by a bullet from Cummins's gun but was able to continue on to safety when Cummins returned to Miller. Liggett and a posse went to Galena to locate Jesse's body but found nothing.[20]

The rumor was perpetrated in the press with reports of suspicious odiferous boxes being delivered to Kearney and elusive doctors having issued death certificates to friends of the outlaw.

Few people believed that George Shepard had killed Jesse James when it came right down to it. A couple of newspapers presented a theory that perhaps Shepard was involved in a scheme with Jesse whereby people would believe Jesse was dead. This would allow Jesse to go underground and leave outlawry behind. Cole Younger heard the rumor in Minnesota. Younger was asked if he believed that Jesse was dead. He answered, "I believe it is true if George Shepard says it's true." But Shepard was vague when he was questioned about the matter. None of those who actually knew Jesse believed that he was dead. Robert Pinkerton became one of Shepard's detractors. He was quoted in the newspaper as saying, "He [Jesse] is totally devoid of fear, and has no more compunction about cold-blooded murder than he has about eating his breakfast. I don't believe Shepard would dare to shoot at him."[21] The entire Shepard incident is strange indeed. When one considers that George Shepard was not only a former James-Younger Gang member but also was a leader of one of the irregular units with whom Jesse had wintered in Texas, it gets even stranger. Quantrill and Anderson's men were certainly not known for their betrayal of one another.

Frank James was doing very well in his new home state of Tennessee while Jesse was alternating between winning and losing his money. He was living with his family on the Jeff Hyde farm and had taken a job at the Indiana Lumber Company.[22] Frank's approach to meeting strangers was quite different from Jesse's. Frank felt as if he would draw less suspicion if he were to act as if he had nothing to hide. He befriended various law enforcement officials in the area and didn't hesitate to talk to anyone. Ben and Annie Woodson were fast becoming part of Nashville's society, although they didn't entertain and didn't speak much about the past. Jesse took a job at the Lambert Mocker Barrel Factory at 296 North Front Street in the spring. Jesse appears in a photo taken of the employees of the company along with Frank James and Bill Ryan. Frank must have changed employers as the barrel factory appears to be aligned with the Indian Lumber Company, they are evidently two different companies. John D. Howard is listed in the 1880 Nashville Directory as living on Burns Avenue, down by the racetrack at this time.[23] Jesse's employment, as usual, didn't last long.

Jesse and Ed Miller returned to Missouri again in the summer of 1880. Their reason for heading north isn't clear. Tucker Bassham had provoked suspicion a short time before by carelessly flashing the money he had made from the Glendale robbery. Bassham was soon questioned by the local sheriff as to how he had come by so much money. He admitted that he had been one of the robbers of the Chicago & Alton Railroad.[24] Bassham was promptly sentenced to ten years in prison. Why Jesse would return to Missouri at a time when Bassham might finger him as having been the leader of the gang that committed the robbery is interesting. The egotistical Jesse perhaps felt that his known presence in the state would inspire Bassham to keep his mouth shut. Jesse didn't like too many people knowing about his activities. He no doubt quickly realized he had made a mistake by relying on the unproved loyalties of men such as Bassham and Miller. They had come to be part of his new gang only because of their association with guerrilla friends of Jesse and not because he had known them personally over the years. Perhaps Jesse had made a huge mistake by bringing them into the gang. Such was definitely the case with Bassham, but what about Ed Miller? Jesse was the only one who could answer that question, but it was not a question that would be of much consequence for very long. Ed Miller disappeared during Jesse and Miller's return trip to Missouri. Some accounts speculate that Jesse was paranoid and feared Miller would expose him as the leader of the robbery. If this were so, Jesse may have shot and killed Miller before Miller could turn himself in and turn state's evidence. Jesse's cousin Clarence Hite told the story that Jesse and Miller got into an argument on their way to Missouri. Hite claimed Miller took a shot at Jesse and knocked off his hat. Jesse then shot and killed Miller. He buried Miller's body at the side of the road east of Norborne, Missouri.[25] Miller's disappearance remains a mystery to this day.

Jesse was in the company of Dick Liddil and Bill Ryan when he returned home to his family in Nashville in July. Frank James was extremely irritated that Jesse had brought members of his new gang to Nashville. Frank was upset to think that there was a good chance that Jesse's questionable new friends might blow Frank's cover. One slip and they could ruin his chances for continuing to enjoy the new life he had been able to create. Jesse agreed to his brother's demand that he at least get rid of the alcoholic Bill Ryan. Jesse sent Ryan to stay with Frank and Jesse's cousins in Adairsville, Kentucky, some forty miles away.[26] Maybe if Ryan were out of Frank's sight, he would be out of Frank's mind as well.

Jesse picked up Ryan in Adairsville the following September. The pair headed for Mammoth Cave, Kentucky. They wasted no time. The two of them robbed a Glasgow tourist stage halfway between Mammoth Cave and Cave City on September 3, 1880. Jesse and Ryan pretended to be moonshiners in need of cash to help them escape from revenue agents. The drama continued when the robbers made a list of the passengers' names. They promised each one that their money would be returned to them when the moonshiners experienced better luck. Watches, jewelry, and some $1,000 in cash was taken that day. The governor of Kentucky offered a $500 reward for apprehension of the robbers as Jesse and Ryan made their way back to Nashville. Law enforcement officials subsequently arrested Dr. Thomas Hunt of Scottsdale, Kentucky, in connection with the robbery. They allowed Hunt to go free when it was revealed that his arrest was clearly a mistake.[27]

Jesse was on a roll. Two weeks later, on September 15, he robbed the payroll of the Dovey Coal Mines at Mercer, Kentucky. Bill Ryan and Dick Liddil accompanied him. Evidently, Jesse's intelligence was off. The outlaws had obtained information indicating the payroll was large and the expected delivery would be thousands of dollars. They netted less than $15. This robbery was hardly worth the effort, but then little effort had gone into planning it. Jesse was losing his touch. He just didn't operate the way he had when things had been good for the James-Younger Gang. This new gang couldn't hold a candle to the old one. Jesse must have been painfully aware that his glory days were far behind him.

Jesse returned with Dick Liddil to Missouri for a short period of time in November. He may have been homesick and in need of a visit to his mother and family. William H. Wallace had been elected prosecuting attorney of Jackson County during the election of 1880. Wallace's platform had promised that he would do everything within his power to put an end to the outlawry of Jesse James and his friends. Jesse was likely amused—and challenged. The *Sedalia Daily Democrat* reported in its January 7, 1881, edition that one of its reporters had spoken with Jesse in Denver, Colorado. The reporter claimed that Jesse had told him that he had served as a Mississippi delegate to the Republican national convention of 1880 and had voted for U. S. Grant's third-term nomination. An interesting notion.

Jesse was back in Tennessee by the end of the month. This time he was accompanied by former guerrilla Jim Cummins. Cummins had been implicated in the Glendale robbery and was eager to quietly disappear until things calmed down. Jesse and Zee were by this time living with their children in the small rooms of a boarding house owned by a woman named Kent on Summer Street. Cummins moved in temporarily with Frank and Annie. Cummins didn't like the way Jesse was acting. He thought Jesse was especially nervous and unpredictable. He didn't want to stay with Jesse and Zee. Cummins refused to live with Bill Ryan, as well. Ryan, he said, was always drunk and not pleasant company.[28] Cummins had known Frank and Jesse at least since the war and had been a close friend of Ed Miller as well. Cummins knew that Miller had not been seen in some time. He began to think that Jesse may have murdered him. Cummins began to act increasingly ill at ease when he was around Jesse. Jesse could not help noticing his old friend's awkward behavior. Jesse joked to Dick Liddil that they ought to get rid of Cummins. Liddil was quick to relay that bit of information to Cummins. Cummins left Tennessee immediately. He later wrote:

> On my way to Kentucky I stopped at George Hyatt's [Hite] and there I saw the brown horse that Ed Miller was riding when he was killed. When I arrived at Bardstown, Ky., I learned that Ed Miller and Jesse James had left there together for Missouri. I told Donnie Pence that I believed that Jesse James had killed Ed Miller. . . . Then I returned to Edsville [Edgefield] in the night and asked Jesse to come out, saying that I had a horse I wished him to look at. My intentions were to kill him as he came out the door. Jesse said he would see the horse in the morning. I told Jesse that

he had a good reason for not coming out; that he had killed Ed
Miller; that I had found Ed's horse and had learned at Bardstown
that he and Ed had started to Missouri together. I told him that I
never wanted to meet him as a friend, and that I intended to let
every one of Ed's friends and relatives know just how he lost his
life. This I did when I arrived in Missouri.[29]

Jesse could not have been happy with this development. Out
of his sight, Cummins was a loose cannon. Both Jesse and Frank
were worried that Cummins might reveal that they were now
living in Nashville. The James boys decided to leave Tennessee
for Alabama while they waited anxiously to see what would
happen next. Jesse moved his family to a small house at 903
Woodland Street where Zee and the children were placed under
the watchful eye of Dick Liddil. A short time later, an incident
occurred while Jesse was out of town. Liddil shot at a man
throwing rocks at the door of Jesse's house. Jesse arranged for
his family to be moved to 711 Fatherland Street.[30] Everyone
seemed to be safe for the time being.

Jesse and Frank returned to Nashville sometime in early
March. Jesse was back in Alabama with Dick Liddil and Bill
Ryan on March 11, 1881. Paymaster Alex Smith of Muscle
Shoals was robbed of over $5,000 that day. Two weeks later,
Frank's uneasiness proved to be right on the money. An inebriated Bill Ryan claimed he was a robber named Tom Hill. Ryan
pulled a gun on a customer named James McGinnis in a back-
room saloon at Earthman's Grocery Store in Whites Creek. Ryan
was almost immediately fingered as having likely been a participant in the Muscle Shoals robbery. He was loaded with money
and had been repeatedly broadcasting that he was an outlaw.
Ryan was arrested after he had been tied to a chair by McGinnis
and the bartender. He was soon on his way to the county jail for
further investigation.[31] Dick Liddil read about Ryan in the *Nashville Banner* the day after Ryan was arrested. Liddil quickly relayed the news to Jesse and Frank.[32] Jesse and Frank
immediately suspected that Ryan would reveal everything he
knew. They made plans to leave Nashville at once.

EIGHTEEN

⌒⌒⌒⌒

Back to Missouri

"Good-bye, old fellows, this is the last time you will ever see or hear of the James Boys."
—Jesse James, according to the *Kansas City Times*, September 8, 1881

JESSE AND FRANK realized that even if they left the state, they were not protecting their families. Their wives and families would still be subject to intense questioning if anything should develop from Ryan's capture. It was decided that Zee, Annie, and the children would also be better off out of Tennessee. They were quickly put aboard a train bound for Nelson County, Kentucky. The women would stay with family until their husbands could decide what further action would need to be taken.[1] Jesse and Frank stole horses from outside town and headed to the Adairville home of their Uncle George Hite. They also paid a visit to their old friend Donny Pence. They no doubt asked Pence to keep an eye on their families. Donny Pence was once a fierce, irreverent guerrilla soldier. Now he was Sheriff of Nelson County.

Bill Ryan was extradited from Kentucky to Missouri to await trial. Tucker Bassham had already been pardoned. A deal had been cut whereby Bassham's freedom would be exchanged for his testimony against Ryan. Bassham had already informed the law that he had assisted Jesse James, Ed Miller, Dick Liddil, Bill Ryan, and Wood Hite in the Glendale robbery.[2] The authorities evidently felt that Ryan had even more to tell about the activities of his friend Mr. James. Ryan was questioned extensively before any plans were made to rush to convict him.

Jesse and Frank took separate routes to Clay County. They undoubtedly stayed with either their mother or their sister Sally. While home in Missouri, Jesse read that a flooding of the Missouri River near Kansas City had caused an engine of the Hannibal & St. Joseph Railroad to fall into the water on April 23. A New York–Kansas City express car was scheduled to stop in the town of Randolph to allow the people who had been passengers on the train to transfer to other transportation. Jesse felt that the timing was right. He and Frank could rob the express car while those in charge of the train were busy doing other things and their attention was elsewhere. Jesse's strategy was for naught. The situation changed by May 4, and Jesse was forced to cancel his plans.[3]

Clarence Hite escorted Zee and the children to Kansas City. They arrived on May 1 and took up temporary residence with Zee's sister. Annie and little Robert visited with General Jo Shelby in northwest Missouri for a few days. Then they traveled on to the home of Annie's father in Independence.[4] Frank had returned to the area through St. Louis and soon reclaimed his family. Jesse rented rooms at the Doggett House on Sixth and Walnut Streets in Kansas City. He used the alias of J. T. Jackson.

Jesse rented a little house on Woodland Avenue, between Eleventh and Twelfth Streets, on June 1. His landlord was former newspaperman D. R. Abeel.[5] Next door lived John Murphy. Jesse's neighbor was the father of Jackson County Marshal Cornelius Murphy. Jesse more than likely enjoyed the irony and was challenged by the marshal's close proximity. Jesse E. told the story of how Marshal Murphy would sometimes gather a posse and set off in search of Jesse and Frank James. The outlaw remained cool as a cucumber, according to his son. Jesse E. related, "One day my father went over to Mr. Murphy and he wished him luck in his hunt for the James boys."[6] Jesse wore

no disguise. He pretended to be a grouchy eccentric who steered
away from any involvement with his neighbors. Groceries were
delivered to the household and any other needs were taken care
of quietly. It was rumored that he was a gambler when those in
the neighborhood noticed that Jesse seemed to be gone from
home frequently. Mr. Jackson certainly didn't seem to hold any
regular job. Jesse E. later recalled his lonely childhood by remembering the time he spent at the Woodland Avenue house.
He remembered that next door on the other side of the house
lived another little boy about his age, future Jackson County
deputy Harry Hoffman. Little "Tim" had wanted to play with
his new neighbor, but his parents encouraged him to stay in his
own yard instead. "My mother said we would be leaving soon
and I would find another little boy to play with. My father always
painted a bright future for me, of going to school, meeting other
children, riding horses on a farm. I didn't know at the time that
there was any reason why the future might not work out just that
way."[7] An incident that may have occurred sometime during this
time frame must have made Jesse uncomfortable. Zee told the
story of how once when Jesse had been traveling on a train, the
conductor noticed that the tip of Jesse's finger was missing when
he handed over his ticket. On the return trip he was asked by
the same conductor if he was Jesse James. Jesse James, he was
told, was also missing the tip of his finger. Of course, Jesse
denied it, but he must have been pleased at the recognition.
Jesse's relocation surely cost him money that he did not have to
spare. Frank James likely needed money, as well. The two men
soon came to the decision that they would make another appearance on the tracks of a Missouri railroad.

Jesse and Frank made plans to rob the Chicago, Rock Island
and Pacific Railroad near Chillicothe, Missouri, on June 8. They
would use Wood Hite and Dick Liddil this time. A heavy rain
caused the roads to quickly flood and made the necessary escape
dangerous. This forced the plan to be aborted. The outlaw band
then rode to the Gallatin area as Jesse attempted to come up with
another scheme in a more accessible location. If he was able to
come up with a plan, this, too, was put on hold. An abscessed
tooth caused Jesse to return to Kansas City.[8] Jesse recovered by
July 14. Jesse, Liddil, and Hite attempted to rob another train

near Gallatin that day. They somehow missed boarding the train and that scheme was called off as well. The idea for quick cash was only postponed until the next day, despite all of the failures.

Jesse somehow heard that William Westfall was now a conductor for the Chicago, Rock Island and Pacific Railroad. Jesse believed Westfall to have been aboard the train that carried the Pinkertons to the bombing of the James-Samuel house. A Chicago, Rock Island and Pacific train was brought to a stop outside the small town of Winston, Missouri, on July 15, 1881. Five outlaws jumped aboard as the train pulled out of Kansas City. Two of the robbers jumped up into the express car while the others climbed aboard the passenger cars. Westfall stood in one of the passenger cars. He was shot in the back without any warning whatsoever. The outlaw who fired the bullet walked up to Westfall as he lay on the floor. He shot the conductor again. A passenger named Frank McMillan was shot and killed after he somehow became involved in the incident. Dick Liddil later testified that he was one of the robbers. Liddil said that he had been in the company of Jesse and Frank James and Clarence and Wood Hite. Liddil claimed that Jesse had been the one who had killed Westfall. Liddil said Frank was guilty of shooting McMillan.[9]

Jesse and his gang disappeared into the woods after the robbery. They reached the Crooked River by daybreak, according to Liddil. Liddil split off from the others there. Jesse, Frank, and Hite entered the town of Lawson where they ate dinner at someone's farm. Then they returned to Clay County. They camped out on the James-Samuel farm and were fed by their family. Clay County Sheriff James R. Timberlake rode around the Samuel farm early on the Sunday morning of July 17. He didn't realize that he was very close to where the boys were lying asleep on the ground. Had he but known. . . . Zerelda Samuel was spotted in Kearney the following day, but she was seen returning from Kansas City on Tuesday evening. Zerelda dealt with the question as to whether or not her sons were in the county by informing those who asked that they were both dead.[10]

Authorities were once again faced with the prospect of locating the robbers. Governor Thomas Crittenden reacted in an unprecedented manner. For years the officials of the state of

Missouri had been pressured by newspapers and local authorities to do something about the continued robberies that took place throughout the state. The newspapers now again put up a hue and cry that the government was doing little to stop the continued outlawry. Various newspapers suggested their own remedies including rewards of up to $100,000. Also suggested was the installation of time locks on express safes and armed guards on all trains. Someone even suggested sharpshooting wheat growers be brought in from the North. The pressure was on. The law could not rely on the words of common thieves to deliver the outlaw leader to them even though they had members of Jesse's gang in custody. By this time it was unlikely that Ryan or the others even knew Jesse's whereabouts.

It was not within a state official's authority to offer any kind of reward for either information regarding the robbers of any private entity or the delivery of their bodies. Crittenden was clever. He enlisted the assistance of Colonel Wells H. Blodgett. Blodgett was the attorney for the Wabash Railroad. Crittenden and Blodgett conducted a meeting with the officials of various railroad and express companies. It was agreed that those companies would provide Crittenden with funds that would be awarded to individuals who might help them locate the James brothers and their associates. Five thousand dollars each offered as bait should anyone be able to deliver Jesse and/or Frank James to the sheriff of Daviess County. An additional $5,000 would be awarded if either man should be convicted of the Winston or Glendale robberies or the murders of cashier Sheets, conductor Westfall, or passenger Frank McMillan. Five thousand dollars per man was also offered for any of the men who accompanied the James boys during this excursion.

Intervention by a governor in the pursuit of the perpetrators of a local crime was of course unusual at best. The newspapers had a field day debating the merits of Crittenden's action. Crittenden was under a tremendous pressure to do all he could to ensure that Missouri not return to the "outlaw state" that it had been labeled during the reign of the James-Younger Gang. Crittenden must have felt his intervention necessary. A monetary incentive might inspire those who had information about the robbery to come forward. The newspapers debated the ethics and

legality of the state becoming involved in the hunt for the outlaws. Several editors suggested that Crittenden had little choice
in the matter. The *St. Louis Chronicle* complained on July 27
that it was likely that the criminals would not be caught due to
the competition of the various officials for the reward. The *St.
Louis Globe-Democrat* argued on August 2 that the state had
little choice but to become involved as long as there were bushwhackers and descendants of bushwhackers.

Jesse and Frank went to the office of real estate agent H. C.
Sailers on the morning of August 30, 1881. They attempted to
rent a house on East Ninth Street.[11] Frank had sent Annie and
Robert to visit family in California while the heat was on. Now
he decided that he wanted them back with him. The rental house
was large enough for several people to live comfortably should
Frank decide to live with Jesse after his family returned. Sailers,
however, did not want a large party in the house. He objected
to their turning a third bedroom into a kitchen. The two men left
without renting the house but returned later that afternoon. Jesse
and his family were allowed to lease the house after they paid a
month's rent. Clarence Hite and Frank helped Jesse move his
family into their new residence almost immediately.[12]

The new James Gang immediately came under suspicion for
the robbery of the Davis and Sexton Bank in Riverton, Iowa.
This event took place on July 11. It was later determined that
the culprits were a small gang of penny-ante robbers lead by an
outlaw named Poke Wells.[13] The authentic James Gang was by
no means out of the robbery business, however.

Another robbery was planned in Independence on September
6, 1881. Jesse's well-laid plans once again failed him during the
night of September 7. The plan had been to bring an eastbound
Chicago & Alton train to a halt near Blue Cut, Missouri, according to Clarence Hite. History should have made Jesse leery
of any thoughts of criminal activity on that date. When two trains
roared by within minutes of each other, the gang didn't know
which of the trains held the most money. The first plan was
abandoned.[14] At 9:00 P.M., a St. Louis express came through and
the boys waved it down with a red lantern. The robbery took
place five years to the day after the Northfield fiasco. Dick Liddil
and the Hites were likely involved. Frank James may have par-

ticipated as well. A new member of the gang was a young man from Richmond, Missouri, named Charlie Ford. Ford had likely been introduced to Jesse by Dick Liddil. Liddil had been seeing Ford's sister, Martha Bolton.

The boys broke open the express car and commanded messenger H. A. Fox to open the safe. Fox was beaten with pistol butts while the passengers were verbally assaulted. The leader of the gang wore no physical disguise. In addition, he brazenly announced that he was Jesse James. If this robbery was indeed committed by Jesse and his new gang, they had certainly abandoned the diplomacy and finesse the James-Younger Gang had employed. When engineer Choppey Foote refused to obey orders, he was threatened. The outlaw who stood before him claimed that the gun that was aimed at his head was the same gun that had been used to kill conductor Westfall. Brakeman Frank Burton heard the approach of another train. Burton broke away from his captors in an attempt to somehow issue a warning that the first train was stopped on the tracks. Bullets were fired at Burton as he ran down the tracks, attempting to avoid a collision between the two trains. He yelled his intent to the robbers and eventually they stopped shooting at him. Foote later stated that after the men realized there was no more money to be had, the leader of the band returned him to the front of the train. There he was given two silver dollars. The outlaw told the engineer that he was "a brave man and I am stuck on you, here is $2 for you to drink the health of Jesse James tomorrow morning." The bandit leader suggested he have his men take away the stones they had placed on the track to stop the train. Foote declined the help. Foote later claimed, "I was so tickled to get out of the scrap so smoothly that I told him not to mind the stones, we could take them off ourselves if he would only take himself and party off. He laughed and said, 'All right, Pard, good night,' and started up the bank with his men behind him."[15] The engineer was wished a good night and the outlaws disappeared into the darkness on foot. One of them hollered back that this would be the last time anyone would see the boys of the James Gang. Hite later stated that the group walked back about a half mile into the woods. They stopped there to divvy up what they had taken from the train. Each man received about $140. Jesse auctioned the jewelry that had been taken and divided that money as well. Jesse kept a nickel-plated watch for himself. Then the boys divided into two groups. One group traveled north. The other tracked back into Kansas City to return to Jesse and Zee's house. They likely crossed paths with a posse that had boarded in Kansas City to ride back to the site of the robbery. Once again, their luck held and they were not spotted.

The words spoken during the robbery certainly sound as if they could have been pronounced by Jesse. Jesse wouldn't be the only suspect, however. A group of young men from the Blue Cut area were arrested and jailed several days later in connection to the robbery. One of them confessed and implicated two others.[16] John Bugler, Creed Chapman, and John Mott stood trial later that month. They testified that they had been working with Jesse James and Dick Liddil but had been denied any of the booty from the robbery. Prosecuting Attorney Wallace didn't believe them. Wallace entered a nolle prosequi in April. Few of the officials thought the boys were guilty, anyway. Visions of Jesse danced in their heads. Jesse in the meantime returned with Frank and Clarence Hite to the Ninth Street house. The three of them holed up there for about two weeks. Annie and Robert eventually came back from California to rejoin Frank. The family first paid a visit to Zerelda Samuel's farm, then Annie and the toddler were put on a train bound for the East.

Jesse and Frank James were on the minds of other people as well during the end of September. Bill Ryan finally came to trial. During the war, an area south of Clay County and just a few miles north of Lee's Summit called the Crackerneck had been a stronghold for Confederate sympathizers and guerrillas. The Youngers had come from the outer boundaries of the area. The Shepards, Bill Ryan, and Tucker Bassham had lived there as well. Ryan was greeted by a roomful of his Crackerneck associates and supporters when he entered the court to begin his trial for train robbery. The intimidation was palpable. Witnesses had already been warned by various former friends of Ryan that there would be retribution for any negative testimony. Associate prosecutor John Southern had even received a death threat. Some of the employees of the railroad who had pertinent information to disclose refused to testify. But not Tucker Bassham.

Bassham went to great lengths to explain to the prosecution how Bill Ryan had encouraged him to work with Jesse James. Ryan had delivered an edict from Jesse when Bassham balked at the idea. Jesse ordered Bassham to participate in the proposed Glendale robbery along with himself, Ryan, Dick Liddil, Ed Miller, and a man named Bob. Bob was later identified as being Wood Hite. Bassham testified that he had been given a gun so that he could take part in the robbery. He claimed he watched as Jesse and Ed Miller robbed the express car. He later received $900 for his efforts. Ryan was quickly convicted and sentenced to twenty-five years in prison. Bassham was rewarded for his testimony by having his home in the Crackerneck burned to the ground. He quickly left the area for parts unknown. That was probably a very good idea. Missouri law enforcement, however, had scored a victory.

Jesse was not happy with the Ninth Street house for some reason. Perhaps he felt a certain degree of suspicion by his neighbors at the comings and goings of strangers at odd times of the day and night. Additionally, since Ryan's conviction, he felt justifiably paranoid. He made up his mind to leave the house after it nearly fell over during a storm. He moved his family to 1017 Troost Avenue on October 1. The Jameses remained there only a month. Jesse once again either experienced paranoia or had some reason to believe that someone suspected who he might be. He and his family made plans within a short time to once again leave their home. Charlie Ford helped Jesse and Zee pack their belongings. They first traveled to Atcheson, Kansas. They were living in a house on a hill overlooking the serene town of St. Joseph, Missouri, by November. The house was small but very cozy and located apart from its neighboring abodes. Jesse claimed to be Tom Howard while Zee continued to use the name Josie. Little Jesse was still called Tim. Jesse rented the house from a city councilman.[17] Zee was happy in St. Joseph. She must have been delighted when Jesse began to make noises about giving up the outlaw life and settling down.

Jesse may have been thinking about retiring, but his antics over the past few years with his new gang were not forgotten. His name would frequently appear in the newspapers. It was noted that the chivalry of the James-Younger Gang had been

The house where Jesse was killed, St. Joseph, Missouri. *Pony Express National Association*

replaced by the coarse and provocative actions of the new James Gang. Public sentiment began to turn against Jesse for the first time in his career. Jesse now appeared a desperate man rather than a seeker of reprisal from the enemies of the war years to many of the citizens of Missouri. The motive that once seemed to clearly butt heads with those who had beaten and restrained the pro-Confederate society now seemed to be nothing more than pure greed. On a personal level, Jesse was adrift within his own emotions and interactions with those not his family. The business of robbery had been far easier and certainly more enjoyable when Jesse and Frank had relied on the loyalty and trust of the Youngers. The men that had replaced those dependable friends were small-time thieves. They seemed to be involved on impulse and sometimes only for the glory of riding with the infamous Jesse James. They were certainly not trustworthy. Jesse grew increasingly distrustful and anxious. He began to constantly look over his shoulder as he waited for another of his own men to betray him. There seemed no way to go but down. Every robbery was especially risky now—a risk not from the selected victims and the law but from within the very confines of his own organization. Zee would surely be relieved if he were to give up outlawry for good. His children could only benefit by having a father who was not constantly being sought by various law enforcement agents. Jesse's sister Sally later confirmed to Jesse Jr. that his father had decided to put an end to his outlaw career.[18] The trouble was that he didn't really know how. Jesse knew that he would still need to somehow confront the crimes he had committed in the past. The likelihood that he would be acquitted of those transgressions was minimal.

Clarence Hite was arrested in Kentucky for his participation in the Winston robbery in February 1882. Hite was returned to Missouri for arraignment. Jesse's cousin pled guilty to the charge. He was sentenced to twenty-five years in the state prison. There seemed to be no evidence to level any charges in conjunction with the Blue Cut robbery. Bassham and Ryan had confessed to their life of outlawry with Jesse. Jesse grew increasingly suspicious of the rest of the men with whom he was involved now that Clarence Hite had been arrested. Dick Liddil had been a good friend to Jesse. But Liddil's awareness of the disappearance of Ed Miller caused him to realize that Jesse was distrustful of those other than his family. Liddil felt that it probably would not be long until Jesse felt that he was a liability and killed him, too.[19] Liddil left Jesse in March. He returned to Missouri where he stayed at the home of widow Martha Bolton. Jesse's cousin Wood Hite was already boarding with Mrs. Bolton. Hite was said by their mutual friends to be in love with the widow. Liddil found that he was interested in the attractive woman himself. An unwelcome animosity grew between the former partners and friends as each of the two men vied for the lady's attentions. Before long, an argument broke out with deadly consequences. Wood Hite was soon dead at the hand of Dick Liddil—with help from Mrs. Bolton's little brother, Bob Ford. Liddil was nobody's fool. He quickly reasoned that there would be hell to pay when Jesse heard of the death of his cousin. Jesse would likely find out the truth and would not in any way be favorable to hearing Liddil's side of the story. There seemed to Liddil to be only one way to go. Liddil decided that he had no choice but to turn state's witness against Jesse. It would be foolish to remain unprotected and risk the consequences of a confrontation with the virulent outlaw.

Liddil had also been involved with a woman named Mattie Collins while he had been courting Martha Bolton. Liddil now sent Miss Collins to Governor Crittenden to talk about cutting a deal. He wanted any and all charges against him dismissed if he told all he knew of Jesse's activities over the past few years. Martha Bolton decided to take the notion a step further since Liddil was proposing an amnesty for himself. She would seek pardons for her brother Charlie as well. Soon Martha was talking to the governor, too. Crittenden would not guarantee pardons for the men of the James Gang. He did promise the two women that he would use his influence to see that the outlaws would not be punished for their crimes. Dick Liddil was satisfied with this compromise. He surrendered to Sheriff James Timberlake of Clay County on January 24, 1882. Timberlake confirmed the terms of surrender with Governor Crittenden and brought in Kansas City Police Commissioner Henry H. Craig to assist him. Liddil spilled his guts when he was interrogated. The law obtained most of the information they needed and laid initial plans that they felt would ultimately lead to the prize: the capture of Jesse James. To this end, Liddil's surrender was not made public until March 31 when Crittenden announced that Liddil was in custody. Crittenden told the press that any members of the James Gang who would surrender, confess to their crimes, and provide information regarding the others, except for Jesse or Frank James, would be granted the influence of the governor to prevent punishment. An attractive incentive indeed.

NINETEEN

✁

The End

"Ma, if we don't meet again, we'll meet in heaven."
—Jesse James, according to testimony given by his mother Zerelda

BY 1882, JESSE was tired and paranoid. He had survived the War between the States but seemed unable to put the trauma of the experience behind him. Jesse had been an outlaw for nearly sixteen years. He had paid an enormous price for surrendering to his consuming need for retribution and revenge. The anxiety of constantly being on the run and looking over his shoulder had created a paranoia that even he could not deny existed. He was isolated and lonely. Jesse hadn't seen his brother Frank in months. Even Frank was tired of living in Jesse's incessantly isolated world.

Jesse had dragged his devoted wife Zee and their young children all over the Midwest in search of a home. He was constantly seeking a place where they might not be recognized nor would he be identified as America's most sought-after felon. Jesse felt that any one of his current associates might try to deliver him into the hands of his enemies. Or even worse, they might try to kill him themselves. There was an impressive price on his head.

The temptation must have been immense for the penny-ante criminals with whom he was currently keeping company. Life was getting too hard. Some eleven robberies and several murders later, Jesse was exhausted. Jesse loved adventure, but being an outlaw was no longer fun. He was ready to retire. Returning to his roots held the promise of a consistent, more tranquil life. Moving his family to the alluring riverside town of St. Joseph had been a good idea. Jesse was somewhat at peace in the little house on the hill as the patriarch of the Thomas Howard family. But he still couldn't relax completely. He knew that as long as he remained in Missouri he had to be careful that his true identity was not discovered. He had thought about relocating Zee and the children to Nebraska. He had family and many friends there. He was eager to put outlawry behind him and begin life anew with those he loved.[1]

On February 15, 1882, a man named J. D. Calhoun placed an ad in Nebraska's *Lincoln Journal*. Calhoun had no idea that a response would come from the infamous Jesse Woodson James. The notice was enticing and to the point:

FOR SALE—A very fine 160 acres. adjoining the town of Franklin, Franklin Co. Corners with depot grounds. Living springs: beautiful creek runs through it. 90 acres in body of finest bottom land: balance natural young timber. Mill within a mile. As good educational, religious, railroad and other facilities as any point in western Nebraska. $10 per acre. Address or call on JD Calhoun, Lincoln, Neb.

Jesse sent a letter to Calhoun:

Dear Sir,

I have noticed that you have 160 acres of land advertised for sale in Franklin Co. Neb. Please write at once and let me know the lowest cash price that will buy your land. Give me a full description of the land etc.

I want to purchase a farm of that size provided I can find one to suit. I will not buy a farm unless the land is No. 1.

I will start on a trip in about 8 days to Northern Kansas and South Nebraska and if the description of the land suits me I will look at it & if it suits me I will buy it from the advertisement in the Lincoln Journal. I suppose your land can be made a good farm for stock and grain—Please answer at once.

Respectfully

Tho. Howard

No. 1318 Lafayette St.

St. Joseph Mo

March 2nd '82[2]

Riverton, Iowa, was again marked as the scene of a crime when the National Bank was robbed on March 10, 1882. Some Midwest historians believe that Jesse was involved in this one, too. Jesse was certainly available to participate. He was in the Iowa-Nebraska area about that time, but no evidence has been found to further substantiate his having been a part of the robbery team.[3]

Jesse visited his mother and her family in Clay County at the end of March 1882. He brought Charlie Ford with him. Ford's younger brother Bob had been allowed to accompany Jesse as well. Twenty-year-old Bob Ford had been pestering Jesse to let him ride with him on one of his outlaw adventures. Bob had no experience in bank robbing. His claim to fame was having stolen a few horses while he was a teenager. Charlie had been with Jesse during the Blue Cut robbery and encouraged Jesse to let young Bob join the gang. Jesse said he would consider it. Jesse was surprised to find that Zerelda Samuel had no use for the Ford boys whatsoever when he showed up in their company at his mother's farm. Zerelda thought Charlie was sneaky-looking. Even the good-looking and outgoing Bob Ford could not charm her. Zerelda told Jesse plainly that she did not feel he should trust the Fords. She suggested that he get rid of them as soon as possible.[4]

Jesse's half-brother, John Samuel, had been wounded in a shooting incident and was laid up at home. That might have been why Jesse spent the night at his sister Sallie's. The Ford brothers camped somewhere nearby. They probably spent the night in the Kearney schoolhouse.[5] Jesse disclosed to his sister that little Jesse E. had been hounding him to get a dog. It so happened that Sallie's dog had just had puppies. Jesse lovingly selected

one of the pups to take back to his son in St. Joseph.[6] Sallie
spoke to her brother about the dangers of his being seen in Missouri. She said many of those who he had thought were his
friends would be more than happy to turn him in for the reward
that was being offered. Jesse laughed. He said that he was very
confident that he would soon be allowed a fair trial. Jesse told
his sister that if he was convicted, he would serve his time. His
family would then be free to live in Clay County. He would
build a home on some land and live out the remainder of his
days in peace if he was acquitted. As to those who he thought
were his friends but perhaps were not anymore, Jesse told his
sister that he would have to win their friendship back when he
came home to stay.[7] Jesse prepared to leave in the morning. He
had the little puppy tucked up into his coat. Zerelda again warned
her son against trusting Charlie and Bob Ford. Jesse laughed as
he mounted his horse to return to St. Joseph. He told his mother
that if they didn't meet again on this earth, they would meet
again in heaven. Zerelda could only shake her head and worry.
Jesse's words were too similar to the words Robert had written
to her just before he died.

If Jesse was going to buy J. P. Calhoun's land, he needed some
cash by which to do it. He made plans to rob a bank in Platte City,
Missouri, on April 4. He would use Charlie and Bob Ford as his
only accomplices.[8] The Ford brothers stayed with Jesse and Zee in
their St. Joseph home during the days they planned the robbery.
Jesse was completely unaware that Bob Ford had conferred with
Governor Crittenden. He had no idea Ford had arranged a pardon
for himself and his brother. The governor had also committed to a
reward of $10,000 if Ford should capture Jesse James, dead or
alive.

The surrender of Dick Liddil was announced in the press on
March 31. Unfortunately for Jesse, this news would not reach
him until several days later. Zee cooked a large breakfast for
Jesse and the Ford brothers on Monday morning, April 3, 1882.
Bob Ford had annoyed Jesse when he started to talk about the
upcoming robbery at the table in front of Jesse's wife and children. The mood didn't get any better when Jesse opened up the
morning paper to read that Liddil had surrendered. Jesse finished
his meal and suggested that the men move into the parlor. Jesse

Sallie Samuel Nicholson, Jesse's half-sister.
The Jesse James Farm

stretched and removed his guns after he entered the living room. Jesse was always on the alert and remained armed even while in his own house. Taking his guns off was completely out of character for him. Charlie and Bob were immediately suspicious. The two brothers looked at each other uncomfortably as Jesse looked around the room. His eyes fixed on a sampler that hung on the wall. The message read "In God We Trust." He moved a straight-backed chair over to stand on while he straightened and dusted the frame with a feather duster. Jesse had turned his back on Charlie and Bob Ford. Unarmed and unaware, Jesse heard the sound of a trigger being cocked. He turned his head slightly to the right as he reacted to the disturbing sound. He didn't have time to turn around. Jesse's head hit the wall as a bullet from Bob Ford's Smith & Wesson .45 Model 3 slammed into it. Jesse toppled from the chair and hit the floor.[9] Zee and the children ran into the room. They found Jesse dead at the age of thirty-four.

As Zee held her dead husband in her arms, Charlie and Bob Ford rushed out the door. They ran to wire Governor Crittenden with the news of what Bob had done. Then they immediately surrendered themselves to the St. Joseph police. Neighbors approached the house on the hill when they heard the gunshot. They were told by Zee that her husband Tom Howard had been murdered. Zee was too overcome with emotion to continue the charade, however. She soon admitted that the man in her arms was none other than Jesse James.

The people of St. Joseph crowded around the James house to get a glimpse of the dead outlaw and his family once they heard the incredible news. Assistant Coroner James Heddens was directed to remove Jesse's body and take it to the Sidenfaden funeral parlor at ten o'clock. The task of positively identifying the man who lay on the slab commenced. A young man named J. W. Graham worked at the St. Joseph photography studio of James W. Porch. Young Graham asked his manager, R. C. Smith, if he could go over to the funeral parlor and take photographs of the dead outlaw. He suggested that such photographs would bring a pretty penny. With Smith's blessing, Graham got permission from St. Joseph City Marshall Enos Craig. Smith photographed Jesse as he lay bound by rope to a wooden plank. The photos would be in high demand and make quite a bit of money for the studio.[10] The distraught Zee James was taken to the nearby Patte House to stay with her children until family could arrive. A near-hysterical Zerelda James Samuel arrived by train the next morning. When she was asked by the police if the dead man was her son, the distressed mother cried, "Would to God that it were not!"[11]

Also arriving in St. Joseph that morning were Sheriff Timberlake, Commissioner Craig, and Prosecuting Attorney Wallace. Timberlake brought with him two men from Clay County who had served with Jesse James during the war to help identify the body. Harrison Trow and James Wilkerson recognized their former comrade immediately. Timberlake had, of course, known Jesse for years. A Clay County farmer named William Clay also

Mary James, Jesse's daughter. Taken days after her father's assassination, 1882. *The Armand De Gregoris Collection*

Jesse Edwards James, Jesse's son. Taken after the murder of his father, 1882. *The Armand De Gregoris Collection*

made the trip with Timberlake for this purpose, as did Mattie
Collins.[12] It was easy to tell that the man who had been killed
was Jesse. Additionally, those who had known Jesse knew that
he had blown the tip off the middle finger of his left hand. The
body of the victim clearly displayed this wound as well as scars
from the two serious chest wounds that Jesse had obtained during

the war. There was no doubt from those in authority that the man lying dead in front of them was Jesse Woodson James.

An autopsy was performed by James Heddens along with doctors George Catlett, Jacob Geiger, and William Hoyt. The man in front of them was determined to be 5'10" tall, with blue eyes and a slender build. His sandy hair had been dyed a dark brown. His fair complexion was offset by a dark, full-face beard. He was dressed in a brown cashmere business suit with a white shirt. The brain was exposed when the doctors removed the cap of Jesse's skull. It was confirmed that the bullet entered the occipital bone immediately behind the right ear and traveled upward. The bullet remained embedded in the skull behind the left ear. The brain and skull were shattered and large pieces of bone bisected the cerebellum.

A coroner's inquest was called for three o'clock that afternoon. Facts and witnesses to the event were presented to a panel of six St. Joseph residents in the circuit courtroom. The jury announced, ''We the jury find that the deceased is Jesse James, and that he came to his death by a shot from a pistol in the hands of Robert Ford.''

The St. Joseph police quickly made their way to Jesse and Zee's little house. They confiscated any items that may have been taken by theft. There were a couple of horses and saddles found in a nearby stable that were identified as being stolen. It was later determined that the horses had been taken by Charlie and Bob Ford.[13]

Governor Crittenden sent a wire from Jefferson City. He asked the St. Joseph police to release Jesse's body to his widow in order to enable his family to return Jesse to Kearney for burial. Jesse was placed aboard a special Hannibal & St. Joseph Railroad train. His remains were accompanied by his wife, children, and mother. Zerelda Samuel raged at Sheriff Timberlake, ''Oh, Mr. Timberlake! My son has gone to God, but his friends still live and will have revenge on those who murdered him for money!''[14] Even though he knew that Frank James remained at large somewhere out in the vast unknown, Timberlake was not threatened. Jesse's body was taken to the Kearney Hotel where hundreds of people passed by to view the remains of America's best-known outlaw.

Jesse's body was taken by carriage to the Mt. Olivet Baptist Church on the afternoon of April 6. Jesse's funeral was preached by Reverends R. H. Jones and J. M. Martin in a service that commenced at three o'clock.[15] Jesse's body was brought to the front of the church by his pallbearers Benjamin Flanders, Liberty mayor J. T. Ford, J. B. Henderson, deputy sheriff Reed, Charles Scott, and James Vaughn.[16] A surprise pallbearer was Sheriff Timberlake. Hundreds of people from all over the area attended the funeral. Included were Jesse's friends, family, and those merely curious to see the famous outlaw in person. Many of those present waited anxiously to see if Jesse's brother would turn himself in so that he could attend the funeral. Frank James didn't show. Reverend Jones read from the Book of Job and from verses four and five of the Thirty-ninth Psalm. Reverend Martin preached a sermon based on Matthew's words, "Therefore be ye also ready; for in such hour as ye think not, the Son of Man cometh." Those in attendance were warned that the suddenness of death they had witnessed should be a warning to all sinners. After the service Jesse's casket was taken to the James-Samuel farm. Jesse was buried near the coffee bean tree. Engraved on his tombstone was the legend, "Devoted Husband and Father, Jesse Woodson James. Sept. 5, 1847, murdered Apr. 3, 1882 by a traitor and coward whose name is not worthy to appear here."

One person attended the funeral that did not mourn the deceased. Mrs. Daniel Askew, the wife of the Jameses' neighbor who was said to have worked with the Pinkertons in the raid on the farmhouse. The widow still believed that it was Jesse who killed her husband in retribution for his involvement and claimed, "I attended the funeral for one reason, and that was not out of respect. I wanted to make certain it was Jesse in that coffin, and to curse him to hell."

Zee James was left alone and in poverty. Charlie Ford talked to a newspaper about Jesse's lack of money: "He may have had $600 or $700. Jesse never made the big hauls people suspected him of having made. When a big haul was made there were big gangs to divide among. He did best taking country banks, which he took on three or four men to work. Besides they lived as fast

Zerelda Samuel, standing by Jesse's family farm gravesite. *The Jesse James Farm*

as their means would permit. Money flew, they cared not how.''[17]

On April 10, an auction was arranged whereby Zee could sell some of her family's furniture and personal items belonging to Jesse. The auction netted a mere $117.[18] It was hardly enough to sustain Zee and the children for very long. Zee's washtub brought seventy-five cents, and the coal hod and coal brought in a dollar. A broom and scrubbing brush went for a quarter.[19] *St. Joseph Herald* reporter Frederick F. Shrader bought Jesse E.'s puppy for his son at a price of $15. One item that Zee would not be auctioning, however, was the beautiful gold watch Jesse had been wearing at the time of his death. The watch was engraved. It bore the legend, ''To Judge Roundtree, with best wishes from Gov. J. Proctor Knott.'' Jesse's possession of Judge Roundtree's watch tied him directly to one of the robberies of which he had been accused. The item was confiscated to be returned to the man from whom it was stolen. Also returned to Judge Roundtree was his daughter's diamond ring. Zee had been wearing it at the time of Jesse's death.

All of those who had been involved with the assassination of Jesse denied participating in any way with Bob Ford. They also denied having entered into any agreement with the Ford brothers in relation to killing Jesse James. Crittenden claimed that he had known that Bob Ford was with Jesse and had plans to betray his friend. He said he did not know the whereabouts of Ford or Jesse and did not know the particulars of the betrayal. Bob Ford himself later addressed the issue. He wrote a letter to the *Missouri Republican* dated February 12, 1884. The return address was given as the St. James Hotel, St. Louis:

Dear sir, if you think these lines are worth publishing you will oblige me very much by so doing.

I wish to answer the dirty lieing remarks made by a member of the post Dispatch in wich he accuses Govener Critenden of a dishonorable act in hiring Thugs to assassinate Jess James in presents of his wife & children. in the first place I don't know who the Pup has reference to.

I am the one who removed the lamented Jess & am freed of it but I was not hired by Gov. Critenden or any one else or did I act under any bodys instruction.

I had the proper orthority to bring Mr. James to Justice which I did but did it in no ones presence but my Brother Chas. & I did it whith my own Revolver which I payed for but had no assuance of any pardon in case I did it. but the would be smart news paper man seems to know more abut the mater than either the Governer or my self. I only did what thousands of others were trying to do but failed & did not have to rob any body or steal any horses to get the chance to do it. & the man that calls me an assassin is a CONTMPTABLE SNEAK & if he wishes to resent it he will find me at the St James Hotel in this city.

hoping you will oblige by publishing these lines I remain

Very Respectfully
Bob Ford[20]

On April 17, Bob and Charlie Ford were indicted on charges of murder in the first degree by a St. Joseph grand jury. They pled guilty and were sentenced to hang. The Ford brothers had little reason to worry. Governor Crittenden granted both full and unconditional pardons later that afternoon when he received word of their sentence.

No one seems to know what became of the reward money. It doesn't appear that the Ford brothers received much of it. That fact could be because the reward may have been divided among several of those who had played a role in the conspiracy. Crittenden wrote in his autobiography that "the proclamation of a reward accomplished its purpose in less than one year at a cost not exceeding $20,000, not one cent of which was drawn from the state."[21]

Newspapers delighted in the reporting of the murder and its various consequences and implications. Heavily discussed and debated was the appropriateness of the governor of the state of Missouri being so directly involved in the assassination of one of its citizens. Crittenden made no apology for any of his actions. He claimed that the Fords should be praised rather than condemned for their role in the drama. John Newman Edwards naturally was outraged. He wrote several caustic articles. His most severe admonition was published in the *Sedalia Daily Democrat* on April 13 when he took to task Bob Ford and Mattie Collins for their betrayal of a loyal friend. Among other vitriolic words of sorrow and disgust, Edwards wrote, "Why the whole State reeks today with a double orgy, that of lust and that of murder. What the men failed to do the women accomplished. Tear the bears from the flag of Missouri. Put thereon in place of them as more appropriate, a thief blowing out the brains of an unarmed victim, and a brazen harlot, naked to the waist and splashed to the brows in blood." The *Independence Sentinel* expected Edwards to be outraged. They published their own editorial on the same day in response to the accusation that Edwards had once been given the gift of a gold watch from Jesse as a sign of his appreciation for Edwards's continual support. The paper stated, "We are not surprised that the Sedalia Democrat should raise a fearful and doleful howl over the execution of its friend Jesse James, as the incident of the presentation of the magnificent gold watch must still be fresh in the memory of its gift editor.'' Edwards carefully admitted that while he had been offered the gift, he had refused it because it was not his practice to accept gifts. As the newspapers continued to rehash Jesse's life and death, Edwards raised several hundred dollars through his newspaper for the benefit of Zee and the children. The *Daily Democrat's* competitor, the *Sedalia Bazoo*, then sponsored a drive for the widow of Conductor Westfall. Jesse was as popular in death as he was during his lifetime.

The fact that the governor of Missouri appeared to be intricately involved in the orchestration of the assassination of one of the state's citizens did not sit well with a lot of people. Frenzied editorials both in support of Crittenden and against the governor were filed. Two resolutions were proposed by Republican representatives to Missouri's House commending Crittenden. Both were declared out of order by the presiding officer. Other proposals demanded that Crittenden account to the House as to how he had disposed of the public funds in his charge. He was also asked for an accounting of the funds paid by the Hannibal and St. Joseph Railroad Company as rewards in conjunction with information leading to the "capture" of Jesse James. These proposals were shot down as well. Some Democrats as well introduced resolutions that would support Crittenden, but they, too, were declared out of order.

Conjecture and deliberation continues to this day about the murder of Jesse James. What is hard to explain is why Jesse, paranoid and suspicious, would take off his guns and turn his back on untried and surely less-than-trustworthy acquaintances. All who knew him knew that Jesse was tired of the outlaw life. Perhaps he deliberately chose to end it the only way he knew how. Jesse's last words to his mother, words that mirrored those of his father before his own untimely death, cannot be forgotten. Those words may have been spoken deliberately as Jesse contemplated putting into motion a scenario that would ultimately lead to his own death. That Jesse James would finally be defeated by a so-called friend by being shot in the back would only contribute to his already larger-than-life legend.[22]

TWENTY

⌘⌘⌘⌘

Frank Goes It Alone

"There was a gang known as the James boys; I belonged to it at one time."
    —Dick Liddil's testimony at the trial of Frank James, July 1883

THE HOUSE WHERE Jesse James had met his end was swamped by visits from the curious. They came from all over the country in the days after Jesse's murder.[1] The owner of the house charged ten cents admission. Relic hunters tore through both the interior and exterior of the little house on the hill. Farther south, hundreds of people visited the Samuel farm in Kearney, asking to call on Jesse's grave. Zerelda took pleasure in talking with most of them. She especially relished the opportunity to deliver her thoughts on the characters of the Ford brothers. Dr. Samuel later said that he could sow the entire farm with flowers from all of the flower seeds that were sent to Zerelda. People from all over the country wrote to her asking that she plant the seeds on Jesse's grave. Over 25,000 people would visit the farm within the next decade. The Ford brothers lost no time in telling their stories to the press as Jesse's supporters mourned him. Bob and Charlie appeared pleased with themselves for ridding Missouri of its number-one criminal. The power and leadership abilities of the outlaw chief were discussed with authority, even though Bob Ford had known Jesse only a short time. Bob claimed: "[In the beginning] What Jesse said went. . . . He ruled with an iron rod and I regard it as common practice among outlaws to have for a leader a man whom they fear, dread and obey."

Ford told a tale that would have astonished any of the people who knew her when he was asked about Zee's influence over Jesse: "She was the head devil, and her suggestions came down as from the holy of holies. Unseen, unknown, she was the unbidden source of the most gigantic scheme of plunder that was ever sought to be consummated."

Bob then spoke of how Jesse's outlaw days were numbered at best:

> Jesse, however, had outlived his greatness as a bandit, though not as an individual robber. As a leader he was dead. There were but few who would place themselves in his clutches. Even his brother, Frank, kept continuously hundreds of miles away; Dick Liddil went back on him; so did Shepard. It was his tyranny among his fellows that wrecked his empire. The day was when the clatter of Jesse James' horse's hoofs was the signal for a hundred highwaymen to mount and away. Now, there is none—no, not one—of the drilled bandits of the West who will move a tap. And hence, I have no fear. There will be more rejoicing among outlawry at his death than among law-abiding citizens.[2]

Dime novels and limited-edition books continued to tell Jesse's story. Most of them were outrageous accounts of daring and adventure. Jesse was fast becoming an industry.

Zee James had no idea what to do or where to go without her beloved Jesse. She took her children to live in a small rented house in Kansas City. She was nearly destitute. Zee had always been a proud woman. She refused to be taken in by members of her husband's family or her own relatives throughout her bereavement. People wasted no time in coming forward with their personal stories of Jesse, whether factual or fictional. Even some of Jesse's relatives were getting in on the act by the following year. The *Louisville Courier-Journal* published a story in March 1883 about Jesse having had an affair with his cousins' stepmother, Sarah Norris Peck Hite. It was claimed that the affair caused a great deal of bad blood between Jesse and the Hite family. The Hite family filed a $25,000 suit against the newspaper for defamation of Sarah Hite's character. The newspaper won the suit when Governor Crittenden testified that Sarah's husband George had told him the same story when he visited the governor in his Jefferson City office. A story having larger, farther-reaching consequences began almost immediately. The enormous "Jesse didn't really die" movement started in the months following Jesse's death. The claims were made despite Jesse's corpse having been identified by several impartial persons while he lay in Sidenfaden's funeral home. Additionally, dozens of those who had known him throughout his life had viewed his body before his funeral in Kearney. This would be a problem that the family of Jesse James would deal with for the rest of their lives.

Zee tried to think of ways to raise money to feed and clothe her children. She was soon approached by representatives of the publishing world. They were eager to coerce Zee to tell her story and reveal Jesse's secrets. Zee eventually signed a contract with one of the more persistent publishers. She gave only one interview before she changed her mind and reneged on the agreement.[3] Jesse's life as an outlaw would remain their own business. The private and recalcitrant Zee then hired on with a theatrical company in a desperate attempt to somehow earn money for her family. She was to appear on stage as the widow of Jesse James for public exhibition. An article in a newspaper reported that a journalist had encountered Zee on her way to Denver to exhibit her skills as a "shootist."[4] She appeared in only two shows. Few people could bring themselves to gawk at the pathetic and obviously needy wife of their dime-novel hero. Zee's career on the boards would end as abruptly as it had started. She would live in near poverty until her son Jesse Edwards was old enough to earn a paycheck.

Jesse E. was not unaffected by having witnessed the death of his father. In a story written about Zee, a newspaperman related how Jesse E. made his adoration of his father known during a

meeting Zee had with attorney Colonel Haire. Jesse E. displayed
some of Jesse's innate characteristics. Zee had been discussing
with Haire the fact that she feared someone would somehow
make off with Jesse's guns. They were now quite valuable and
she was afraid someone would steal them and sell them for
profit. Zee asked Haire to put them in a safe place for her. Seven-
year-old Jesse E. snatched the gun out of the attorney's hand.
The little boy proclaimed, "No you won't take these pistols!
They belong to my papa!" Haire ignored Jesse E. and continued
his conversation with the boy's mother. He absentmindedly
started to slip the other gun into his pocket. The small boy
cocked the hammer of the pistol he was holding and snapped it
right at Haire's head. Lucky for the astonished attorney, the gun
was unloaded. Jesse E. ran to get cartridges when the gun didn't
fire. The boy would have attempted to load the gun and shoot
Colonel Haire if he had not been stopped by his alarmed mother.[5]

The Youngers gave no public comment on Jesse's death. They
had claimed years before that they were not friendly with him.
There was little now to say and so they said nothing. Cole
Younger did initially question the validity of the reports of the
murder. He sent his sister Henrietta, who was living in St. Joseph
at the time, to confirm that Jesse was dead. Younger must have
wondered about Frank James. He no doubt had assurance from
mutual friends that Frank would be all right.

Frank James was all right. He and his family were in Lynchburg, Virginia, when Jesse was killed.[6] Frank had been told by
his family that Jesse had plans to give up outlawry. He must
have known in his heart that it would have been impossible for
his younger brother to live a normal life. Only Frank had been
able to steer clear of any illegal activities when Jesse and Frank
had been living in Nashville. Frank had enjoyed living among
the finer denizens of the city and pretending to be one of them.
No, Frank had no desire to return to outlawry now that Jesse
was gone. He also knew that the attention of those who had
arranged for the murder of his brother would soon be on him.
He was the only member of the notorious James-Younger Gang
still at large. Frank thought things through and soon reached a
very important decision.

Frank discussed his idea with his friend John Newman Edwards. Both men agreed that the time had come for Frank James to surrender. It was agreed that it would be prudent for Edwards to approach Governor Crittenden on Frank's behalf. The outlaw and the newspaperman composed a letter to Crittenden requesting that Frank be allowed amnesty. Crittenden replied to Edwards that he could not grant Frank a pardon, but he was willing to assure a fair trial if Frank would surrender. Crittenden indicated that he would decide if further action was necessary on his part if Frank received a verdict of guilty. In light of things that would happen in the future, it is likely that there was more to Frank's orchestrated surrender than the few letters exchanged between Edwards and Crittenden. Any additional agreements would be kept between the parties involved.

On the morning of October 4, 1882, Frank and Edwards met with Governor Crittenden and a select group of state officials and newspapermen. Edwards announced, "Governor Crittenden, I want to introduce you to my friend Frank James."[7] Frank removed his holster and offered it to Crittenden. He said, "Governor Crittenden, I want to hand over to you that which no living man except myself has been permitted to touch since 1861, and to say that I am your prisoner."[8] Arrangements were then made for Frank James to be delivered to the sheriff of Jackson County.

Frank remained in his jail cell in Independence for several weeks although he could not have been more comfortable were he a guest of one of the city's finer hotels. He was allowed to furnish his cell with books, a comfortable chair, and whatever else might bring him serenity. He visited with friends and lived a peaceful existence the entire period of his incarceration. Would the same treatment have been given Jesse had he chosen to surrender? Frank remained calm and gracious. He felt that the chances he would be convicted on any charges brought against him were minimal due to the passage of time and the questionable availability of witnesses. Sentiment in favor of Frank James being pardoned was popularly expressed. Those who desired to put the war of rebellion behind them admitted that they had been the members of the Missouri population who had quietly supported Jesse and Frank and the actions of the James-Younger Gang.

Frank was first charged with an 1867 Independence bank rob-

Frank James, c. 1910. *The Jesse James Farm*

bery. No mention was made of Jesse in the indictment. The robbery at Blue Cut was added to Jackson County's charges against
him. The only testimony against Frank was word-of-mouth accusations. Prosecutor William Wallace had no choice but to dismiss the first charge. The Blue Cut indictment would be dealt
with later. Several other county law enforcement agencies appeared in Independence. They were delighted to have Jesse
James's brother behind bars where they themselves could appear

to serve him with papers concerning robberies in their jurisdictions. The governor of Minnesota sent no formal representation. He requested in writing that Frank be arrested and extradited to Minnesota where he could be placed on trial for the Northfield robbery. Crittenden refused. He replied that Frank would first have to answer to all charges that would be brought against him in Missouri.

Frank was then charged with the Gallatin robbery, the murder of cashier John Sheets, the Winston robbery, the murder of conductor William Westfall, and passenger Frank McMillan. Frank was transferred to Daviess County to await trial there before he answered the Blue Cut robbery charge in Jackson County. A successful prosecution would be impossible without witnesses. Those who would come forward to accuse Frank James face to face were few and far between. This would have been one of the advantages Jesse would have enjoyed. The prosecution reviewed their options. Jesse's buddy Bill Ryan was currently serving his time in the Missouri penitentiary. He could be of no help to them. Rumors had been circulating that Jesse and Frank's cousin Clarence Hite had provided Wallace with inside information in exchange for a pardon. Whether the claim was truth or fiction would never be known. Hite died of tuberculosis a short time after Frank's surrender and the issue was dropped from speculation.

The prosecution's eyes then fell upon Dick Liddil. Liddil had already admitted to having been a member of Jesse's new gang. He proved his willingness to cooperate when he made himself available to answer questions about the robberies in which he participated. Liddil claimed to have held back nothing during his trial. His alibi placed him in Kentucky at the time of the Muscle Shoals robbery. He declared firsthand knowledge that Jesse James, Bill Ryan, and Frank James had robbed the postmaster.[9]

The trial against Frank James for the murder of train passenger Frank McMillan began on August 21, 1883. Former Missouri Lieutenant Governor Charles P. Johnson, commissioner of the supreme court of Missouri, was to serve as Frank's representation. The jury that was ultimately selected consisted of twelve Democrats, several farmers, and two Confederate veterans. Rumors were rampant that the jury had been stacked in favor of the defendant.

Dick Liddil attested that he had participated in the Winston robbery when he was called as a material witness. He said he had been accompanied by Frank and Jesse James and Wood and Clarence Hite. Liddil claimed that he himself had not entered the passenger car. He said, "Frank talked to me about the robbery afterward. He said he thought they had killed two men. Jesse said he shot one, he knew, and that Frank killed one. He saw him peep in at the window and he thought he killed him."[10] Some of those who had been passengers on the train were called. None of them could positively identify Frank as being the man who pulled the trigger, although they believed the murderer of McMillan to have been a man who looked a great deal like him. Other witnesses were called in an attempt to place Frank either in the area or in the company of the other accused robbers near the date of the robbery. The defense then presented witnesses who claimed that Frank could not have been present. They had seen him elsewhere during that time.

Frank himself took the stand. He claimed that he was living a peaceful life in Tennessee until the arrest of Bill Ryan. Within weeks the couple and their son moved to Lynchburg, Virginia. While Frank had been living in Lynchburg, he read that his brother Jesse had been killed.[11] Frank's mother was called to testify that Frank had not been with Jesse and his group when they visited her farm. Zerelda claimed, "I have not seen Frank for seven years till I saw him at Independence."[12] Frank's family attempted to make it perfectly clear that Frank had participated in no wrongdoing. They did not offer alibis for Jesse, however.

In a surprise move, Governor Crittenden was called as a witness for the defense. Crittenden testified that Dick Liddil had initially told him that Jesse was the one who murdered McMillan, not Frank. Crittenden related how Liddil had told him that Frank had questioned Jesse after the incident as to why he shot someone when it had been agreed that no one would be killed. Liddil said Jesse said that he had done so to create a common bond among the men to secure their loyalty.[13] When all was said and done, it was clear that the only one who could connect Frank directly with the robbery was Dick Liddil. And Liddil was a man who was both an outlaw and a traitor to his friends.

The closing rhetoric consisted mainly of various orations about the war and its consequences. The jury deliberated for three and a half hours and eventually returned a verdict. Frank James was not guilty.

Prosecuting Attorney Hamilton moved for nolle prosequi in regard to the murder of Westfall since Frank had been acquitted of having been involved in the murder of McMillan. A continuance was granted in the matter of Sheets's murder. Frank was returned to Jackson County where he was released on bond on December 13 but was promptly rearrested and sent back to Gallatin. He was again released on bond a few days later. Governor Crittenden worked out an agreement whereby Frank would appear in court to answer the state of Alabama's charges after the Missouri courts were through prosecuting him.

Frank would now be made to stand trial for his involvement in the Blue Cut robbery. Prior to this trial, Crittenden had upheld the ruling of the state supreme court that the testimony of a convicted felon was not admissible in court. Dick Liddil would not be allowed to testify against Frank James. Crittenden continued to support Frank James by dropping all charges made against him in regard to the Blue Cut robbery. Evidently the governor had a very guilty conscience when it came to the James family.

On April 17 of that year, Frank was arraigned in Huntsville on charges pertaining to the Muscle Shoals robbery of 1881. Liddil once again failed to convince the jury that he was a reliable witness. The defense called witnesses who had lived in Nashville during the time that Frank James lived in that city. They all affirmed that Frank had been in Nashville using the name B. J. Woodson on the day in question. After a short deliberation, the jury once again found Frank James not guilty.

Frank was arrested minutes after he was declared innocent of the Alabama robbery. This time he would face charges of having been involved in the Rocky Cut robbery of 1876. Crittenden gave Frank James a present. The charges against him in regard to the Rocky Cut robbery were dropped. Frank James was now a free man, once and for all. People couldn't help but wonder if the notorious Jesse James would have fared as well.

TWENTY-ONE

∽∾∽∾

Life After Jesse

*"I don't believe in grudges or revenge. I believe in letting bygones
be bygones and forgetting old grievances."*

—Jesse Edwards James

FORMER MISSOURI CONFEDERATE Warren Carter
Bronaugh paid a visit to Cole Younger at the Stillwater prison
in the late summer of 1885. Bronaugh later claimed that it was
only after he obtained a letter of introduction to the prison's
warden and met Cole Younger that he realized that Younger had
been the soldier who saved his life during the war. This would
have been a touching scenario were it not for the fact that a letter
that Bronaugh wrote to Frank James after the alleged meeting
suggests that Frank James may have solicited Bronaugh's help
in regard to his old and loyal friend. Bronaugh wrote that he had
a great deal more to tell Frank about his visit but would wait
until they met in Clinton.[1] Regardless of the circumstances,
Bronaugh teamed up with the Youngers to do everything within
his power to assist them in their parole efforts. He would remain
active in this cause for the next six years.

Cole Younger spoke to a reporter from the *Cincinnati En-*

quirer, in an article published on April 17, 1889. Younger went to great lengths to convince all concerned that everyone who had been involved in the Northfield robbery was now dead. Those who had speculated that Jesse had been one of the robbers could interpret Younger's statement as an affirmation of that belief. Since Frank James was still alive, Younger's remark indicated that Frank had not been involved. Few people believed it.

Frank James was a free man for the first time since 1861. He had grown accustomed to constantly looking over his shoulder. He never knew what the future might bring. Adjusting to a life without those elements was extremely difficult. Why he did not attempt to start life anew by returning to his roots in Clay County or by attempting to recapture those enjoyable days he had spent in Nashville is anybody's guess. Frank drifted throughout the Midwest, taking employment in a variety of less-than-challenging jobs. He first found work as a shoe salesman at a store in Nevada, Missouri. He had moved on to work for the Mittenthal Clothing Company in Dallas, Texas, by 1886.[2]

In the meantime, twelve-year-old Jesse Edwards had taken a job as an office boy for the Crittenden and Phister Real Estate Company. He had previously worked part-time at the Bee Hive Department Store in Kansas City. Most people would have raised their eyebrows at the knowledge that the boy was working for the son of the man who had been responsible for his own father's death. Jesse's mother and grandmother, however, had agreed to the employment. There was little else to say.[3] Jesse worked for Tom Crittenden, Jr., on a part-time basis for the next six years. Zee had tried hard to provide for her family in the years since Jesse's murder. She found that the expense was overwhelming as the children grew older. Eventually, her brother Tom Mimms invited Zee and the children to live with his family. This move relieved some of the pressure from the young widow. It also allowed Jesse E. to complete his education and enter law school.

John Newman Edwards decided in 1888 to assist the Youngers much the same way as he had the James brothers. Edwards prepared one his flowery petitions championing the release of the Youngers on parole. He claimed that the Youngers were respectable men who had been compelled to their crime by the extenuating circumstances of the War between the States. Edwards pointed out that they had been model prisoners since they had been imprisoned in Stillwater. They were now "old men" who posed no threat to the people of Minnesota or Missouri.[4] Edwards's petition was endorsed by the majority of the membership of the Missouri legislature. It would not get past the governor of Minnesota. Governor William R. Merriam had a personal reason for denying the Youngers their freedom. His father John had been a passenger on the train that had been robbed at Gad's Hill. The elder Merriam was likely one of those who had been embarrassed by the gang that night. Merriam told Bronaugh, "I cannot pardon these men. My duty to the state and my personal prejudice against them make it impossible."[5]

Bob Younger had developed pulmonary tuberculosis while incarcerated. Former Union Army officer E. F. Rogers and Confederate officer Stephen C. Reagan helped Bronaugh accumulate over 163 letters from prominent citizens in the states of Minnesota and Missouri. They asked that Bob be allowed to return to Missouri to die. All efforts to send the young outlaw home failed. Bob Younger died in prison on September 16, 1889, at the age of thirty-four.

Frank James continued his search for peace and contentment. With Annie and Robert in tow, he next took a job in Paris, Texas. He worked as a wrangler for livestock dealer Shep Williams. Working for Williams during the next two years had Frank and his family on the road traveling throughout Texas, New Orleans, and Louisiana. They even stayed a short time in Guttenberg, New Jersey. The traveling was evidently not in line with Frank's plans for his family. In 1894, he became employed as a doorman at Ed Butler's Standard Theatre in St. Louis. Frank supplemented his income by taking a second job during the racing season at fairgrounds in Missouri and Kentucky. His job was to drop the timer's flag during the horse races. Frank would work at Famous Footwear selling shoes or at Famous Department Store as a floorwalker in the off season. The Frank James family would remain in St. Louis for several years.

Although the curious had sought out Jesse's boyhood home from the time of his murder, they were descending on the James-Samuel farm in droves by 1895. The *Kansas City Star* later reported that over 3,500 people had traveled to the farm between that year and 1898. Zerelda enjoyed the company. She especially liked having the opportunity to talk about the son whom she missed terribly. Zerelda had a pole that she called a memory cane. On the pole she tied hundreds of ribbons that had been given to her by visitors to the farm. Their names, addresses, and the date on which they spoke with her were written on the ribbons. The pole provided the aging mother with an object by which she could find comfort and additional companionship.

A group of prominent civic leaders from Northfield and Faribault attended the first public meeting of the newly formed Minnesota parole board on July 12, 1897. Faribault mayor A. D. Keyes told all assembled that if the Youngers were to be paroled, they should answer three questions. Had Frank James participated in the Northfield robbery? What was the name of the man who was the last to leave the bank? And who had been the rider of the dun horse? Minnesota's current governor David Clough responded to Keyes's questions by saying that Frank James was not the person who was under consideration. Keyes responded with the comment, "It is not an element of good citizenship to conceal a murderer."[6] Cole and Jim Younger were again denied parole.

In 1898 an incident occurred that once again rocked the James family and put them back in the newspaper headlines. The Missouri Pacific Railroad's Number 5 train was robbed at Leeds, near Kansas City, on September 23. The robbery occurred about 9:40 P.M. as the train made its way from Kansas City to Wichita and Little Rock. A group of men stopped the train by waving a red lantern. They then detached the express car and engine and moved them down the track about a mile. Here they dynamited the safe in an attempt to open it. The tremendous explosion ended up destroying the entire car. Not much was available to be salvaged except twenty-nine silver dollars.

Jesse Edwards James was arrested and charged with being a participant in the Missouri Pacific robbery a few weeks after the robbery. Jesse E. was brought to trial in February 1899. He was represented by Thomas Crittenden's former secretary, Finis C. Farr. Jesse E. was acquitted on February 28. He was asked if he was bitter for having been suspected of the crime if only by his bearing of the infamous name of Jesse James. He claimed, "I can honestly say that I bear no ill will toward anyone. You see, some of my best friends are men who were Federal soldiers who fought my father and were fought by him in honorable warfare. I'm sure that if my father were living today, he would be a friend to these former enemies, too." Jesse's son seemed not to have inherited his father's belief in retribution and revenge. It had to be clear to Jesse E. and to his family that he would never be able to outrun the shadow cast by his infamous father. Nor would his mother. Zee James suffered a complete physical breakdown during this turbulent time in the life of her son. She later told a reporter, "Just think, that by his arrest all my work for twenty-two years has been torn down and put to naught. How I guarded and watched that boy in order that no stigma could be discovered on his character. And how he obeyed me always. . . . They arrest my boy because his name was Jesse James. That is what I have prayed against."[7]

Jesse E. tried to ignore the blemish placed on his good name. He had devoted his young life to his mother and had grown into a fine young man. At 8:00 P.M. on January 24, 1900, about fifty people celebrated with him as he married a lovely young woman. Stella was the daughter of Martha and Alfred M. McGown.[8] The wedding took place at the home of the bride's parents at 415 Landis Court in Kansas City. Reverend Dr. S. H. Werlein of the Kansas City Methodist Church South presided over the ceremony. One of the couple's friends, Harry Hawley, sang a song that had been written especially for the occasion by Hawley's accompanist, Charles N. Daniels.[9] Frank and Robert James were among the friends and family in attendance. Also celebrating were the attorneys who had helped to acquit Jesse during the train robbery proceedings.

Zee James was too ill to attend the wedding. She had remained silent, ill, and alone with her memories in the small house she shared with Jesse E. and Mary in Kansas City. Zee had not been well since the murder of her husband. Her health had taken a turn for the worse throughout the ordeal of her son's trial. She became bedridden for the next eleven months due to sciatic rheumatism and nervous prostration. Zee lapsed into a coma a week before her death on November 13, 1900.[10] Those who knew Zee well felt that although she had serious physical symptoms, the

Jesse Edwards James, c. 1900. *The Jesse James Farm*

true cause of her death was a broken heart.[11] Her daughter-in-law, Stella, would describe the stoic woman with tender and loving words. ''She had been a devoted and courageous mother who had guided her children tenderly and watched over them prayerfully, determined that they should grow up respected citizens.''[12] Zee had become a member of the Troost Avenue Methodist Episcopal Church during her time in Kansas City. Her funeral was held there with Reverend M. B. Chapman officiating. Zee's pallbearers were the men who had served as her son's attorneys during his trial for train robbery: L. S. Banks, T. T. Crittenden, F. C. Farr, E. P. Swinney, Frank P. Walsh, and R. L. Yeager. Reverend Chapman upheld Mrs. Jesse James as a fine Christian example. He claimed, "In all of the trials which filled her tempestuous life, she never did an unworthy act."[13] "What a Friend We Have in Jesus" was once again heard by the friends and family of Zee Mimms James. This hymn was the same song that was sung during the funeral of her beloved husband. Zee was temporarily interred in a vault at the Elmwood Cemetery in Kansas City.

Zee was nearly destitute at the time of her death. Her only real asset was her little house. Jesse E. sold the house the following year for $1,300 in order to pay off his mother's outstanding debts. Jesse E. received $293 and his sister Mary $75 when Zee's estate was settled.[14] Mary James was a lovely young woman who had dedicated her life to caring for her mother and brother. She married Clay County farmer Henry Barr on March 6, 1901, at the home of her aunt, Sallie Nicholson. The couple lived in a beautiful house near Kearney called Claybrook.[15]

In 1901, Frank James was approached by a group of Democrats who asked him if he would be interested in holding the position of doorkeeper for the state legislature. Frank saw such an appointment as a means by which he could regain respectability. Perhaps he could even lose some of the stigma that had been attached to him over the past couple of decades. Frank received fifteen votes in the Democratic caucus. Then those who had sponsored him withdrew their support. They had second thoughts about associating with an outlaw, no matter how famous he was. Frank suffered his defeat by indulging himself in his love of Shakespeare and the classics. He signed on as an actor with a traveling theatrical company. Frank appeared in a few productions including *Across the Desert* and *The Fatal Scar*.

The Youngers were finally paroled on July 10, 1901. Cole was now fifty-seven and Jim fifty-three. Warden Henry Wolfer arranged employment for the two with the P. N. Peterson Granite Company of Stillwater and St. Paul. Cole and Jim Younger would sell tombstones for their living.

Mary James Barr, c. 1915, at the James farm. *The Jesse James Farm*

Zerelda Samuel aged gracefully. Her long years of secrecy and stress apparently were at an end. Throughout her life she had been as independent as they come, but she had also often relied on her two eldest sons. Now Jesse was dead and Frank was trying to find his way in a world in which he had never freely moved. Zerelda turned to another of the young men she had raised. Perry Samuel was a black man who had been born into the Samuel family. There has been much speculation from writers and historians over the years that Perry was in fact Reuben Samuel's son by one of the former slave women who remained in the employ of the Samuel family after the war. Perry was very good to Zerelda. He took care of the business of running the farm and helped Zerelda with any personal business in which she might ask him to become involved. Perry tended to her every need and drove her wherever she needed to go. He was her loyal and trusted friend.

Reuben Samuel's mental capacities had continued to diminish over the years, especially as he became elderly. He had taken good care of the household chores for Zerelda. He continued to be a loving and solicitous husband. Jesse E. and Stella were surprised when one day John Samuel called to talk to them about Reuben's state of mind. Zerelda had reported that Reuben had hit her. This was something he had never done before.[16] Reuben then took to a rocking chair on the porch. He seemed to have virtually given up on living any kind of a normal life. Zerelda and the family decided that it would be best for Dr. Samuel if he were placed in a home for the mentally impaired in St. Joseph.

Frank James soon tired of the nomadic life of an actor and returned to his roots. He and his family moved to the James-Samuel homestead with Zerelda. Frank would now oversee the operation of the farm. The ever-enterprising Zerelda Samuel had been giving tours of Jesse's grave to strangers who stopped by to see the birthplace of America's most famous outlaw. Pebbles from the top of the grave were sold for twenty-five cents to the curiosity seekers. Zerelda would hold court expressing her opinions of Northern aggression and those who would harass the fine boys who opposed such action. The elderly woman loved talking to reporters. One time she told a story of the earlier years:

> Some of the detectives that came prowling around had narrow escapes. They used always to come when they thought my boys were away, but two of them missed it once and came very near getting killed. Jesse was at my home one day when I saw two men coming down the road. They stopped at the gate and hallooed. Jesse stepped just inside the door to the stairway leading to the attic and stood there with his revolvers in his hands. Jesse said, "Go to the door, Mother." I opened the door and one of the men said they were cattle buyers, and asked me if we had any fat cattle. "The cattle you are looking for are in the house; come in and get them!" I shouted. They talked together awhile in whispers and then went on.[17]

Frank had very little to do with the tourists. He would usually make himself busy elsewhere when they showed up at the farm. Occasionally, he would talk to one or two of them. But he would never speak to them about his outlaw years.

On June 29, 1902, Jesse and Zee James's bodies were finally united in death. Jesse was removed from his grave at the James-

Samuel farm and Zee was brought from Kansas City. They both were buried at the Mt. Olivet cemetery in Kearney. Jesse E. supervised the disinterrment of his father at the farm.[18] Frank James was in Kearney at this time but was suffering from a bout of the flu. The morning of the reburial brought rain, so Frank elected to remain at his hotel in town with his mother. Jesse E. watched as his father's remains were revealed. The coffin had disintegrated and all that remained were Jesse's bones, his hair and beard, and the black suit in which he was buried. The brave young man picked up his father's skull in order to see for himself that Jesse had been shot in the back of the head as he remembered it. A small hole behind the right ear assured Jesse E. that his memory was accurate and that the skull he was holding was that of Jesse James.

Jesse's remains were placed in a new coffin and taken inside the farmhouse. Back at the hotel, Frank provided a country dinner for the pallbearers. He had helped Zerelda Samuel and Jesse E. to select the men. Within a few hours, Jesse was on his way to his final resting place, accompanied by pallbearers John "Hicks" George, Hiram George, Jacob "Frank" Gregg, William Gregg, Warren Welch, and James "Sam" Whitsett. Zerelda Samuel must have been saddened to have her son's burial site moved away from her constant care, but it was time. Jesse's daughter Mary bought a house adjoining the cemetery. She could now keep an eye on Jesse's grave and hopefully prevent too much vandalism from souvenir hunters who might chip away at his headstone. This was the headstone that had stood above his grave on his family's farm. It would now announce to visitors of the Mt. Olivet Cemetery that Jesse Woodson James was a resident.

History has shown that it is very difficult to keep the monuments marking Jesse's grave intact. The James-Samuel family had been able to guard the original marker placed on Jesse's grave while he was buried at the farm. It wasn't long after Jesse was moved to Mt. Olivet that souvenir hunters began to chip away at his stone. The stone was ultimately destroyed by visitors to the grave who wanted mementos of America's most famous outlaw. All but the base of the monument, which now is on display at the James Farm Museum, disappeared. A new stone was erected in June 1960. Family members erected a replica of the original monument in 1989. A Confederate veteran's marker was placed with both headstones during a public dedication ceremony on August 5, 1989.

Jim Younger had been unable to return to Missouri or marry the woman he loved due to the terms of his parole. He put a bullet in his head on October 19, 1902. There were now only two members of the James-Younger Gang still living. Cole Younger was granted a conditional pardon on February 4, 1903. He got together with his old wartime buddy Frank James soon after his return to Missouri. Neither man had a great deal of wealth and talk soon turned to how they might take advantage of their celebrity. Wild west shows were very popular and soon the two old friends had enlisted in a production to be called The Great Cole Younger and Frank James Historical Wild West Show. Younger would serve as the manager. Frank signed on as master of ceremonies. The show included "Russian Cassocks, American Cowboys, Rough Riders, Indians, Mexicans and broncos." It opened in the Pinkerton's hometown of Chicago.[19]

The wild west show toured throughout the Midwest. It soon became obvious that many of those connected with the production were carny types who found it near to impossible to stay out of trouble. Two of the "Rough Riders" got into a fight shortly after the show arrived in Memphis on May 24. Eugene Scully was arrested on charges of carrying a loaded pistol and assault with intent to kill after he shot Charles Burrows in the leg. Ten other employees were arrested for their involvement in an illegal gambling operation by the time the production hit Nashville.[20] The newspapers accused the old outlaws of degrading themselves even further by having anything at all to do with such a shoddy production. Since Frank and Younger had publicly claimed to have become involved with the show as a means to earn money for their retirement, they found it easy to threaten to terminate their involvement. They claimed that their paychecks were few and far between. This was a claim that was unfortunately true. The embarrassing quest for recognition escalated when the show eventually arrived in Younger's former hometown in St. Clair County. Frank, Younger, and a third man scuffled in the streets of Osceola. They of course drew a crowd, and their altercation resulted in the arrest of the third man. It was soon determined that the fracas had been a hoax. It had been staged to draw attention to that evening's performance of the wild west show.[21]

Frank James and Cole Younger gave many promotional interviews during their association with the wild west show as they toured the country. Younger held court espousing his family's prestigious roots and his own wartime heroism. Frank was constantly asked about Jesse. He refused to say anything about the brother he had loved and lost. Both men, in an obvious attempt to draw to the show those who had held northern sympathies during the war, claimed to "love everybody."[22]

Eventually, an embarrassed Frank James and Cole Younger demanded the withdrawal of their names from all advertising. The owners of the company staging the show threatened a lawsuit. Frank and Younger threatened the same. The production continued with Frank and Cole resuming their roles. There was another dispute by the time the production arrived in Illinois in November. One of the owners accused Younger of stealing funds. Cole may have been old, but he was still Cole Younger. He leveled his illegal pistol at his accuser and quietly informed him that Cole Younger and Frank James would no longer be a part of the production.[23] Frank James had grown tired of life on the road. He bought a small ranch and moved with his family to Fletcher, Oklahoma.

By 1910, Perry Samuel was married and had moved away from the James-Samuel farm. Eighty-six-year-old Zerelda Samuel found that the succession of housekeepers her family hired failed to take care of her in the manner to which she had become accustomed. She was too used to the devotion of her husband, children, and the faithful Perry Samuel. Zerelda stayed in two different Kearney hotels during the winter months. After that she tried living with a local couple who had invited her to stay with them in their home. She wasn't happy there, either. Zerelda was eventually invited by Jesse Edwards and his bride Stella to live with them for a while. That made her happy. Zerelda's presence in their home was taxing on the young couple, but they loved her too much to ever say or do anything that might make her feel unwelcome. Zerelda was used to being waited on. She often tried the patience of those in her new home as her demands were vocal and many. Jesse E. and Stella loved her just the same. They tried to make Jesse E.'s grandmother comfortable and happy. As something of a publicity stunt, Zerelda had been given a lifetime pass on one of the railroads after the death of Jesse. She was allowed to use the pass for herself and her family members. The railroad officials didn't deny her the obvious pleasure she took in continually inviting all members of the James-Samuel family and any friends and neighbors who might want to accompany her into Kansas City or wherever she might be traveling. Zerelda visited Frank and Annie in Fletcher during the winter of 1910. After a couple of months, Zerelda decided that she would like to try living at her home in Clay County once again. Annie insisted on accompanying her back to Missouri. Zerelda and Annie boarded a St. Louis and San Francisco passenger train and began the journey back to Missouri. On February 10, 1911, Zerelda suffered an apparent heart attack or stroke while on the train. Zerelda Cole James Simms Samuel was dead. She was buried at Mt. Olivet near her adored martyred sons, little Archie and Jesse. Stella James may have summed up the spirit of Zerelda when she wrote in her autobiography, "Had Zerelda Samuel lived in our day, she could well have been a leader among women. She fought for what she believed in, and, like a general, once she was in a fight, she gave her all."[24]

Frank James decided that he would once again try living on the family homestead after the death of his mother. It would, after all, be a good place to hand down to his son Robert when the time came. Jesse E. was enjoying a fine career as an attorney. He wasn't interested in farming. Frank had decided that he could find the peace he had so desperately sought amid the flourishing fields and cottonwood trees of his youth. Jesse E. visited Frank at the farm regularly. He would often ask questions in an attempt to get to know the father who had been taken from him at such an early age. Frank would speak only in the third person when Jesse E. would mention some of the tall tales and stories that he had heard or had been told. The elderly uncle would often cage his answers with, "The Frank James I knew . . ."[25] Even his brother's son would remain uninformed in regard to any of Frank and Jesse's outlaw escapades.

Cole Younger bought a house for himself and a niece in Lee's Summit. He became bored once he was out of the limelight and decided to hit the lecture circuit. He traveled around the country speaking of "What My Life Has Taught Me" and selling copies of his so-called autobiography. Younger eventually returned home where he enjoyed long hours of sitting comfortably on the porch of his home. He would entertain assembled groups of neighborhood children with stories from his own youth or the war. Frank visited his friend every once in a while. The two men would have private conversations about the old days. A revival meeting was held during the fiftieth anniversary of the raid on Lawrence. Cole Younger walked to the front of the meeting and proclaimed himself a sinner and a Christian.[26] Frank James must have been amused, but he himself was no stranger to religion. His friend John Phillips would shortly claim, "When at peace with the world, he [Frank] sought to make his peace with God. His religion was not in tithes or burnt offerings, but of the heart. It was a matter between him and God. Who so mean spirited as to question his sincerity? Who but a Publican would wrap himself in a cloak of self-righteousness, and say there is an ascension robe for Frank James? Only the recording angel holds the balance sheet of the wrongs he did and those he suffered, and knows what is written in the Lamb's book." It is too bad that those words were spoken after Frank's death, for he surely would have enjoyed every one of them.

Frank evidently changed his mind about welcoming visitors to his farm. By 1914, he was often seen outside in the yard entertaining strangers who dropped by to pay their respects. A crude hand-painted sign designated the Clay County farm as the "Home of the James', Jesse and Frank James." A fifty-cent admission was charged. Frank continued to remain mum on the subject of his outlaw years, however. Many novels were continuing to be written that blew the factual escapades of the James boys all out of proportion. A reporter asked Frank how accurate he felt they were. Frank replied, "If I admitted that these stories were true, people would say: 'There is the greatest scoundrel unhung!' And if I denied em, they'd say: 'There's the greatest liar on earth!' So I just say nothing."[27]

On February 18, 1915, Frank's heart gave out. He was sev-

enty-two years old. He may have additionally suffered a stroke.
Frank's wife Annie didn't say much publicly but did claim that
"A better husband never lived."[28] When Cole Younger was told
of the death of his closest friend, he sat alone in his room, lost
in his memories.

People came from all over the Midwest to pay tribute to Frank
James, but it had been decided by the family that the funeral
would be private. Certainly no reporters would be admitted. The
funeral would bring Frank almost full circle. It was held at the
James-Samuel farmhouse where he had grown into his manhood.
Judge John Phillips extolled his former client's virtues by saying,
"In important respects, Frank James was a man of admirable
qualities. Without the adventitious aid of academic education, or
very inspiring associations, his wonderful mentality, keen acu-
men, and thirst for knowledge, enabled him to absorb such information about men, books and nature as demonstrated that had
opportunity and dame fortune seconded his gifts, he would have
achieved a brilliant career and honorable fame. From a close
observation of his real character in later life, I feel a positive
conviction that the troublous, tragic life that befell him was neither of his liking or inclination. He deserved and coveted better
things." Quoting the Koran, Phillips expressed his belief that
"He that dies pays all debts."[29] Robert James took his father's
body by train to St. Louis in the company of his cousin Jesse E.
It was cremated as Frank had requested. On the way home, Robert dropped the metal from the coffin into the Missouri River.
Annie placed Frank's ashes in a vault at the New England Safe
Deposit Co. and Kearney Trust Company in Kansas City. Later
they would be removed to be interred beside Annie's at Hill
Cemetery in Independence, near the site of the Rock Creek
School House where Annie had taught school.

Cole Younger had been ill and confined to his room throughout the winter. Jesse E. visited Younger regularly, accompanied
by their mutual friend, Jackson County Marshall Harry Hoffman.
Hoffman had lived next door to Jesse E. and his family when
they were boys in Kansas City. The year after Frank's death,
Cole Younger informed the two young men that he was going
to die. He had some things he wanted to tell them. The three of
them talked privately for several hours. Younger swore Jesse E.

and Hoffman to secrecy should anyone ever ask what he had told them. He spoke of the outlaw days and of Northfield. Younger did not come right out and say who it was that had killed cashier Heywood. He did tell the young men who it was that had ridden the dun horse. This was the horse said to have carried the murderer. Jesse E. clearly understood that the killer of Heywood had been his Uncle Frank. Jesse would always keep this information to himself, eventually confirming the fact only to his family.[30] Hoffman later revealed what he had been told by writing the "true account" of Cole Younger's life, as related to him by Younger, titled *The Youngers' Last Stand*. Cole Younger died in the company of his family on March 21, 1916, at the age of seventy-two.[31]

Jesse E. attempted to end the saga by telling what he believed to be the true story of his father's life in 1920. Jesse E., Harry Hoffman, and writer-director Franklin Coates were signed by a company named Mecca Pictures to create a movie based on the life of Jesse James. All did not go well. The three men canceled their contract over some type of personal dispute. A production company named Mesco Pictures approached Jesse, offering to continue the project under their production company banner. Thomas T. Crittenden served as vice-president of the company and Hoffman was the general manager. The capital of the company was $250,000. Twenty-five hundred shares of common stock were made available at a par value of $100. Interestingly, Jesse E. proclaimed in the prospectus that the story was completely accurate. This was a claim that would prove to be false by the time the final picture was completed. Jesse E., his friends, and family had the opportunity to invest in the production since the stocks were common. Unfortunately, Jesse and the others bought shares of the offered stock. They had no way to predict the future revenue of the production.

Mesco had another idea. The powers that be felt it would be a huge box office draw if Jesse E. were to portray his father. When Jesse E. balked, the producers offered him $50,000. Stella James later wrote that Jesse E. was a successful attorney but he had four daughters to put through college. He felt obligated to accept the offer.[32]

Jesse James Under the Black Flag commenced production

with Jesse E. in the lead. A cast of amateur actors supported him, including Margurete Hungerford and Diana Reed. One small consolation to Jesse E. was that Stella would play herself and Harry Hoffman would portray their mutual friend, Cole Younger. The picture was filmed in the area around Kansas City. Jesse E. portrayed both himself and his father in flashback scenes. Postproduction commenced in Chicago after the filming was completed. There the picture hit a snag. The production ran out of money. Houses and farms were mortgaged to complete the picture. Included was the home of Jesse E. and Stella. Jesse E. felt terrible that he had encouraged his friends to invest in the production. It now looked as if it might not make any money at all. He felt he had no choice but to continue to be involved with the production. He committed to tour with the picture for four months throughout the East in order to garner publicity and exposure. He was to be paid $25.00 a day plus expenses. A voucher found with the contracts that he signed indicates that Jesse E. was paid only a total of $32,400 for both starring in the picture and promoting it.[33]

Jesse E.'s time on the road with *Under the Black Flag* cost him dearly. His mental and physical health took a beating. He was a wreck by the time he arrived back home. The picture was a complete failure and lost great amounts of money. Jesse E. felt compelled to personally repay the money his friends and family had lost in the venture.[34] Eventually, he would even be forced to sell his house. Jesse E. was unable to return to his law practice for a year after his return from promoting the movie. He entered a hospital when his health did not improve. He remained there for several months. Finally, Jesse E. was able to leave the hospital. His daughters left college and took jobs to help support him emotionally. The family took up residence in a house outside Independence. Jesse was sufficiently recovered to once again practice law by October 1926. But within two years, he felt unable to continue and closed his practice. Jesse never fully regained his health. He followed the path traveled by his mother. Like Zee James, Jesse E. remained a broken man throughout the remainder of his life. He died on March 16, 1951, another victim of the legacy of Jesse Woodson James.

AFTERWORD

JESSE JAMES IS a megastar. His legend continues to grow and prosper more than a hundred years after his death. Films, television documentaries, books, songs, plays and even an operetta celebrate this most famous of America's bad-boy heroes. The study of Jesse and his gang also continues to be fascinating fodder for historians, researchers, and journalists. Two significant discoveries came to light in 1996 through the efforts of teams of those who would delve deeper into the story of Jesse Woodson James.

Historian Ralph Ganis came upon some interesting material while examining the lives of two young men from North Carolina. Twenty-six-year-old Lorenzo Merriman Little left Montgomery County, North Carolina, in 1853 to relocate with friends and relatives to Toulomne County, California. A study of his travels indicates that he may have become friendly with Cole Younger during that time. Younger was in California at the end of The War between the States. It appears the two men had mutual friends who were involved with some of Younger's Confederate activities while he was on assignment on the West Coast during the final days of the war. Little returned to Montgomery County in late February or early March with enough money to finance the purchase of several acres of land. Ganis is of the opinion that there is good reason to believe that Little may have participated in the Liberty bank robbery. Little traveled to Nashville in the late 1870s with the son of a Confederate soldier named Andrew Moorman "Mome" Diggs. Both Little and Diggs can be seen in a photograph taken of the employees of the Lambert Mocker Barrel Factory—the same photo that clearly shows Jesse and Frank James as employees.

The characters of both Little and Diggs demonstrate that they were men who had no compunction about doing as they pleased, regardless of the cost or consequence. Both have lengthy criminal records that include instances of assault and battery. Diggs was eventually sent to the state penitentiary for murder.

Many of the robberies that were accredited to the gangs of Jesse James contained small nuances that made them appear to have been perpetrated by Jesse and his friends. Jesse becomes an unlikely suspect in most cases when one examines the physical circumstances, however. Robberies that appear to be copycats may have been the work of operatives of Jesse James. Jesse may have tutored several of his buddies in the fine art of bank and train robbing. The distances between robbery sites coupled with the dates these sites were chosen to be robbed may have provided Jesse with more than a little assistance as he built his legend. Jesse would have valid and believable alibis for the dates of the robberies. He could also enjoy the fact that the newspapers helped build his reputation as a robber extraordinaire as they accredited robberies all over the country, many simultaneously, to the humble Missouri farm boy. Little and Diggs may have been two of those operatives. The Corinth, Mississippi, bank robbery, for instance, was committed by robbers wielding knives. Although Jesse threatened Joseph Heywood with a knife, no other instance of knifes over guns has been recorded in regard to Jesse's gangs. "Mome" Diggs assaulted a man with a knife and was known to carry a knife as an additional weapon. When one looks at the photos of Little and Diggs, it can be seen that Little resembles Cole Younger. The men who robbed the bank at Corinth used knives and one of them was said to have looked like Cole Younger. Could Little and Diggs have been the robbers? Might they have been responsible for some of the other robberies believed to have been committed by Jesse and his gang? It appears certain that Little and Diggs knew Jesse and Frank, at least through their association at the barrel factory.

Further research into the copycats may provide us with more answers as to there being a Jesse-sponsored second gang.

Another bit of research into the life of Jesse would find national exposure and interest. A fifteen-member forensic team headed by Professor James Starrs of George Washington University conducted an in-depth study of the DNA of Jesse James in 1995. Nebraska researcher Emmett C. Hoctor had proposed the study to Dr. Starrs the previous year in an effort to answer a question once and for all. Was it indeed Jesse who had been killed on April 5, 1882? Why such a question needed to be addressed in the first place is a story unto itself.

At the time of Jesse's death, it was difficult for most people to believe that the infamous Jesse James could be the victim of one of his gang members in his very own house. Jesse was known to be daring, clever, and smart. How could he allow such a thing to happen to him? Was it carelessness? Was it suicide? Or was it all one huge plot to make the public believe Jesse was dead when in fact he was not? Many people chose to believe the latter, despite the fact that Jesse's body had been identified by dozens of people who had known him throughout his life. With the speculation that Jesse had paid someone to assume his identity in death came the pretenders. The pain they would cause the true family of Jesse James and the confusion they would wreak for generations to come would be the only events in their lives that would make them noteworthy.

One of the first such pretenders was a man named John James. John James gathered information about the real Jesse in the Clay County town of Excelsior Springs. The man was claiming to be the one and only Jesse Woodson James by 1932. James attested that the man who had been killed in St. Joseph in 1882 had been a man by the name of Charlie Bigalow. James had been able to garner further information from a childhood friend of the real Jesse named "Aunt Margaret." Soon some of the officials of Excelsior Springs were putting James up in a hotel and national publicity declared him to be the surviving outlaw himself. James had somehow gathered affidavits from old-timers that attested to his claim. A Los Angeles newspaper asked Stella James, Jesse's daughter-in-law, to go to Missouri and confront the impostor in a public hearing. Stella took the newspaper up on their offer and

attended a meeting whereby ''Jesse'' was asked a variety of
questions. Since Jesse E.'s book had been published by this time,
James knew the answers to many of the questions put to him
about Jesse's life. He did not know such things as the name of
the half-brother who had been killed in the Pinkerton explosion
or which arm Jesse's mother had lost in that tragedy. It was soon
determined that John James was indeed an outlaw. He was on
parole for having killed a man in Illinois. James continued his
charade even after his public defeat. Finally, his sister attested
to the Superior Court of California that John James was not Jesse
James nor was he of a sound mind. James died in the Arkansas
State Hospital for the Mentally Ill in 1947.

The most famous of the Jesse impostors appeared in 1948.
One hundred-one-year-old J. Frank Dalton now claimed that he
was the outlaw Jesse James. He stated that he had employed a
stand-in in order to make the public believe he was dead and
had been living in Oklahoma. Dalton was quite feeble and easily
led. He was taken under the wing of an entrepreneur named
Orvus Lee Houk. Houk soon announced that he was Dalton's
grandson, thus making him a descendant of Jesse James. Houk
told ''Jesse's'' story to a writer named Del Shrader, who published a book titled *Jesse James Was One of His Names*. In the
book we are introduced to not only a competent, long-living
outlaw but a man who was influential to the formation of RKO
Film Studio, fought with Maximilian, and astral traveled to save
time as he engaged in his many adventures. Stella James was
surprised and appalled to see that Dalton was using the same
affidavits that John James had gathered. Dalton petitioned to
have his name legally changed to Jesse Woodson James, but was
denied by the Missouri court. This ''Jesse'' was displayed at
fairs and other sites of merriment around the country throughout
the remainder of his life. In 1967, a man named Rudy Terrelli
picked up Dalton and his story. Terrelli claimed that ''Jesse''
had been a frequent visitor to the Eastern Missouri cave that
Terrelli owned and was operating as a tourist attraction. Terrelli
offered $10,000 to anyone who could prove that Dalton was not
Jesse James. Stella James and Jesse's granddaughters Ethelrose
and Estelle took the promoter up on his offer. They sued him
when he refused to pay them. The trial was held in May 1970

in Union, Missouri. The decision was in favor of the real-life Jesse's family. The decision was appealed but upheld by the St. Louis Court of Appeals in 1972. When J. Frank Dalton died in 1951, he was buried under a tombstone declaring him as Jesse Woodson James.

If that had been the end of the story, there would be no real need to conduct a DNA study some forty years later. But the saga continued. So-called descendants of Dalton, or Jesse James as they claimed, emerged with contentions that Dalton was truly Jesse James and that he had told them of millions of dollars of booty that he had buried. Others came forward saying that their families had hidden the truth for over a century. Their grandfather, not Dalton, was really Jesse James. Others came forward claiming to be the real Frank James. And the story grew and grew.

The James family grew weary of the continued claims and felt compelled to do nothing more than dismiss them as the tall stories they were. They knew that Jesse Woodson James had died in 1882, and there was little more to be said. When Hoctor expressed the interest of Professor Starrs to conduct the DNA study to Jesse's great-grandson, retired Superior Court Judge James R. Ross, the family conferred and eventually agreed. Perhaps science could silence the pretenders.

Dr. Starrs worked with the James family and historians to locate seventeen true descendants of Jesse James in order to obtain their written approval to exhume the outlaw's grave. Once that was accomplished without objection, Clay County Circuit Court Judge Vic Howard approved the order with the stipulation that the remains be returned to the grave within ninety days of the exhumation. Jesse's grave was unearthed by a team of professionals under the direction of Dr. Starrs on July 17, 1995. Dozens of national and international television reporters and newspapers followed the events of the next few days. The dig was conducted under the watchful eyes of no other than the Pinkerton Security Agency!

The exhumation took longer than expected. Dr. Starrs and his assistants at first hoped to find Jesse's casket closer to the surface than was later revealed. It was determined that little of the casket remained by the time it was unearthed two days later. The glass top was revealed along with silver handles and an unreadable nameplate. As to the body of Jesse itself, only a few arm, leg, and foot bones were found. Six portions of Jesse's skull were eventually revealed as well as fourteen teeth. Items that would prove helpful to the identification of the remains in the grave were two reconstructed gold teeth, a black onyx stone, a button, and a .36 caliber bullet found in chest bone material.

Jesse's remains were then scattered across the country in search of information that would prove conclusively that Jesse's body was who his family said it was as well as to determine other factors integral to the James legend. Scientists at Penn State University, Florida State University, Kansas State University, George Washington University, the Kansas City Crime Laboratory, and the University of Colorado prepared to study Jesse James. Blood samples were taken from Robert Jackson, great-grandson of Susan Parmer and Mark Nikkol, Susan's great-great-grandson as mitochondrial DNA can only be passed through the female. The complete study would take more than six months. James Starrs revealed the team's findings on February 23, 1996, in Nashville.

The in-depth analysis confirmed that the DNA profiles of Susan James Parmer's descendants were consistent in every way with that of the remains that had been studied. The man in the grave was thirty to forty years old. He was between 5'8" and 5'10". The two gold teeth matched Jesse's family's knowledge that he had gold restorations of two of his teeth. The photo of Jesse in his original casket clearly shows a tie pin with a black stone. Additionally, the .36 caliber bullet was found in the precise spot among the bones where Jesse's wartime wound would have been. It had been shot from an 1851 model handgun. The pieces of the skull showed that a bullet had entered the back of the head behind the right ear. The bullet had not passed through the skull. The remains in the grave were conclusively proven to be that of Jesse Woodson James.

It had been time to rebury Jesse in October as the scientists and Jesse's family cooperated with the court order to return the remains to the grave within ninety days. As would be expected with anything having to do with Jesse James, the planned funeral and reburial immediately met with controversy. Jesse had been a member of the First Baptist Church of Kearney, but the church refused the request to host Jesse's second funeral. They knew all too well that there would be a media circus and they wanted no part of it. William Jewell College, having been organized in part by Jesse's father, initially agreed to host the service. When they were told that the service would include the use of the Confederate flag, the administration forbade the use of any Confederate symbols. Members of the family were outraged. Jesse's great-grandson, retired judge James R. Ross, made his feelings very clear. "He [Reverend James] undoubtedly turned over in his grave with your discriminatory and bigoted acts," Ross wrote to the school administration. Eventually, the Knights of Columbus Hall agreed that their community hall could be used to hold the funeral.

On the morning of October 28, visitors filed past Jesse's new poplar-wood coffin as it lay draped in the Stars and Bars at the Fry Funeral Home. Floral arrangements from the Sons of Confederate Veterans and various Jesse-related historic societies such as the nonprofit James-Younger Gang organization and the Friends of the James Farm surrounded the casket. In front stood a portrait of the deceased that had been painted by artist George Warfel. Butternut Confederate uniforms adorned the honor guard that stood at attention holding period rifles and muskets. Jesse's six great-grandchildren—Betty Barr, Fred Barr, Donald Baumel, Diane Fairchild, James Lewis, and James Ross—were present as well as some of sister Susan's descendants. Also present was Thelma Barr, the wife of Jesse's grandson Lawrence, who has served as the family's genealogist for decades.

In the afternoon, over 700 people filed into the community hall to witness or participate in the funeral as a white, horse-drawn hearse waited outside. The brief ceremony would be sponsored by the Missouri Division of the Sons of Confederate Veterans. The service began with a processional led by honorary pallbearers Bill Breckenridge, Gary Chilcot, Donald Hale, Lee Pollack, David Smith, James Starrs, Phillip Steele, and Wilbur Zink. After a welcome by Dr. Charles E. Baker of the Centerpoint Independent Church of Birmingham, Alabama, "What a Friend We Have in Jesus" was sung by the congregation. This hymn is reported to have been Jesse's favorite hymn. Music was provided by Kathy Barton, Bob Dyer, and Dave Para. Dr. Charles E. Baker was currently serving as chaplain-in-chief of the Sons of Confederate Veterans. He prepared for his sermon as Reverend John Killian of the First Baptist Church of Bolbo, Alabama, read from the book of Job. Reverend Killian served as Military Order of Stars and Bars pastor. "Rock of Ages" was then sung by the congregation. Dr. Baker then spoke of Jesse and of the importance of Christianity. He made note that all of those in attendance on this day had one thing in common with those who had attended Jesse's first funeral. Everyone must die. "Amazing Grace" was sung, followed by a eulogy presented by Robert L. Hawkins, III, the past commander-in-chief of the Sons of Confederate Veterans. After the common doxology, the recessional was led by ancestors of Confederate veterans. The all-male group included Keith I. Daleen, James Chris Edwards, William Earl Faggart, Fred H. Gillham, Sr., Judge Frank W. Koger, Representative Jerry McBride, William Philyaw, and J. E. B. Stuart, IV.

The private graveside ceremony was brief. Dr. Baker read from the Book of Psalms, made some brief remarks, and said a prayer. An honor guard from the Fifth Missouri Infantry reenactor group fired a salute. The Stars and Bars, United States Flag, Missouri Flag, Missouri Battle Flag, and the first Confederate Flag were presented by a color guard under the command of Robert L. Koffman.

Jesse was once again interred to rest in peace. The folklore, facts, names, dates, and legend, however, would continue to expand and thrive. Jesse Woodson James wasn't just a Western folk hero, he was a man for all time.

NOTES

Chapter One

1. John James was born in Hanover County, Virginia, in 1775. He married Mary (Polly) Poor March 26, 1807. John and Mary moved to the Big Whippoorwill Creek area of Logan County, Kentucky, in 1811. The couple had eight children: Mary was the mother of Zerelda Amanda Mimms, the future wife of Jesse Woodson James. William was an ordained Methodist minister and merchant. John R. was a dentist. Elizabeth married businessman Tillman Howard West and together with her husband organized the Methodist Episcopal Church, south of Kansas City. Robert Sallee was the father of Frank and Jesse James. Nancy G. married George B. Hite. Their sons would ride with the James Gang. Thomas Martin founded the T. M. James Co., which imported fine china. Drury Woodson was a prominent San Luis Obispo County pioneer, builder of the Hotel De Paso Robles, and owner of the La Panza Ranch near Santa Margarita, California. Beamis, Joan M. and Pullen, William E., *Background of a Bandit: The Ancestry of Jesse James*, 7–16; James, Stella, *In the Shadow of Jesse James*, 8.

2. James Cole was born September 8, 1804, in Woodford County, Kentucky. He married his cousin Sallie Lindsay, who was born April 15, 1803. Sallie Lindsay Cole and her second husband, Robert Thomason, had four children together. Elizabeth was married to Thomas Patton. Martha Ann married Robert Mimms, Zee Mimms James's brother. Mary Alice was married to Marrett Jones Scott. A fourth child, a son, was born to the couple, but his name seems not to have been recorded. Jesse Richard Cole was born November 29, 1826. He married

Louisa G. Maret on December 23, 1846, in Clay County. He died November 16, 1895. Ibid. 58, 68.

3. Ross, James R., *I, Jesse James*, 12.

4. Grandson Jesse Edwards's wife Stella claimed that Zerelda had an exceptional humor and would often play tricks on her family. James, Stella Frances, *In the Shadow of Jesse James*, 59.

5. Jacob Groomer built the log cabin, measuring eighteen feet by thirty-five feet, in 1822. A double-sided fireplace heated its two rooms. Robert Gilmer bought the property from Groomer in 1844 and added a second cabin with attic space. This eighteen-foot cabin stood about eight feet in front of the original, with a breezeway in between the rooms. Clay County Probate Court Records; James Farm *Journal*, October, 1994.

6. Both Clay and Jackson Counties were lovely areas that drew a large number of settlers from the Southern states. President Harry Truman was a resident of Jackson County. President Truman explained to two young award winners that he met in 1949 that the countryside where the James family would eventually reside was broken in two during the election of 1824. The Republicans named their county after GOP candidate Henry Clay. The Democratic supporters named Jackson County after candidate Andrew Jackson. (Richard Fristoe, maternal grandfather of the Younger boys, proposed Jackson's name as he had served with Jackson during the Battle of New Orleans.) Truman told the two boys that the James family lived in the Republican-named county. He was quick to add that they were always loyal to the Democratic party and were "big Democrats." Truman admitted that he had a secret admiration for Jesse James. When one of the boys claimed that he admired both Mr. Truman and Mr. James, the president quipped, "A lot of people haven't liked either one of us." He evidently sympathized with Jesse and Frank as he claimed, "The James boys were pushed so hard they began to fight back," something to which Mr. Truman felt he could relate. The *Kansas City Times*, Drew Pearson column, June 18, 1949.

7. *Kansas City Journal*, April 6, 1882. Interview with William James.

8. James, Stella, *In the Shadow of Jesse James*, 38.

9. Clay County probate court records.

10. James, Stella, *In the Shadow of Jesse James*, 38.

11. William A. Settle, Jr., *Jesse James Was His Name*, 203. Dr. Settle read the letters that were kept in a safe-deposit box by Robert's grandson, Robert James.

12. Settle, William A., *Jesse James Was His Name*, 8.

13. An inventory of Robert James's assets filed after his death in 1851 included fifty-one books on subjects including philosophy, Latin, history, literature, public speaking, Greek, grammar, mathematics, theology, chemistry, and astronomy. Also listed as assets were six head of cattle, three horses, a yoke of oxen, thirty sheep, and seven slaves. Clay County probate court records.

Chapter Two

1. With this document, Congress recognized the title "War between the States" as proper when referring to the 1862–65 conflict; with appreciation to Marvin Katzen, Charleston, S. C.

2. The marriage of Zerelda James and Benjamin Simms forged a genealogical connection between two families, which would be interlaced in history. Simms's niece, Augusta Peters Inskeep, married Coleman Purcell Younger. Coleman was the brother of Henry Washington Younger, the father to the outlaw Youngers. Many books concerning the history of the James-Younger Gang have claimed that the James brothers and the Younger boys were cousins, but such is not the case. The relationship between the Simms-Younger and James family is only through the shirttail relationship of Zerelda James, Benjamin Simms, Augusta Peters, and Coleman Younger. The Youngers were first cousins to the Dalton outlaws. The Youngers were also vaguely related to the outlaw Johnny Ringo through the marriage of Augusta Peters and Coleman Younger. Ringo's mother was Mary Peters Ringo, the sister of Augusta Peters. Histories have erroneously recorded that Jesse and Frank James were related by blood to those parties as well.

3. The records of Dr. Absolam Kerns, Clinton, Missouri, 1853.

4. Sarah Louisa Samuel was born on December 26, 1858. She married William Nicholson on November 28, 1878, and lived near the James-Samuel farm until her death on July 14, 1921. Sallie had three sons. John T. Samuel was born December 25, 1861, and married Norma Lena Maret on July 22, 1885. The couple had no children. John died in 1934. Fanny Quantrill Samuel was born October 18, 1863, and married Joe C. Hall. Fannie and Hall had three children. Fannie died on May 3, 1922. Archie Peyton Samuel was born on July 26, 1866. Beamis, Joan M., and Pullen, William E., *Background of a Bandit*, 60.

5. James, Stella Frances, *In the Shadow of Jesse James*, 51.

6. Ross, James R., *I, Jesse James*, 16.

7. Adjutant general's report, State of Kansas, Seventh Regiment Kansas, Roll.

8. Castel, Albert, *William Clarke Quantrill: His Life and Times*, 32–33.

9. Younger Cole, *Cole Younger by Himself*, 16.

10. Loan, Brigadier General Benjamin, letter to Major General Samuel R. Curtis, Central District of Missouri, January 27, 1863.

11. Settle, William A., Jr., *Jesse James Was His Name*, 22.

12. Ibid.

13. Croy, Homer, *Jesse James Was My Neighbor*, 25.

Chapter Three

1. James, Stella, *In the Shadow of Jesse James*, 39–40.

2. It has been suggested by local oral historians over the years that Zerelda miscarried the baby she had been expecting, but daughter Fannie was born to the Samuels on October 18 of that year. It is possible that Zerelda, with a history of miscarriage, may have miscarried a child in the aftermath of a previous raid on her farm.

3. James, Stella, *In the Shadow of Jesse James*, 40.

4. Settle, William A., Jr., *Jesse James Was His Name*, 26.

5. Oath of allegiance and parole papers of Mrs. Z. Samuel and Reuben Samuel of Clay County, dated June 5, 1863, and June 24, 1863.

6. Kate King was also known as Kate Clarke. It has been debated whether or not Kate and Quantrill were married or merely lovers. Quantrill kept her secluded in Howard County, Missouri. Castel, Albert, *William Clarke Quantrill: His Life and Times*, 149, 213.

Chapter Four

1. It was true that Jesse's eyes were never at rest. He suffered from granulated eyelids, which caused him to appear nervous and excitable although for the most part he was remarkably calm. The blinking may have contributed to his high-strung, trigger-happy reputation.

2. Ross, James R., *I, Jesse James*, 36.

3. Edwards, John Newman, "A Terrible Quintet," *St. Louis Dispatch*, 1874.

4. The James family accepts that Jesse's fingertip was indeed a result of an accident on his part. There has been speculation in books written about the guerrillas that the wound was caused from something other than Jesse's own gun. The predominant suggestion has been made that it occurred sometime in battle. Ross, James R., *I, Jesse James*, 36; Love, Roburtus, *The Rise and Fall of Jesse James*, 100; Edwards, John Newman, *Noted Guerrillas*, 350. In *Jesse James Was His Name*, author

William Settle asserts the position that "the finger tip probably was lost in June of 1864 in a battle in which two Clay Countians named Bigalow were killed by the Jameses and others who were commanded by Fletcher Taylor," 31.

5. Yeatman, Ted, "Jesse James' Surrender," *Old West*, Fall 1994.

6. Ibid.

7. Ibid.

8. Ibid.

9. William A. Settle, Jr., interview with Jesse's boyhood friend, Judge Thomas A. Shouse, June 15, 1940.

10. Yeatman, Ted, "Jesse James' Surrender" *Old West*, Fall 1994. On December 13, 1866, Arch Clement rode into Lexington, Missouri, with a group of men. Union Major Bacon Montgomery saw to it that an immediate attempt was made to arrest the guerrillas. When soldiers entered the saloon where Clements was drinking, Clements met them with bullets. He ran out the door and mounted his horse. Clements was engulfed in a fusillade of fire while riding down Franklin Street. Clements's dead body revealed that he had been hit approximately thirty-three times. Hale, Donald R., "Was Archie Clements Missouri's First Bank Robber?" *Quarterly of the National Association for Outlaw and Lawman History*, Vol. XIX, No. 2, April–June 1995.

11. *Liberty Tribune*, February 5, 1865.

12. Hoctor, Emmet C., "Rusticating in Nebraska: 1862–1882," talk given to the Friends of the James Farm annual meeting, April 11, 1992.

13. Ross, James R., *I, Jesse James*, 54.

14. James, Stella, *In the Shadow of Jesse James*, 38.

Chapter Five

1. Ross, James R., *I, Jesse James*, p. 55.

2. This subject has been debated in various books. According to James R. Ross, Jesse's great-grandson, the family accepts that Jesse planned the robbery. Author's conversation with James R. Ross, 1990.

3. Pinkerton, William, "Train Robberies, Train Robbers and the Holdup Men," address to the Annual Convention of the International Association Chiefs of Police, Jamestown, VA, 1907.

4. Statement of Greenup Bird, *Liberty Tribune*, February 16, 1866.

5. Younger, Cole, *Cole Younger by Himself*, 54.

6. Liberty *Tribune*, March 2, 1866.

7. Ibid.

8. Statement of Cole Younger to Harry Hoffman, 1915; The United States Treasury Department responded to a request made to Senator

Harry S. Truman by William F. Norton of Liberty for a full accounting of the cashing of the bonds taken during the Liberty bank robbery. A complete list of the denomination, serial numbers, date of redemption, and source of receipt was provided. Forty thousand dollars worth of the bonds were redeemed by 1868. Two thousand dollars were left outstanding. Welsley, Mr. W., letter to Wm. F. Norton, April 11, 1942. Historian Ralph Ganis has been examining information that another of the Liberty bank robbers may have been a man named Lorenzo Merriman Little. Ganis's research has turned up substantial evidence that Little knew Cole Younger. Ganis believes that Little was brought into the gang by Younger and may have participated in some of the robberies of the James-Younger Gang.

Chapter Six

1. Settle, William A., Jr., *Jesse James Was His Name*, 53–54.
2. *Lexington Caucasian*, October 31, 1866.
3. Ibid.
4. Ross, James R., *I, Jesse James*, p. 75–78.
5. *Liberty Tribune*, March 8, 1867.
6. Younger, Cole, *Cole Younger by Himself*, 61.
7. *Liberty Tribune*, March 29, 1867.
8. History of Ray County, MO, Missouri Historical Company, St. Louis, 1881, 388.
9. *Richmond Conservator*, May 24, 1867.
10. Ibid.
11. *Richmond Conservator*, June 1, 1867.
12. Wybrow, Robert, *From the Pen of a Noble Robber: The Letters of Jesse Woodson James, 1847–1882*.
13. *Richmond Conservator*, November 30, 1867.
14. Ibid.
15. Ibid.
16. Cummins, Jim, *Jim Cummins the Guerrilla*.
17. *Richmond Conservator*, November 30, 1867.

Chapter Seven

1. James, Jesse W., letter to the editor of the *Nashville Banner*, July 5, 1875.
2. Younger, Cole, *Cole Younger by Himself*.
3. James, Jesse W., letter to the editor of the *Nashville Banner*, July 5, 1875.

4. Documents displayed at the Liberty Bank Museum, Liberty, Missouri.

5. James, Jesse W., letter to the editor of the *Nashville Banner*, July 5, 1875.

6. Younger, Jim, letters to a friend, 1890–1901.

7. McCoy had been with the First Missouri Confederate Infantry until they were almost completely eliminated during the battle of Shiloh.

8. Jackson, Gary, letter to author, August 19, 1993. Alex Henderson bought a nice farm in Robertson County, Tennessee, shortly after the Russellville robbery. Two of Henderson's brothers, Wick and Henry, were said to have been bank robbers. They were eventually killed by law enforcement agents. Wick Henderson was killed in Adairville, Kentucky.

9. *Louisville Courier*, March 24, 1868.

10. *Louisville Daily Journal*, "Bank Robbery at Russellville, KY," March 21, 1868.

11. Ibid.

12. Ibid.

13. *Louisville Daily Journal*, March 28, 1868.

14. Ibid. George Shepard, who is called John in the article, was described as "a Missourian and is said to have belonged to the infamous Quantrill party that committed so many deeds of blood and rapine during the war . . . is about forty years old . . . married to a very beautiful young lady named Miss Sanders."

15. James, Jesse W., letter to the editor of the *Nashville Banner*, August 4, 1875.

16. Younger, Cole, *Cole Younger by Himself*, 62.

17. Spicer, June, great-granddaughter of Josie and John Jarrette, interview with author.

Chapter Eight

1. *St. Joseph Gazette*, December 9, 1869.

2. *St. Louis Globe-Democrat*, "The Only Living Witness Tells How Jesse James Held Up a Bank in Gallatin, Mo., 73 Years Ago," October 17, 1942.

3. *Liberty Tribune*, December 17, 1869.

4. *St. Louis Globe-Democrat*, "The Only Living Witness Tells How Jesse James Held Up a Bank in Gallatin, Mo., 73 Years Ago."

5. *Liberty Tribune*, December 17, 1869.

6. Ibid.

7. Ibid.

8. *St. Louis Globe-Democrat*, "The Only Living Witness Tells How Jesse James Held Up a Bank in Gallatin, Mo., 73 Years Ago."

9. *Liberty Tribune*, December 17, 1869.

10. *St. Joseph Gazette*, December 7, 1868.

11. James, Jesse W., letter to Governor McClurg dated June 1870, published in the *Kansas City Times*.

12. James, Jesse W., letter to Governor McClurg dated July 1870, published in the *Kansas City Times*.

13. *Liberty Tribune*, July 22, 1870.

14. Ibid.

15. Several historians have suggested in recent years that it was perhaps the drug addiction that made Jesse act paranoid and irrational at the time of his death. It is noteworthy that the 1996 DNA study revealed that Jesse had no excessive amount of drugs in his system at the time of his death.

16. Miller, Rick, *Bounty Hunter*, 39.

Chapter Nine

1. "James Robbery Integral Part of Wayne History," newspaper article, publication and date unknown.

2. *Osceola Republican*, June 8, 1871. William A. Settle, Jr., mentioned in the notes to his book *Jesse James Was His Name* that when he interviewed Henry Clay Dean's grandson, Dean Davis, on March 23, 1945, Davis told him that his grandfather believed it was Frank James who interrupted his speech. Such action, however, is more indicative of Jesse's personality.

3. "James Robbery Integral Part of Wayne History."

4. *Osceola Republican*, June 8, 1871.

5. Clelland D. Miller was born on January 9, 1850, in Holt, Clay County, Missouri. He was the oldest of five sons born to Emeline and Moses Miller. Miller joined Bill Anderson's guerrilla unit on October, 22, 1864, at the age of fourteen. He was captured four days later during the battle that claimed the life of Anderson. Miller was imprisoned in the Jefferson Barracks prison until April of the following year. Miller's body was preserved in a keg of alcohol and put on exhibit throughout Minnesota after his death in Northfield. Eventually, Miller's family won their appeal to obtain his body, and he was laid to rest in the Muddy Fork Cemetery in Holt.

6. "James Robbery Integral Part of Wayne History."

7. *Chicago Times*, in *Kansas City Evening Star*, July 21, 1881.

8. Transcript of the trial of Clelland Miller, Wayne County, Iowa, 1871.

9. James, Jesse W., letter to the editor of the *Kansas City Times*, October 1872.

10. Younger, Jim, letters to a friend, 1899–1901.

11. *St. Louis Daily Missouri Republican*, May 1, 1872; *The Kentucky Explorer*, November 1988. The Youngers' paternal grandfather, Charles Lee Younger, was quite a man. Family legend has it that he fought Indians alongside Daniel Boone and drove a huge team of mules from Kentucky to Missouri. He fathered eighteen children by four women. One of these women was his mistress, Parmelia Dorcus Wilson. Charlie Younger died on November 12, 1854. His will stipulated that his eight children by Parmelia were free to change their names from Wilson to Younger. Evidently, when Cole arrived in Corydon, he decided that since the Wilsons were using the Younger name, he was free to use theirs.

12. *The Kentucky Explorer*, November 1988.

13. Ibid.

14. *Neosho Times*, in the *St. Louis Republican*, October 12, 1882.

15. Younger, Cole, *Cole Younger by Himself*, 62.

16. James, Jesse Woodson, letter to the editor, *Nashville Banner*, dated July 5, 1875.

17. *Kansas City Times*, September 27, 1872.

18. Ibid.

19. *Kansas City Times*, October 15, 1872.

20. James, Jesse W., letter to the editor of the *Kansas City Times*, 1872.

21. *Pleasant Hill Review*, November 26, 1872; Younger, Cole, *Cole Younger by Himself*, 64.

22. *St. Louis Missouri Republican*, May 28, 1873.

23. Younger, Jim, letters to a friend, 1899–1901.

Chapter Ten

1. Charlie Pitts was one of twelve children born to a couple living near Commerce, Oklahoma. He was born in 1844. Pitts went in search of his fortune by the age of fourteen. He ended up in Missouri, where he was hired on as a farmhand of an affluent Jackson County farmer named Washington Wells. Pitts does not seem to have served as a guerrilla, but folklore has it that he aided and abetted that movement during the war. Pitts spent time in the Ozark region after the war and on the Cherokee reservation in Indian County. Pitts used the alias of

Samuel Wells when he rode with the James-Younger Gang. He may
have married a woman named Emma Henderson in 1874. While a
marriage certificate exists, it is impossible to determine if this was
indeed the Charlie Pitts in question.

2. Bill Chadwell was born William Stiles in Monticello, Minnesota.
There is little else known about him. Chadwell lived for a time in St.
Paul. He was arrested there for stealing a horse and served jail time. It
is thought that at this time he changed his name to Chadwell.

3. Adair Community Service Club, *Welcome to Adair*, date unknown; *Kansas City Times*, July 23, 1873.

4. *New York Times*, July 23, 1873. John Rafferty's family received
no compensation for the engineer's death other than a small gold pin.
Wilson, Jackie, curator of the Jesse James Museum, Adair, letter to
author, August 18, 1989.

5. *New York Times*, July 23, 1873.

6. *Adair News*, April 22, 1954. One of the boys mentioned was
Jack McCall. McCall later traveled to the Black Hills. There he was
involved with Calamity Jane and Wild Bill Hickok.

7. James, Jesse W., letter to the editor of the *St. Louis Dispatch*
dated January 1874.

8. One newspaper related a story about a man who was friendly
with Arthur McCoy. McCoy's wife was mentioned as being a member
of the Dent family who were "famous for their relation to President
Grant." copy of article in possession of author, newspaper and date
unknown.

9. *Little Rock Gazette*, January 18, 1874.

10. *Little Rock Gazette*, February 18, 1874.

11. Pinkerton, William, "Train Robberies, Train Robbers and the
Holdup Men," address given to the annual convention of the International Association of the Chiefs of Police, Jamestown, VA, 1907.

12. *St. Louis Globe-Democrat*, February 2, 1874.

13. *St. Louis Times*, February 2, 1874.

14. Arthur McCoy has sometimes been mentioned as having participated in the Gad's Hill robbery, but McCoy died three weeks before
the event.

15. *St. Louis Times*, February 4, 1874.

16. Ibid.

17. Eden, M. C., "Missouri's First Train Robbery."

18. Younger, Jim, letters to a friend, 1899–1901.

Chapter Eleven

1. *Liberty Tribune*, March 20, 1874; Kansas City *Times*, March 14, 1874. Whicher's first name has been a subject of disagreement among James researchers for many years. He has been called James, John, and Joseph. The author has chosen to refer to him as James due to the facts contained in his hometown obituary.

2. James Whicher was twenty-six years old at the time of his death. He was a resident of Iowa City, Iowa, and had recently married Millie A. Hildebrand. Whicher had been a sailor prior to going to work for Pinkerton. He had retired from that career after a fall from a masthead. Whicher's body was taken to Chicago, Illinois, where he was buried at the Graceland Cemetery. Fitzgerald, Ruth Coder, James Farm *Journal*, publication of the Friends of the James Farm, 1988.

3. Ibid.

4. *St. Louis Republican*, in *Liberty Tribune*, December 25, 1874.

5. Coroner's inquest into the death of John Younger and Edwin Daniels, March 1874, St. Clair County, Missouri, testimony of Louis J. Lull.

6. Coroner's inquest into the death of John Younger and Edwin Daniels, March 1874, St. Clair County, Missouri, testimony of Theodrick Snuffer.

7. Coroner's inquest into the death of John Younger and Edwin Daniel, March 1874, St. Clair County, Missouri, Testimony of G. W. MacDonald.

8. Yeatman, Ted P., "Allen Pinkerton and the Raid on Castle James," *True West*, October 1992.

9. *Kansas City Times*, interview with Cora McNeill, 1897.

10. *Liberty Tribune*, March 27, 1874.

11. James, Stella, *In the Shadow of Jesse James*, 123–124.

12. Ibid., 33.

13. Ibid., 124.

14. *St. Louis Dispatch*, June 7, 1874.

15. James, Stella, *In the Shadow of Jesse James*, 32. At the coroner's inquest into the death of Jesse James, Zee testified that she and Jesse were married on April 24, 1874, at Kearney, and that they had honeymooned in Texas for about five months.

16. *Kansas City Star*, July 16, 1944.

17. Settle, William A., Jr., *Jesse James Was His Name*, 92.

18. *Kansas City Daily Journal of Commerce*, January 29, 1875.

19. Younger, Jim, letters to a friend, 1899–1901.

Chapter Twelve

1. *Lexington Register*, August 31, 1874.
2. Ibid.
3. Ibid.
4. *Kansas City Times*, September 9, 1874.
5. *New York Times*, September 15, 1874; courtesy Chuck Parsons.
6. Settle, William A., Jr., *Jesse James Was His Name*, 73.
7. Younger, Jim, letters to a friend, 1900–1901.
8. *Lexington Caucasian*, October 17, 1874.
9. Younger, Cole, *Cole Younger by Himself*, 63–65.
10. Settle, William A., Jr., *Jesse James Was His Name*, 75. New information developed by historian Ralph Ganis suggests the strong possiblity that the Corinth robbery may have been the work of Jesse's associates Little and Diggs.
11. *Kansas City Times*, December 10, 1874. Jesse was generous with whatever money he obtained through robbery. He would often bring gifts to his family when he visited. He brought his little brother Archie a wood recorder and once gifted his sisters with silk he had purchased in New York. He gave his sister Sallie a beautiful hand-tooled saddle. Sallie couldn't recall Frank ever giving members of his family gifts. James, Stella, *In the Shadow of Jesse James*, 51.
12. Ross, James R., *Jesse James Was His Name*, 166. Author interview with James R. Ross.
13. Billy Judson continues to be a controversial figure. Jesse's great-grandson Judge James R. Ross stands by the family's belief that Judson was, indeed, a member of the gang. No other documentation or suggestion of his having been a member of the gang has been found by the author. Billy Judson was an alias used by F. W. Wickizer, according to Judge Ross. Wickizer died in 1935 while living in Arlington, California. His son, Russell A. Wickizer, was a justice of the peace in San Bernardino, California, at that time. Wickizer wrote a manuscript of his adventures with the James-Younger Gang that was willed to Judge Ross's mother, Josephine Frances James Ross. Mrs. Ross entered into a written agreement with Wickizer whereby his manuscript would be used in conjunction with Mrs. Ross's personal knowledge to prepare the book *Jesse James*. The book was never published. Judge Ross wrote to the author, "Obviously neither Jesse nor Frank put in writing that Billy Judson was a member of the gang. As I'm sure you know, there is no statute of limitations for murder in Minnesota. How then can I be so sure of everything I wrote in my book regarding Billy Judson?

Because Frank James told Jesse Jr. (my grandfather) and my grandfather told me of Frank's statements to him." Ross, Hon. James R., letter to author, July 22, 1996.

14. Letter addressed to "My Dear Friend" said to have been authored by Jesse W. James.

15. *St. Louis Republican*, December 12, 1874.

16. Yeatman, Ted, "Allan Pinkerton and the Raid on 'Castle James,' " *True West*, October 1992.

17. Settle, William A., *Jesse James Was His Name*, 77.

18. *Liberty Tribune*, February 5, 1875.

19. Yeatman, Ted, "Allan Pinkerton and the Raid on 'Castle James.' "

20. Ibid., material provided to Yeatman by Fred R. Egloff.

21. Egloff, Fred R., "The Greek Fire Bomb," *True West*, October, 1992.

22. *St. Louis Dispatch*, January 27, 1875.

23. Clay County Circuit Court records, File No. 449. Robert J. King probably was an alias of Robert J. Linden, the man who likely threw the bomb. Linden's next assignment was Pennsylvania's Molly Maguire coal field case. Linden became head of Philadelphia's police department by the late 1890s. Yeatman, Ted, "Allan Pinkerton and the Raid on 'Castle James.' "

24. James, Jesse W., letter to the editor, special to the *Nashville Banner*, dated August 4, 1875.

25. *Journal of the House, Twenty-eighth General Assembly of Missouri*, 1875.

26. Yeatman, Ted, "Allan Pinkerton and the Raid on 'Castle James.' "

27. Letter written to "Jim" believed to have been authored by Jesse W. James, dated June 10, 1875.

28. Yeatman, Ted, "Allan Pinkerton and the Raid on 'Castle James.' "

Chapter Thirteen

1. Yeatman, Ted P., *Jesse James and Bill Ryan in Nashville*.

2. Ibid.

3. Eden, M. C., "Revolvers vs. Croquet Mallets and an Irate Lady," *The Brand Book*, Vol. 15, No. 4, July 1973.

4. Ibid.

5. Letter to "My Dear Friend" said to have been authored by Jesse W. James.

6. A later correspondence claims that Dr. W. M. Vertrees of Nashville was the doctor who delivered Jesse Edwards. Dr. Vertrees later said that "Mr. Howard" gave him a Colt .38 revolver for delivering his son. *The Westerner*, Issue No. 12, August 1989.

7. *St. Louis Republican*, September 16, 1875; *Huntington Advertiser*, September 21, 1875.

8. Ibid.

9. *Louisville Courier-Journal*, September 15, 1875.

10. *Huntington Advisor*, September 23, 1875.

11. *Wheeling Intelligencer*, September 27, 1875.

12. The *Huntington Advisor* wrote that "Keene" provided them with some biographical information. He said he was born December 18, 1849, and had been raised in Pike County, Illinois. He also claimed to have served two years in the Confederate Army. *Huntington Advisor*, October 28, 1875.

13. James, Jesse W., letter to the *Nashville American*, dated September 21, 1875.

14. *Kansas City Times*, February 1876.

Chapter Fourteen

1. Younger, Jim, letters to a friend, 1899–1901; the account of "Maggie."

2. Yeatman, Ted, "Jesse James in Tennessee," *True West*, July 1985.

3. Younger, Jim, letters to a friend, 1899–1901; the account of "Maggie."

4. Ibid.

5. Ibid.

6. Ibid.

7. Ibid.

8. Ibid.

9. *Booneville Daily Advertiser*, July 8, 1876.

10. *Booneville Daily Advertiser*, July 11, 1876.

11. *Booneville Daily Advertiser*, July 25, 1876.

12. Settle, William A., Jr., *Jesse James Was His Name*. McDonaugh, James, letter to Governor C. H. Hardin, August 6, 1876.

13. *Kansas City Times*, August 13, 1876.

14. *Kansas City Times*, August 14, 1876.

15. Letter reprinted in the *St. Louis Globe-Democrat*, August 24, 1876.

16. Hoctor, Emmett, " 'Safe Retreat'—Found!" National Associa-

tion and Center for Outlaw and Lawman History *Quarterly*, Vol. XV, No. 4, Oct.–Dec. 1991.

17. Ross, James R., *I, Jesse James*, 12.

18. Younger, Cole, *Cole Younger by Himself*, 76.

19. Ibid., 77.

Chapter Fifteen

The chronology and detailing of the events at Northfield were drawn together through the use of several sources. Included were the unpublished letters of Jim Younger, Cole Younger's account in *Cole Younger by Himself*, Dallas Cantrell's book *Younger's Fatal Blunder*, George Huntington's *Robber and Hero*, and the various accounts in the area newspapers.

1. Younger, Cole, *Cole Younger by Himself*, 77.

2. Mollie Ellsworth gave an interview to the *St. Paul Pioneer Press* on September 20, 1876. She mentioned that she knew one of the men who stayed at the Nicolette House was Jesse James. She had met Jesse several years before when he had been seeing a woman named Hattie Floyd in St. Louis.

3. Hobbs, J., statement given September 11, 1876.

4. Younger, Cole, *Cole Younger by Himself*, 78.

5. *Minneapolis Tribune*, September 1876.

6. *Rice County Journal*, September 14, 1876.

7. Vought, T. L., Account of October 1876.

8. *The Southern Minnesotan*, "The Gettysburg of the James-Younger Gang," publication and date unknown.

9. Ibid.

10. Younger, Cole, *Cole Younger by Himself*, 77.

11. *Mankato Free Press*, December 1876.

12. Cantrell, Dallas, *Youngers' Fatal Blunder*, 22.

13. Younger, Cole, Account given to Dr. A. E. Hedback.

14. Huntington, George, *Robber and Hero,* 18.

15. Huntington, George, *Robber and Hero,* 19.

16. Ibid.

17. *Minneapolis Tribune*, September 8, 1876 .

18. Ibid.

19. Ibid.

20. Ibid.

21. It has not been determined if Jesse or Frank were actually injured during their flight from the streets of Northfield. When one considers that they later encountered a medical doctor and did not ask for a

medical opinion regarding any wounds, it seems doubtful that they received any kind of serious bullet wound during the aftermath of the robbery.

22. It stands to reason that in their haste to retreat, some of the weapons of the dead robbers were left behind in the street. Paul Chilgren of Northfield claims that a pistol has remained in his family since September 7, 1876. The pistol was dropped by one of the outlaws and retrieved from the street by merchant C. P. Ofstos. The pistol is a .38 rimfire with a five shot cylinder; Chuck Parsons, "The Answer Man," *True West*, September 1983. Jesse favored rimfires. A .45 Smith & Wesson rimfire was given to an Oklahoma museum by Perry Samuel after Jesse's death; Davis Gun Museum, Oklahoma.

23. Younger, Cole, *Cole Younger by Himself*, 85.
24. Hoffman, Harry, *The Youngers Last Stand*.
25. Ross, James R., and Barr, Betty, interviews with author.
26. Younger, Cole, letter to Dr. A. E. Hedback.
27. Ibid.
28. Younger, Cole, *Cole Younger by Himself*, 80.

Chapter Sixteen

1. Dispatch of S. B. Brockway to J. A. Winter, September 14, 1876.
2. Younger, Cole, *Cole Younger by Himself*, 87.
3. Huntington, George, *Robber and Hero*, 52.
4. Ibid.
5. *The Southern Minnesotan*, "The Gettysburg of the James-Younger Gang."
6. Younger, Cole; statement to Harry Hoffman.
7. Ibid.
8. *The Southern Minnesotan*, "The Gettysburg of the James-Younger Gang."
9. Cantrell, Dallas, *Youngers' Fatal Blunder*, 50.
10. *Sioux City Democrat*, date unknown.
11. Ibid.
12. *St. Paul Pioneer Press*, September 20, 1876.
13. Document in the possession of the Northfield Historical Society.
14. Account of Charles Armstrong, June 21, 1945.
15. *Faribault Democrat*, September 22, 1876.
16. *Kansas City Times*, October 15, 1876.

Chapter Seventeen

1. *Kansas City Times*, October 24, 1876.

2. *Liberty Tribune*, December 1, 1876.

3. The location of both Jesse and Frank James after the Northfield raid has been the fodder for much speculation, debate, and folklore. The reported activities of the brothers place them in places as diverse as Colorado, California, Wyoming, New Mexico, and Nebraska. They have been said to have taken Indian brides as wives, formed outlaw bands with army deserters, gambled, and fathered numerous children. All of this makes for good storytelling and the subsequent folklore has passed down several interesting stories for generations. It is doubtful that most of it is true.

4. Yeatman, Ted P., "Jesse James in Tennessee," *True West*, July 1985.

5. Ibid.

6. The twins are buried in a cemetery in Johnsonville, Tennessee, according to writer Phillip Steele.

7. These aliases were given to Missouri law enforcement agents by Dick Liddil upon his surrender.

8. Judge John Phillips in his eulogy of Frank James as published in the *Kansas City Star*, March 28, 1915.

9. John P. Helms made available to the *Nashville American* all of the letters that Jesse had written to him concerning this matter after the surrender of Frank James. Excerpts were published in the *Nashville American* in October 1882.

10. Yeatman, Ted P., "Jesse James in Tennessee."

11. Ibid.

12. Yeatman, Ted P., letter to author, September 11, 1994.

13. *Nashville Tennessean*, July 21, 1995.

14. *Missouri Republican*, October 1882. Mangum, William Preston, "Frank and Jesse James Raced Horses between Their Holdups," National Association and Center for Outlaw and Lawman History *Quarterly*, Vol. XIII, No. 2, Fall 1988.

15. Magnum, William Preston, "Frank and Jesse James Raced Horses between Their Holdups."

16. *Kansas City Times*, November 4, 1879.

17. Ed Miller greatly admired his brother Clell. It was not until after the death of his wife, Lucinda Pense, and their baby in 1878 that Ed decided to turn to a life of crime and follow in his older brother's footsteps. Miller, C. E. "Ed," letter to author, undated.

18. Magnum, William Preston, "Frank and Jesse James Raced Horses between Their Holdups." One of Jesse's horses, as well as one of Frank's, was listed in *Krik's Guide to the Turf*, published by Henry G. Crickmore out of New York in 1878. B. J. Woodson's Rebel is listed. J. W. Woodson's Jewell Maxey also appears; information obtained from historian Ted P. Yeatman.

19. Fitzgerald. Cummins, Jim, *Jim Cummins' Book*, 86.

20. *Kansas City Times*, November 4, 1879.

21. *Richmond Democrat*, November 20, 1879.

22. Yeatman, Ted P., "Jesse James in Tennessee." Yeatman, Ted P., letter to author, 1993.

23. Ganis, Ralph P., letters and conversations with author, October 1996.

24. Testimony of Tucker Bassham at his trial for robbery, July 1880.

25. Fitzgerald, Ruth Coder, James Farm *Journal*, 1988. Miller family records list Ed Miller's death as being on or about March 10, 1880.

26. Yeatman, Ted P., *Jesse James and Bill Ryan in Nashville*.

27. Yeatman, Ted P., "Jesse James in Tennessee."

28. Cummins, Jim, *Jim Cummins' Book*, 89. An interesting note in the Cummins story is that in 1909, Cummins married for the first time at the age of sixty-three. His new bride was Canadian entertainer Florence Sherwood. Cummins had romanced Miss Sherwood for twelve years. The bride stated, "I got ready at last because I couldn't get him to visit me in Canada. He always said he would never see me again unless I consented to be his wife. Then I got a theatrical offer for Jim and I think I ought to do the best I can for him." The exact nature of the theatrical offer is not evident. *St. Clair County Democrat*, October 31, 1909.

29. Cummins, Jim, *Jim Cummins' Book*, 89.

30. Liddil, Dick, testimony at trial of Frank James.

31. Yeatman, Ted, "Jesse James and Bill Ryan in Tennessee," *Nashville Tennessean*, July 21, 1995. W. L. Earthman built a three-room addition onto his house with the share of the reward money he received for Ryan.

32. Liddil, Dick, testimony at trial of Frank James.

Chapter Eighteen

1. Yeatman, Ted, "Jesse James in Tennessee."

2. *St. Louis Missouri Republican*, September 29, 1881.

3. *St. Louis Missouri Republican*, October 1, 1881.

4. Testimony of General Jo Shelby at the trial of Frank James.

5. Perry, Milton F., conversation with author, 1989.

6. James, Stella, *In the Shadow of Jesse James*, 7.

7. Ibid.

8. Testimony of Dick Liddil at the trial of Frank James.

9. Ibid.

10. *Kansas City Times*, July 20, 1881.

11. James, Stella, *In the Shadow of Jesse James*, 116.

12. Liddil, Dick, testimony at trial of Frank James.

13. *Liberty Tribune*, August 5, 1881.

14. *Kansas City Times*, April 6, 1882.

15. *Kansas City Times*, September 8, 1881.

16. *St. Louis Missouri Republican*, September 12, 1881.

17. Perry, Milton F., conversation with author, 1988.

18. James, Stella, *In the Shadow of Jesse James*, 49.

19. Liddil, Dick, testimony at trial of Frank James.

Chapter Nineteen

1. James, Stella, *In the Shadow of Jesse James*, 49. Jesse's desire to quit outlawry was told to Jesse Edwards by his aunt Sally Nicholson.

2. Wybrow, Robert, *From the Pen of a Noble Robber*, 20.

3. Author's correspondence with Nebraska historian Emmett C. Hoctor, 1996. Mr. Hoctor believes that Jesse participated in the Riverton robbery.

4. Samuel, Zerelda, testimony at coroner's inquest.

5. James, Stella, *In the Shadow of Jesse James*, 49. Statement of Sally Nicholson to Jesse Edwards.

6. James, Stella, *In the Shadow of Jesse James*, 30.

7. James, Stella, *In the Shadow of Jesse James*, 50. Jesse E. strongly believed that his father wanted to surrender in the months before his death. Jesse E. told his wife that Zerelda Samuel and friends of the family had approached three different Missouri governors over the years in hopes of Jesse being allowed to stand a fair trial. Jesse E. claimed that their overtures were disregarded.

8. Testimony of Bob Ford at coroner's inquest.

9. Ibid.

10. *Kansas City Times*, "Jesse James Is Very Definitely Dead, Says a Man Who Photographed His Body," November 12, 1948.

11. *St. Louis Missouri Republican*, April 5, 1882.

12. *St. Joseph Herald*, April 5, 1882.

13. *St. Joseph Herald*, April 6, 1882.

14. *Kansas City Evening Star*, April 6, 1882.

15. *Kansas City Times*, April 7, 1882.

16. A popular misconception is that the J. T. Ford, who served as Jesse's pallbearer, was the father of Bob and Charlie Ford. Although the two men shared the same initials, the J. T. Ford who served as pallbearer was the mayor of Liberty and was not related to the Ford brothers.

17. *St. Louis Weekly Missouri Republican*, April 13, 1882.

18. Ibid.

19. Ibid. This newspaper reported what other items brought: The chair Jesse was standing on when he was shot went for five dollars while five other plain cane chairs went for two dollars a piece. Stone china plates were sold for a dollar each and saucers went for fifty cents. Silverware could be bought for a dollar a piece. The duster Jesse used to brush off the sampler was sold for five dollars, an old wash basin four dollars and seventy-five cents, a jackknife four dollars, a satchel twenty-one dollars, a waistband eleven dollars, a pair of old mittens two dollars, and a "crippled" revolver went for seventeen dollars. Many of these items would continue to grow in value, even within the next few years. Kansas Sheriff Albert Houghton claimed that he had been actively pursuing Jesse and was ready to arrest him even hours before his death. Houghton later bought the chair Jesse was standing on when he was killed for $250. Dora McCormick, the daughter of an antique dealer who bought the chair in 1892, wrote in her diary: "This morning Father purchased the chair that Jesse James was standing on when he was killed. It has a letter with it signed by the family. All day people have come by to see it. Everyone wants to touch it." The following month when Miss McCormick's father sold the chair, Dora wrote, "I feel sorry to see the chair leave but it was depressing to look at. But Sheriff Houghton is obsessed with Jesse James so he'll get more out of it than anyone." *The Westerner*, Issue No. 12, August 1989, 23.

20. *St. Louis Missouri Republican,* April 7, 1882.

21. Crittenden, Thomas, *The Crittenden Memoirs.*

22. Charlie Ford toured a theatrical circuit with his brother Bob in the months after the murder of Jesse James. The pair would recount on stage how they killed Jesse. They were not well received as the heroes they believed themselves to be. Charlie could not stand the stigma attached to having shot a man in the back. He killed himself in May 1884. Bob Ford traveled to New Mexico, then Pueblo, Colorado, after the hoopla of the assassination began to die down. He was known to frequent the saloons and gambling halls in that town. He eventually opened a saloon and gambling enterprise of his own in Walsenberg, Colorado. He stayed there only a short time. When a gold strike ben-

efited the town of Creede, the twenty-eight-year-old Ford tried his luck there. He opened a new saloon called the Creede Exchange that was in the same building as the boarding house he operated. Ford operated the Exchange with his wife Dorothy. Ford was forced to close the Exchange and look elsewhere for his livelihood in April 1892. On June 8 of that year, the day after he opened a large tent that served as a dance hall and bar, Ford was accosted by Hinsdale deputy sheriff Ed O'Kelly. O'Kelly approached Ford from behind and called his name. O'Kelly shot him in the head at point-blank range when the unsuspecting Ford turned around. O'Kelly was convicted of Bob Ford's murder and sentenced to life imprisonment on July 7. He served ten years of his sentence before he was released. O'Kelly never gave his reason for the murder.

Chapter Twenty

1. The house eventually became the property of the city because the owner faulted on the paying of back taxes. It was moved from its location on the hill to a spot next to the Patee House. The house remains in this location today and is open to the public for tours.

2. *Weekly Missouri Republican*, April 13, 1882.

3. Perry, Milton F., conversation with author, 1985.

4. *Omaha Bee*, August 20, 1885.

5. This is from a copy of the newspaper article that the author has in her possession but which is not identified or dated; courtesy Emmett Hoctor.

6. James, Frank, testimony at his trial.

7. *St. Louis Missouri Republican*, October 6, 1882.

8. Ibid.

9. Liddil, Dick, testimony at his trial.

10. Ibid.

11. James, Frank, testimony at his trial.

12. Samuel, Zerelda, testimony at trial of Frank James.

13. Crittenden, Thomas, testimony at trial of Frank James.

Chapter Twenty-one

1. Bronaugh, W. C., letter to Frank James, collection of Lee Pollack.

2. Settle, William A., Jr., *Jesse James Was His Name*, 163.

3. James, Stella, *In the Shadow of Jesse James*, 10.

4. Petition presented to the General Assembly of Missouri, 1888.

5. Bronaugh, W. C., *Youngers Fight for Freedom*, 130.

6. Ibid., 201.

7. *Kansas City World*, October 12, 1899.

8. Stella McGown James came from a prestigious family. Her grandmother was Mary F. Prunty, a granddaughter of Daniel Boone's son Nathan. Stella and Jesse E. had four daughters: Lucille Martha was born December 21, 1900, and married Frank Lewis on September 1, 1931. The couple had one son, James Curtis. Lucille died June 11, 1988. Josephine Frances was born April 20, 1902, and married Ronald Ross on September 2, 1925. Josephine and Ronald had one son, James Randal. Josephine died on March 31, 1964. Jessie Estelle was born on August 27, 1906, and married Mervyn Baumel on May 23, 1921. The couple had two children, Donald James and Diane June. Jessie Estelle died on February 2, 1987. Ethelrose was born July 10, 1908, and married Calvin Owens on October 16, 1937. Ethelrose had no children. She died on December 22, 1991. James, Stella, *In the Shadow of Jesse James*, 25, 73.

9. Stella James writes in her autobiography how by growing up in a household with two females and no father, Jesse E. was adored and spoiled by his mother and sister. Mary James told Stella soon after Stella married Jesse that it was now her responsibility to draw a bath for Jesse, lay out his clothes in the morning, put the collar and cuff buttons in his shirt, and brush his shoes each morning. Stella didn't mind. She adored Jesse E. and was happy to take care of him. James, Stella, *In the Shadow of Jesse James*, 30.

10. Zee James lived out the remainder of her days in a little house at 3402 Tracy Avenue in Kansas City. The house has been moved and currently stands at 1211 East 34th Street. Ibid.

11. James, Stella, *In the Shadow of Jesse James*, 42.

12. Ibid., 43.

13. *Kansas City Journal*, November 15, 1900.

14. James, Stella, *In the Shadow of Jesse James*, 126.

15. Mary Susan James and Henry Barr had four children: Lawrence H. was born October 16, 1902, and married Thelma Duncan. The couple had one daughter, Elizabeth Ann. Lawrence died February 25, 1984. Forster Ray was born October 11, 1904, and married Gertie Essary. Forster and Gertie had no children. Chester A. was born May 27, 1907, and married Beatrice Holloway. The couple had one son, Frederick Arthur. Chester died March 22, 1984. Henrietta was born March 14, 1913, and died October 10, 1913. Steele, Phillip W., *Jesse and Frank James: The Family History*, 53–54.

16. James, Stella, *In the Shadow of Jesse James*, 59.

17. Newspaper publication unknown, Oklahoma City, OK, February 10, 1911, document on file in the Joint Collection, University of Missouri Western Historical Manuscript Collection—Columbia & State Historical Society of Missouri Manuscripts.

18. Jesse E. once operated a candy and cigar store in Kansas City. While there, he made many friends who later hired him to handle legal business for them. He specialized in corporation law, wills, and the like when he did start work as an attorney. Jesse claimed there was no money in criminal practice and so he had little interest in pursuing that option. *Kansas City Star*, March 27, 1951.

19. Flier from The Great Cole Younger and Frank James Wild West Show.

20. *Nashville American*, June 1, 1903.

21. *Appleton City Tribune*, September 22, 1903.

22. *Washington Post*, December 2, 1903.

23. *Knoxville Daily Journal & Tribune*, December 15, 1903.

24. James, Stella, *In the Shadow of Jesse James*, 67.

25. Ross, James R., interview with author.

26. Zink, Wilbur, *From Bandit King to Christian*.

27. Dibble, R. F., *Strenuous Americans*, 46–47.

28. James, Stella, *In the Shadow of Jesse James*, 134.

29. *Kansas City Star*, March 28, 1915.

30. Ross, James R., interview with author.

31. There have been many accounts over the years as to whether or not Jesse Edwards James served as a pallbearer for Cole Younger. Jesse E.'s wife Stella wrote in a letter in regard to the matter: "Jess, Robert, Mae and I went to Mr. Younger's funeral by train from Kansas City. I seem to remember that Jesse was asked to act as pall bearer. But— ask to be excused as he expected to be in the court—on a case. Later he found he would be able to attend the funeral. I do know that Jesse did not sit with the rest of us in the church." James, Stella, letter to B. James George, February 11, 1959, Joint Collection University of Missouri Western Historical Manuscript Collection—Columbia & State Historical Society of Missouri Manuscripts.

32. James, Stella, *In the Shadow of Jesse James*, 95.

33. Ibid., 137.

34. Ibid., 96.

BIBLIOGRAPHY

Books

Appler, Augustus C., *The Guerrillas of the West or the Life, Character and Daring Exploits of the Younger Brothers*, St. Louis, Eureka Publishing Company, 1876

Beamis, Joan M. and Pullen, William E., *Background of a Bandit: The Ancestry of Jesse James*, New Hampshire, Beamis-Pullen, 1970

Brant, Marley, *The Outlaw Youngers: A Confederate Brotherhood*, Lanham, Maryland, Madison Books, 1992

Breihan, Carl W., *Saga of Jesse James*, Caldwell, Idaho, The Caxton Printers, 1991

Bronaugh, Warren Carter, *The Youngers Fight for Freedom*, Columbia, Missouri, E. W. Stevens Publishing Company, 1906

Brownlee, Richard S., *Gray Ghosts of the Confederacy: Guerrilla Warfare in the West, 1861–1865*, Baton Rouge, Louisiana State University Press, 1958

Buel, James William, *The Border Outlaws*, St. Louis, Missouri, Daniel Linahan Publishing, 1881

Cantrell, Dallas, *Youngers' Fatal Blunder*, Naylor Publishing, 1973

Castel, Albert, *William Clarke Quantrill: His Life and Times*, Columbus, Ohio, The General's Books, 1992

Connelly, William E., *Quantrill and the Border Wars*, New York, Pageant Book Company, 1956

Crittenden, Henry Huston, compiler, *The Crittenden Memoirs*, New York, G. P. Putnam's Sons, 1936

Croy, Homer, *Jesse James Was My Neighbor*, New York, Duell, Sloan and Pierce, 1949

Cummins, Jim, *Jim Cummins the Guerrilla*, Denver, The Reed Publishing Company, 1903

Dacus, Joseph A., *Illustrated Lives and Adventures of Frank and Jesse James and the Younger Brothers*, St. Louis, North Dakota, Thompson and Company, 1882

Dibble, R. F., *Strenuous Americans*, New York, Boni and Liveright, 1923

Edwards, John Newman, *Noted Guerrillas*, St. Louis, Bryan, Brand and Company, 1877

Hale, Donald, *We Rode With Quantrill*, Missouri, 1982

Hardy, William P., *Chronology of the Old West*, New York, Vantage Press, 1988

Heilbron, W. C., *Convict Life at the Minnesota State Prison*, St. Paul, W. C. Heilbron, 1909

History of Clay and Platte Counties, Missouri, St. Louis, National Historical Company, 1885

History of San Luis Obispo, California, date unrecorded

History of Jackson County, Missouri, Union History Co., 1888

History of Ray County, Mo., St. Louis, Missouri Historical Company, 1881

Horan, James D., *Desperate Men*, New York, G. P. Putnam's Sons, 1949

Huntington, George, *Robber and Hero*, Northfield, Minnesota, Christian Way Company, 1895

James, Jesse Edwards, *Jesse James, My Father*, Independence, Missouri, Sentinel Publishing Company, 1899

James, Stella Frances, *In the Shadow of Jesse James,* Thousand Oaks, California, The Revolver Press, Dragon Books, 1989

Love, Robertus, *The Rise and Fall of Jesse James*, New York, G. P. Putnam's Sons, 1926

McCorkle, John, *Three Years with Quantrill*, Armstrong, Missouri, 1914

McNeill, Cora, *Mizzoura*, Missouri, Mizzoura Publishing Company, 1898

Miller, George, Jr., *The Trial of Frank James for Murder*, Columbia, Missouri, E. W. Stephens Publishing Company, 1898

Miller, Rick, *Bounty Hunter*, College Station, Texas, Creative Publishing Company, 1988

O'Flaherty, Daniel, *General Jo Shelby: Undefeated Rebel*, South Carolina, Chapel Hill Publishing, 1954

Ross, James R., *I, Jesse James*, Thousand Oaks, California, Dragon Publishing Corp., 1988

Settle, William A., Jr., *Jesse James Was His Name or, Fact and Fiction Concerning the Careers of the Notorious James Brothers of Missouri,* Columbia, Missouri, University of Missouri Press, 1966

Steele, Phillip W., *Jesse and Frank James: The Family History,* Gretna, Pelican Publishing Company, 1987

Triplett, Frank, *The Life, Times, and Treacherous Death of Jesse James,* St. Louis, J. H. Chambers and Company, 1882

Younger, Coleman, *The Story of Cole Younger By Himself,* Chicago, The Henneberry Company, 1903

Newspapers

Adair (Iowa) News, "Adair Woman Recalls the Jesse James Train Robbery of 1873," April 22, 1954

Appleton City (Missouri) Tribune, June 1, 1903

Booneville (Missouri) Daily Advertiser, July 8, 1876; July 11, 1876; July 25, 1876

Chicago Times, July 21, 1881

Cincinnati Enquirer, April 17, 1889

Daily Missouri Democrat, September 1, 1863

Des Moines Sunday Register, "Outlaws Iowa Can't Forget," July 23, 1939

Faribault (Minnesota) Democrat, September 14, 1876; September 22, 1876; October 6, 1876

Huntington (West Virginia) Advertiser, September 21, 1875; September 23, 1875; October 28, 1875

Jackson County (Missouri) News, September 23, 1875

"Jesse James Not a Hero to Native of Northfield, Minnesota," June 26, 1948, publication unknown

"Jesse's Jobs," October 17, 1879, publication unknown

"James Robbery Integral Part of Wayne History," Wayne County, Iowa, publication and date unknown

Kansas City (Missouri) Commercial Advertiser, June 3, 1868

Kansas City (Missouri) Daily Journal of Commerce, January 29, 1875

Kansas City (Missouri) Evening Star, July 21, 1881; April 6, 1882

Kansas City (Missouri) Journal, Interview with William James, April 6, 1882; November 15, 1900

Kansas City (Missouri) Star, March 28, 1915; "Proud Granddaughters of Jesse James, Bandit," May 16, 1937; July 16, 1944; March 27, 1951

Kansas City (Missouri) Times, September 27, 1872; October 15, 1872; October 20, 1872; October 25, 1872; July 23, 1873; March 14, 1874;

September 9, 1874 ; December 10, 1874; January 28, 1875; February
1876; August 13, 1876; August 14, 1876; August 23, 1876; August
25, 1876; October 15, 1876; October 24, 1876, January 9, 1879;
November 4, 1879; July 20, 1881; September 8, 1881; April 5, 1882;
April 6, 1882; April 7, 1882; "Cora McNeill," 1897; "Death of
Mrs. Mary Barr," October 12, 1935; "Jesse James Is Very Definitely
Dead, Says a Man Who Photographed His Body," November 12,
1948; "Jesse James a Truman Hero" from the syndicated Washing-
ton Merry-Go-Round column of Drew Pearson, June 18, 1949;
"Jesse James, Jr. Dies," March 27, 1951

Kansas City (Missouri) World, October 12, 1899

Knoxville (Tennessee) Daily Journal & Tribune, December 15, 1903

Lee's Summit (Missouri) Ledger, March 25, 1874

Lexington (Missouri) Caucasian, October 31, 1866; August 30, 1873;
October 17, 1875

Lexington (Kentucky) Register, "The Outlaws," 1869; August 31, 1874

Lexington (Missouri) Union, September 5, 1863

Liberty (Missouri) Tribune, February 5, 1865; "Statement of Greenup
Bird, Sr.," February 14, 1866; February 16, 1866; March 2, 1866;
March 8, 1867, March 29, 1867, July 24, 1868; December 17, 1869;
July 22, 1870; March 20, 1874 ; March 27, 1874; December 25,
1874; February 5, 1875; December 1, 1876; December 5, 1879;
January 9, 1879; August 5, 1881

Lincoln (Nebraska) Journal, February 15, 1882

"L. M. Demarray Recalls Story of Narrow Escape by T. J. Dunning
and of Raid on Mathews Flock of Chickens," publication and date
unknown

Little Rock (Arkansas) Gazette, January 18, 1874; February 18, 1874

Louisville (Kentucky) Courier, March 24, 1868

Louisville (Kentucky) Courier-Journal, September 15, 1875, September
25, 1875; March, 1883; "Bank Account . . . Pistol Points to James
Gang," 1980

Louisville (Kentucky) Daily Journal, "Bank Robbery at Russellville,
KY," March 21, 1868; "Russellville Bank Robbery," March 23,
1868; "The Russellville Bank Robbery," March 28, 1868

Lowry City (Missouri) Independent, February 19, 1931

Madelia (Minnesota) Times-Messenger, "The Inside Story of the
Northfield Bank Robbery," March 27, 1936

Mankato (Minnesota) Free Press, December, 1876; "The Younger
Gang Comes to Mankato," September 20, 1979

Maryville (Missouri) Tribune, September 3, 1903

Memphis Commercial Appeal, May 26, 1903

Minneapolis Tribune, September 8, 1876; September 25, 1876

Missouri Republican, October 1882

Nashville American, October 1882; June 1, 1903; June 8, 1903

Nashville Evening World, "The Outlaw," April 25, 1882

Nashville Tennessean, "James Mystery Recalls Gang's Nashville Days," July 21, 1995

New York Times, "Daring Railway Robbery," July 23, 1873; "The Iowa Train Robbery," July 26, 1873; "The James Brothers," September 15, 1874

Nodaway (Missouri) Forum, September 3, 1903

Northfield (Minnesota) News, "General Ames Too Modest to Tell Part in Northfield Raid," August 2, 1929

Omaha Bee, August 20, 1885

Osceola (Missouri) Democrat, December, 1873

Osceola (Missouri) Republican, June 8, 1871

Pleasant Hill (Missouri) Review, November 26, 1872

Rice County (Minnesota) Journal, September 14, 1876

Richmond (Missouri) Conservator, May 24, 1867; June 1, 1867; November 30, 1867; December 5, 1879

Richmond (Missouri) Democrat, November 20, 1879

Sedalia (Missouri) Daily Democrat, April 13, 1882; April 23, 1882

Sioux City Democrat, date unknown

St. Clair County (Missouri) Democrat, "J. M. Cummins Marries," October 31, 1909

St. Joseph (Missouri) Gazette, December 7, 1868; December 9, 1869; April 11, 1882

St. Joseph (Missouri) Morning Herald, September 7, 1873; March 27, 1874; April 5, 1882; April 6, 1882

St. Louis (Missouri) Chronicle, July 27, 1881

St. Louis (Missouri) Daily Missouri Republican, May 1, 1872; May 28, 1873; November 21, 1879; September 12, 1881; September 21, 1881; October 1, 1881; April 5, 1882; October 6, 1882; October 7, 1882; October 12, 1882; January 5, 1883

St. Louis (Missouri) Democrat, September 7, 1873

St. Louis (Missouri) Dispatch, November 22, 1873; January 1874; June 7, 1874; November 22, 1874; John Newman Edwards editorial, January 27, 1875; "The Pardoning Power—Amnesty," editorial by John Newman Edwards, March 8, 1875

St. Louis (Missouri) Globe-Democrat, February 2, 1874; February 4, 1874; August 24, 1876; August 2, 1881; September 10, 1893; "Train Robbery," August 11, 1905; "The Only Living Witness Tells How

Jesse James Held Up a Bank in Gallatin, Mo. 73 Years Ago," October 17, 1942

St. Louis (Missouri) Republican, February 2, 1874; December 12, 1874; December 22, 1874, December 25, 1874, September 16, 1875; September 19, 1875; August 6, 1878; April 7, 1882; October 26, 1902

St. Louis (Missouri) Times, February 2, 1874; February 4, 1874

St. Paul (Minnesota) Pioneer Press, September 20, 1876

Washington Post, December 2, 1903; December 6, 1903; April 1, 1915

Weekly Missouri Republican, "Under the Daisies," April 13, 1882

Wheeling (West Virginia) Intelligencier, September 17, 1875; September 27, 1875

White Cloud (Minnesota) Chief, September 3, 1863

Magazines, Articles, Pamphlets, and Presentations

Adair Community Service Club, *Welcome to Adair*, date unknown

Bowman, Don R., "Quantrell, James, Younger, et al.: Leadership in a Guerrilla Movement, Missouri, 1861–1865," *Military Affairs*, Vol. XLI, No. 1, February, 1977

Brant, Marley, *The Families of Charles Lee and Henry Washington Younger: A Genealogical Sketch*, Burbank, California, September, 1986, available through the Friends of the Youngers

Chiarelli, Anne, *Aspects of Slavery in Missouri*, Jackson County Historical Society, date unrecorded

Colliers, "The Borderland," September 26, 1914

Confederate Veteran, Vol. XVIII, No. 4, April, 1914

Constock, Jim, *The West Virginia Heritage Encyclopedia,* Vol. 11, 1976.

Crickmore, Henry G., *Krik's Guide to the Turf*, New York, 1878

Eden, M. C., *"Missouri's First Train Robbery," The Brand Book*, English Westerners Society, Vol. 16, No. 2, January, 1974

Eden, M. C. "Revolvers vs. Croquet Mallets and an Irate Lady," *The Brand Book*, English Westerners Society, Vol. 15, No. 4, July, 1973

Egloff, Fred, "The Greek Fire Bomb," *True West*, October 1992

Fitzgerald, Ruth Coder, "Clell Miller," James Farm *Journal*, 1988

Fitzgerald, Ruth Coder, "John W. Whicher," James Farm *Journal*, 1988

Hale, Donald R., "Was Archie Clements Missouri's First Bank Robber?" National Association for Outlaw and Lawman History *Quarterly*, Vol. XIX, No. 2, April–June, 1995

Hoctor, Emmett C., "Rusticating in Nebraska, 1862–1882," talk given at the annual meeting of the Friends of the James Farm, April 11, 1992

Hoctor, Emmett, " 'Safe Retreat'—Found!" National Association for Outlaw and Lawman History *Quarterly*, Vol. XV, No. 4, Oct.–Dec., 1991

Jackson County Historical Society *Journal*, "Mrs. Jesse James Jr. Recent Visitor at Museum," December 1965

James Farm *Journal*, newsletter of the Friends of the James Farm, Vol. 12, No. 1, April, 1995 ; "Mrs. Jesse James Devout Worker in Revival" date unknown; "Last Visit of Jesse James with His Mother," Vol. 5, No. 5, December, 1985; "James Home History," Vol. 11, No. 2, October, 1994

"James Robbery Integral Part of Wayne History," date and publication unknown.

Jessen, Kenneth, "Bob Ford Gunned Down: Chain of Death Ends in Creede," National Association and Center for Outlaw and Lawman History *Quarterly*, date unknown

The Kentucky Explorer, "A Bank Is Robbed in Columbia," Vol. 3, No. 6, November 1988

Magnum, William Preston, "Frank and Jesse James Raced Horses between Their Holdups," National Association for Outlaw and Lawman History *Quarterly*, Vol. XIII, No. 2, Fall 1988

Mink, Charles R., "General Order No. 11: The Forced Evacuation of Civilians During the Civil War," *Military Affairs*, December 1970

Montgomery, Wayne, letter to the editor, "More on Jesse James' Death," publication and date unknown

National Association and Center for Outlaw and Lawman History newsletter, "Graves of Jesse James Twins Found," Vol. X, No. 1, Jan.–March 1985

Northfield News special publication, "Defeat of the Jesse James Gang," 1981

Parsons, Chuck, "Jesse James Guns," "Answer Man" column, *True West*, October 1983

Pinkerton, William, "Train Robberies, Train Robbers and the Holdup Men," address given to the annual convention of the International Association of Chiefs of Police, Jamestown, Virginia, 1907

The Southern Minnesotan, "The Gettysburg of the James-Younger Gang," date unknown

Warn, Bob, "Historical Bank Raid Centered on Ames Family," Northfield Historical Society, 1977

The Westerner, "Jesse James: A Sheriff's Obsession," Vienna, West Virginia, Issue No. 12, August, 1989

Wybrow, Robert J., "From the Pen of a Noble Robber," *The Brand Book*, The English Westerners Society, London, Vol. 24, No. 2, Summer 1987

Wybrow, Robert J., "The James Gang in West Virginia," *The Brand Book*, The English Westerners Society, London, Vol. 15, No. 2, January 1973

Yeatman, Ted P., *Jesse James and Bill Ryan at Nashville*, Nashville, Depot Press, 1981

Yeatman, Ted P., "Jesse James in Tennessee," *True West* Vol. 32, No. 4, July, 1985

Yeatman, Ted P., "Allan Pinkerton and the Raid on 'Castle James,' " *True West*, Vol. 32, No. 10, October 1992

Yeatman, Ted P., "Jesse James' Surrender", *Old West*, Fall 1994

Zink, Wilbur, *From Bandit King to Christian*, 1971

Zink, Wilbur, *The Roscoe Gun Battle*, Missouri, Democrat Publishing, 1982

Correspondence

Addy, Mildred, granddaughter of Mads Ouren, letter to author, November 1, 1983

Bligh, D. G., to Missouri Governor, March 3, 1875. (Joint Collection, University of Missouri Western Historical Manuscript Collection—Columbia & State Historical Society of Missouri Manuscripts)

Brockway, S. B., to J. A. Winter, September 14, 1876

Bronaugh, W. C., to Frank James, June 13, 1884, collection of Lee Pollack

Ganis, Ralph, to author, August–October 1996

Hoctor, Emmett, letters to author, 1995–1996

Hoffman, Harry, to B. J. George, June 3, 1958; June 25, 1958; undated (Joint Collection, University of Missouri Western Historical Manuscript Collection—Columbia & State Historical Society of Missouri Manuscripts)

Jackson, Gary, to author, August 19, 1993

James, Frank, to W. C. Bronaugh, February 19, 1903

James, Frank, to John Trotwood Moore, June 21, 1903

James, Stella, to B. James George, February 11, 1959 (Joint Collection, University of Missouri Western Historical Manuscript Collection—Columbia & State Historical Society of Missouri Manuscripts)

Loan, Brigadier General Benjamin, letter to Major General Samuel R. Curtis, Central District of Missouri, January 27, 1863

McDonaugh, James, to Governor C. H. Hardin, August 6, 1876

Miller, C. E. "Ed" Miller, to author, undated
Mills, John, to author, November 3, 1982; December 6, 1982
Rawlins, F. M., to author, January 3, 1986
Ross, James R., to author, July 22, 1996
Spicer, June, to author, April 13, 1983
United States Treasury Department, Chief, Division of Loans and Currency, (name undetectable) to Mr. Wm. F. Norton, April 11, 1942
Wilson, Jackie, Jesse James Museum, Adair, Iowa, to author, August 18, 1989
Yeatman, Ted P., letters to author, March 12, 1984; September 26, 1984; May 14, 1987; February 4, 1992; May 24, 1993; July 29, 1995; August 27, 1995; September 11, 1994; September 14, 1995
Younger, Cole, to Harry Hoffman, April 4, 1907; March 7, 1916
Younger, Jim, to a friend, 1899–1901
Younger, Bob, correspondence to "Aunt," 1877–1888

Public Documents of the United States of America

Campaigns and Battles of the Civil War, GPO
Congressional Record of March 2, 1928, re: Senate Joint Resolution No. 41
National Archives Military Records of Coleman Younger
National Archives Military Record of Irvin Walley
National Archives Military Record of John Jarrette
Oath of Allegiance, Mrs. Zerelda Samuels, June 5, 1863
Parole of Reuben Samuel, June 24, 1863
Parole of Mrs. Z. Samuel, June 5, 1863
War Department, *The War of the Rebellion: A Compilation of the Official Records of the Union and Confederate Armies*, Washington, D.C., Government Printing Office, 1880–1902

Public Documents of the State of Missouri

Ford, Robert and Charles, Pardon by Thom. Crittenden, 1882 (Joint Collection, University of Missouri Western Historical Manuscript Collection—Columbia & State Historical Society of Missouri Manuscripts)
Journal of the House, Twenty-eighth General Assembly of Missouri, 1875
Pardon petition for Jesse James, Frank James, Coleman Younger, and James Younger, et al., Missouri Legislature, 1899

Public Records

Adjutant general's report, State of Kansas, Seventh Regiment Kansas, roll

Allen, J. S., affidavit pertaining to the Northfield Bank Robbery, September 11, 1876, Northfield, Minnesota

Bassham, Tucker, testimony at his trial, July 1880

Clay County Circuit Court records, File No. 449

Clay County probate records, estate of Rev. Robert James, Liberty, Missouri

Claims on account, posse, in regard to the Northfield bank robbery, 1876

Complaint, Rice County, Minnesota, Northfield bank robbery, 1876

Coroner's inquest into the death of John Younger and Edwin Daniels, March 1874, St. Clair County, Missouri, testimony of Louis Lull; testimony of Theodrick Snuffer; testimony of G. W. MacDonald

Coroner's inquest, "Heywood and Others," Northfield, 1876

Crittenden, Thomas, testimony at trail of Frank James

Ford, Robert, testimony at coroner's inquest into the death of Jesse James, April 1882

Glispen, Sheriff James, statement of expenses in regard to manhunt, Madelia, Minnesota, 1876

Hobbs, J., affidavit pertaining to the Northfield bank robbery, September 11, 1876, Northfield, Minnesota

Indictment for the Otterville, Missouri, robbery, 1876

James, Frank, testimony at his trial

James, Frank and Jesse, warrant for arrest in regard to the Glendale robbery, 1879

James, Frank, warrant for arrest, 1882

Kerns, Dr. Absolam, Clinton, Missouri, 1853

Miscellaneous documents relating to the Liberty bank robbery on file at the Liberty Bank Museum, Liberty, Missouri

Liddil, Dick, testimony at the trial of Frank James

Parmer, Allen, testimony at trial of Frank James

Pillsbury, J. S., proclamation of September 9, 1876

Samuel, Zerelda, testimony at coroner's inquest into the death of Jesse James, April 1882

Shelby, Joseph O., testimony at the trial of Frank James

Transcript of the trial of Clell Miller for robbery, Wayne County, Iowa, 1871

Vought, T. L., statement of October 1876, Madelia, Minnesota

Wilcox, Frank J., affidavit pertaining to the Northfield Bank Robbery, Northfield, Minnesota, September 11, 1876

Younger, Charles, last will and testament, February 26, 1852

Younger, Cole, parole reports, August 1901–January 1903

Younger, James, parole reports, August 1901–October 1902

Younger, James, certificate of death, 1902

Younger, James, land title, Grayson County, Texas

Younger, Robert, certificate of death, 1889

Younger, T. C., James, and Robert, warrant for arrest in regard to the Northfield robbery, 1876

Younger, T. C., James, and Robert, indictment for the Northfield robbery and murders, 1876

Younger, T. C., James, and Robert, transfer papers from Faribault to Stillwater State Prison, 1876

Manuscripts and Accounts

Armstrong, Charles, account of June 21, 1945, Madelia, Minnesota

Bird, Greenup, statement of Liberty bank robbery, 1866

Bradford, George, 1877

Edwards, John Newman, "A Terrible Quintet," *St. Louis Dispatch*, 1874

Hobbs, George, account given September 11, 1876

Hoffman, Harry, *The Fog Amidst the Rumors Cleared Away* (Joint Collection, University of Missouri Western Historical Manuscript Collection—Columbia & State Historical Society of Missouri Manuscripts)

Hoffman, Harry, *The Youngers Last Stand*

Palmer, G. M., account given in 1938, Mankato, Minnesota

Pinkerton, William A., "Train Robberies, Train Robbers, and the 'Holdup' Men." Address at Annual Convention of International Association of Chiefs of Police, Jamestown, Virginia, 1907

Pomeroy, Charles, account of 1876

Samuel, Perry, account given to Harry Hoffman, undated (Joint Collection, University of Missouri Western Historical Manuscripts Collection—Columbia & State Historical Society of Missouri Manuscripts)

Vought, T. L., account, 1876

Traverse, Kitty, account given 1878, St. Paul, Minnesota

Younger, Cole, account given to Dr. H. E. Hedback, 1897

Younger, Cole, *What My Life Has Taught Me*

Younger, Cole to Harry Hoffman, 1915

Interviews

Barr, Betty—great-granddaughter of Jesse James
Barr, Lawrence—grandson of Jesse James
Barr, Thelma—granddaughter-in-law of Jesse James
Fitzgerald, Ruth Coder—Clell and Ed Miller family
Hall, Carolyn—Hall/Younger family
Miller, C. E.—Clell and Ed Miller family
Nicholson, John—great-nephew of Jesse James
Owens, Ethelrose James—granddaughter of Jesse James
Perry, Milton F.—James historian, former curator of James Farm
Ross, James R.—great-grandson of Jesse James
Smith, Nora Lee—Hall/Younger family
June Spicer—great-granddaughter of John and Josie Jarrette
Whipple, Ruth—Duncan/Younger family

Clipping Collections

Joint Collection, University of Missouri Western Historical Manuscript
    Collection—Columbia & State Historical Society of Missouri Man-
    uscripts, "James Boys' Mother Dead," publication and date un-
    known; "Curious Letter by Slayer of Jesse James Defends the
    Integrity of Gov. Crittenden," date and publication unknown
Hoctor, Emmett C., "About Polk Wells," publication and date un-
    known; "Mattie Collins," publication and date unknown; *Omaha
    (Nebraska) Bee*, "The Bandit's Spouse, 1885; Jesse James' Widow,
    St. Louis Globe-Democrat, date unknown; "Why Jesse James Was
    Not Taken Prisoner," publication and date unknown

INDEX